The Dirty Game

The Dirty Game

Uncovering the Scandal at FIFA

ANDREW JENNINGS

CENTURY

1 3 5 7 9 10 8 6 4 2

Century
20 Vauxhall Bridge Road
London SW1V 2SA

Century is part of the Penguin Random House group of companies
whose addresses can be found at global.penguinrandomhouse.com.

Penguin
Random House
UK

First published by Century in 2015
(First published in Great Britain by Andrew Jennings in 2014)

www.randomhouse.co.uk

A CIP catalogue record for this book is
available from the British Library.

ISBN 9781780895420

Printed and bound by Clays Ltd, St Ives PLC

MIX
Paper from
responsible sources
FSC® C018179

Penguin Random House is committed to a sustainable future
for our business, our readers and our planet. This book is made
from Forest Stewardship Council® certified paper

As always, for the fans . . . and the bears

'Sweet songs never last too long on broken radios'

John Prine, 'Sam Stone', 1971

Contents

This is the updated and refreshed version of *Omertà*, published as an ebook in April 2014 by the author and in Portuguese in Brazil.

Foreword by Románio

 CÂMARA DOS DEPUTADOS
Deputado Federal **Románio** - PSB/RJ

Most reporters do not have the courage of Andrew Jennings. He has the ability and willingness to put what is true on the page, the radio, the Internet and television.

Andrew is one of the guys within journalism for whom I have 100% respect. For all he has done in the fight against FIFA, in publishing his articles and books.

Glad to know that my work here in Congress for which he has provided me with material, has been very positive, I thank him and ask him to keep sending things to me.

Here I am not an Andrew Jennings, but I'm Románio!

I have guts like him and a lot of courage.

Románio de Souza Faria
Former player and congressman

Introduction

May 27, 2015, 6 am. knock . . . knock. 'Please get your clothes on and come out with your hands up . . . Sir.' Seven overfed FIFA executives are being taken from their beds in one of the world's most luxurious hotels, paid for by football, to concrete cells at a Zurich police station, provided by Swiss taxpayers. Hands up? Who knows for sure? FIFA's leaders are not acquainted with obeying laws, anybody's laws. Policemen must be careful.

I knew it was going to happen one day but the FBI wouldn't tell me when they would pounce. More than three years earlier I had handed them the crucial FIFA documents that resulted in the dawn raid on the Baur au Lac hotel. I had to be patient. Very patient.

I knew that the evidence collected by the FBI's New York-based Eurasian Organised Crime squad was being evaluated by the Justice Department in Washington and chewed over by a Grand Jury in Eastern New York. The Brooklyn US Attorney, Ms Loretta Lynch, supervised the secret investigations over the years as they expanded around the world.

The evidence I gave the FBI in August 2011 revealed that Chuck Blazer, an American member of FIFA's leadership cabal living in fabulous opulence in Trump Tower, was stealing millions of dollars every year from FIFA and regional football. He had 'disappeared' himself offshore to avoid paying tax. I discovered he hid his wealth in Caribbean tax havens. The FBI shared my confidential documents with the American tax authorities and, soon afterwards, the grotesquely obese Blazer was arrested in Manhattan riding his mobility scooter.

Days later, Blazer, facing the rest of his life in jail, capitulated and turned state witness, implicating dozens of other FIFA crooks also involved in soliciting bribes to grant marketing and TV rights for their football tournaments.

Blazer was shipped to the London Olympics where he secretly recorded selected FIFA officials and associated low-lifes. One plea-bargained and repaid a staggering $151 million he had siphoned off in kickbacks and skimming contracts. He agreed to wear a wire and entrapped several more prominent FIFA officials, some later arrested in Zurich.

More than a year before I gave them Blazer's documents the Feds had approached me asking for help identifying some of the FIFA crooks. They had seen my TV documentaries and read my first book exposing FIFA racketeering. They knew that I knew a lot and had deep sources in FIFA's darknesses. They appeared to be investigating a money-laundering syndicate.

SHOULD A REPORTER ASSIST THE FBI? It was a no-brainer. European police forces had closed their eyes to the huge amount of evidence that I had already published and shown on TV. I was shunned by British football officials who preferred their privileges, gratefully accepted from President Blatter.

Unexpectedly, I was invited to London by a trusted intermediary to meet what turned out to be FBI Special Agents and Department of Justice officials targeting organised crime. They looked like they could do the job avoided by all other law enforcement, especially in Switzerland.

As I read the drop-dead, 164-page criminal indictment made public by the Justice Department after the Zurich raid I realise that it was my evidence that produced the FIFA cataclysm, the story *du jour* world-wide.

America's new Attorney-General in Washington, only in the post for a month, was none other than Loretta Lynch, who had supervised for years the investigation in New York of FIFA criminality. She announced, 'They were expected to uphold the rules that keep soccer honest. Instead they corrupted the business of worldwide soccer to serve their interests and enrich themselves.' If that wasn't worrying enough for FIFA officials cowering in Zurich and worldwide, she went on, 'This Department of Justice is determined to end these practices, to root out corruption and to bring wrongdoers to justice.'

Ouch!

The officials arrested – and those fearing arrest – will take time to comprehend they have done anything wrong. Bribes and contract kickbacks have been business as usual since the mobbed-up João Havelange arrived as new president of FIFA in 1974. The world's most popular sport has been controlled, increasingly, from the very top by lowlifes with no discernible morality, many wearing impressive FIFA blazers.

The rest of the world of sport, locked outside FIFA's glass palace on a hill above Zurich, could smell the rottenness and booed President Blatter when he dared appear in public. But we didn't know the dirty details. They did, they looked at each other and admired fellow thieves and corrupters, surrounded by a sprinkling of naïfs enjoying an extraordinary lifestyle provided by Havelange and Blatter to keep them obedient. Few are thin men, the majority gorged for decades on lobster, caviar and fine wines.

They came to think that ripping off the game was their God-given prerogative, together with the big leather seats at the front of the plane, the limos, the company of presidents, prime ministers and monarchs. Sometimes, really, being showered with rose petals by little children in India, garlanded with flowers elsewhere by beautiful young women and later in the day, any sexual activities they preferred.

When they face their shaving mirrors today they see victims, persecuted by American imperialism and people lacking class – think of journalists. Their lawyers will explain to them, wearily, that their bribes in US dollars were cleared through the New York banks, automatically triggering a host of indictable crimes.

In the decade I covered police corruption in London I spent time with many major criminals, bank robbers and varied gunmen. They bribed detectives to stay out of jail. They despised them and admired honest officers.

Theirs was a skilled and dangerous occupation, they would tell me, proudly, 'Andrew, I am a professional criminal.' They were more honest than these self-deceiving pimps in FIFA blazers prostituting an honest game for their own enrichment.

Havelange encouraged the corruption and Blatter allowed it to continue. Fat men don't lead palace coups, they exploit the exclusive licence to get fatter. Blatter, in his older years demented by power, failed to keep control. John Gotti would have shot one Executive Committee member a year, to encourage discipline.

IT WENT TERMINALLY WRONG on December 2, 2010. Blatter should have instructed his fellow deviants, gathered at the FIFA table to decide which countries should be granted the World Cups of 2018 and 2022; 'Whoever is bribing you, take their money, as usual. But we cannot go to Qatar. Too hot in the summer and no way can we risk the rage of the fans, the clubs, the TV networks – and the endless sight of coffins being shipped out to Nepal.

'Same with Russia. If the oil price does not hold up and Putin's dream of rebuilding the Soviet empire triggers financial collapse, he cannot afford a World Cup in 2018. They will renege on promised stadiums, hotels and airports. Fans won't want to risk travelling beyond Moscow.'

But Blatter was lethargic, too busy admiring himself in his mirror, enjoying the bliss of homage from a past US president and a future British king.

He permitted his bloodsuckers to lump their votes for two World Cups together, to double the bribes while they were still breathing, fatally over reaching themselves. Arrogant, greedy, confident they were untouchable, they cast votes that would inevitably blow up in theirs and the face of football.

It has taken a long time, maybe too long in one reporter's working life. I am not quick, I am slow and methodical; it took a while in the early years observing these creeps to figure their dirty game. This is it:

Sport generates passion; passion generates money; that money and the officials controlling it are never regulated; organised crime fills the vacuum; fraudsters privatise the sport, selling it to the global brands through their porous marketing companies.

Barefoot kids continue to play without boots or showers or decent kit. The money has gone, sometimes to Cayman, sometimes to Vaduz, removed, surgically.

'MR JENNINGS, you must feel very vindicated' enquired the battalion of foreign film crews when I pitched up in Zurich with my BBC team after the arrests. Yes indeed. Other praise came from Chuck Blazer. As reporters should, I sent him questions in 2011, giving him right of reply to the story I would publish about his rackets.

'You are useless as a journalist,' Blazer fired off from Trump Tower at 16:57:21 on July 17, 2011. I published, then called the Feds.

I have reported from war zones in the Middle East, Chechnya, Central America and London pubs where some drinkers habitually carry guns or knives. I know quivering fear. When FIFA's lowlifes are sent to intimidate me, it is only irritating.

*

'HORNY HOUSEWIVES: Click to unsubscribe.' Engage with those gyrating breasts… and watch your computer die. My morning routine when checking the emails is to erase the invitations from startlingly attractive young women to enjoy their photos and maybe more. They are but a click away. There was a phase of authentic-looking BBC and CNN News Alerts with exclusives like 'British Government Secretly finances ISIS' – direct from the well-paid mittel-European trolls. 'Click for more.' No thanks.

One particular FIFA lowlife became so irritated by my blog that he paid for it to be hit by massive DDoS attacks that, at their peak, froze a substantial chunk of the UK's web traffic and affected up to half of all the Internet traffic coming into the UK. My forensic people determined the attack had been mounted from Russia, Belarus, Ukraine and China. Did FIFA pay? I will ask the Swiss cops. to look deeper into FIFA's invoices and payments.

Before FIFA my previous big sports investigation was corruption at the International Olympic Committee. It took a decade to expose the structural venality at the IOC and reveal it was led by a life-time fascist – Juan Antonio Samaranch – who thought the wrong team won World War Two. Their institutionalised dishonesty was exposed to daylight in the 1999 cash-and-sex-for-votes scandal of how Salt Lake City won the 2002 Winter Games.

No IOC members were arrested, a few nonentities sacrificed and a big-hitting New York PR company brought in to swamp reporters with claims of reform that are now hard to detect. They got away with it.

*

BUT IT IS ALL OVER for the slimy puddle that is what's left of FIFA. The investigations multiply and the Feds have promised more arrests, some may be spectacular. We have had enough of Blatter's highly-paid 'independent investigators' and 'compliance' operators producing reports that he can never publish — mainly because there is little in them. Publication would reveal their uselessness. They twist in the wind to entrance reporters, believing that one day, stark truths will be revealed. Dreaming. They already have been.

Football needs to abandon Blatter's posh palace above Zurich with its unsupportable window cleaning bills. The Swiss cops are rushing to do the job they avoided for 30 years. But it's too late for the rump of officials and 'strategic advisors' to be allowed to re-arrange the boardroom chairs, shred the secret documents listing Blatter's vast 'salary', bonuses, allowances and first-class flights for his girlfriends, then claim all is 'reformed.' And get back into the big leather seats, well protected from the sweaty fans in the back of the plane.

Blatter's authoritarian rule that players, clubs, fans or national associations that go to civil law against his outlaw kingdom will be suspended can be stuffed where the sun don't shine. Protecting the People's Game desperately needs the People's tax payer funded cops and auditors keeping watch. Not sons of Blatter.

On his way to obscurity Blatter can repay from his FIFA pension pot the $29 million that he spent on his hagiography *United Passions*, the worst film ever screened. He may not need a pension where he is going.

Up with the crates of archives, down from the hill to the airport and never go back. Where the plane should land can wait. Meanwhile the fans and smaller clubs need to have national, regional, continental conferences to debate a new, flat constitution that genuinely empowers the grassroots. Who pays? Coca-Cola, McDonalds, VISA and Adidas talk the moral talk. Now they can prove it. They can also pay for uploading every document in the archives. Our citizens have wrested online transparency and Freedom of Information from our governments: It's football's turn. Clubs, national associations and what used to be FIFA, salaries, travel and hotel expenses and per diems. All meetings streamed on the Internet. No hiding places any more. Total transparency. And anything else we can think of.

A new organisation, maybe provisionally called World Football Union, will restore to me the right to attend football's press conferences, taken away by Blatter in 2003 because I knew too much. There could be trouble with the acronym so we must work on it.

Thanks to the BBC's *Panorama* programme, a popular fortnightly magazine in the UK, the producers at ZDF and ARD in Germany, NPR and PBS and CBS Sixty Minutes in America and supportive media in Brazil when the kids needed new shoes.

Now, come with me to meet the Mafia in Palermo, the Rio mobsters who taught João Havelange the arts of fraud and embezzlement, milking the game, and the current gang whose corruption finally gave us the chance us to take our ball home.

Andrew Jennings,
Cumbria, August 2015

Prologue:

In Palermo – learning about the Mafia

Palermo, February 1987: We are in an orange grove outside the city, filming a small industrial building. It is deserted now but until recently was a juice pressing plant. According to claims filed with a subsidy department of the European Union, it was the busiest orange juice pressing plant in the world.

The Mob used it to submit massive fraudulent demands for subsidy on orange juice that had never existed. They bribed and intimidated officials to rubber-stamp their claims – and stole millions of dollars. The scam ended, the mobsters escaped. But this is Sicily and they are everywhere, watching.

A big black saloon car with black tinted windows pulls up alongside me and my film crew. A bulky man emerges and walks towards me. Gesturing over his shoulder at an invisible but obviously important person behind the tinted windows he announces, sharply, 'E says you no film 'ere.'

I pretend not to understand, it gives my cameraman time to grab a few more exterior shots of the disused building. As the guy's eyes began to bulge with anger I grab his hand, shake it firmly, say *'Arrivederci,'* and shout to the crew, 'Time to go!'

It wasn't a good day. Earlier we had driven up to the little town of Altofonte, in the hills above Palermo. We knew it was the home of a Mafia boss who was now their top man in London. The streets were narrow, the high, blank walls closing in on both sides of our rental car. We took a blind turn, swung hard left into another narrow lane – and were faced by four black horses with black plumes on their heads. Oh no! A funeral. We found space to slide by the horses and the glass hearse. We avoided the scowls, didn't dare catch the eye of anybody in the column of mourners walking behind. Without delay, we found another road out of town.

One evening later that week we were escorted by armed police through concrete corridors and thick, blast-proof steel doors in a labyrinth beneath the Palace of Justice in Palermo. Eventually we arrived at the tiny office of Investigating Magistrate Giovanni Falcone. A jovial man whose successes against the Mafia had made him their top target, he took time away from the intelligence reports he was studying, produced a bottle of Scotch whisky and entertained us with information about the gangsters we were investigating.

Five years later the Mob got Falcone and his wife. His car disintegrated when half a ton of explosives was detonated in a culvert under an autoroute from the airport to Palermo.

I completed the film, revealing how the Mafia laundered

millions of dollars from heroin sales in America through banks in the City of London, onward to Bellinzona in Switzerland and finally to Italy. Afterwards, I wanted to know more about how the Mafia operated. I studied essays and reports by senior policemen and criminologists examining the definitions and structures of organised crime syndicates. This became essential preparation for investigating the international sports federations.

I sniffed around FIFA in the 1990s and from 2000 began to focus on Blatter and Havelange. Soon I realised that I was back in the dark ethos of Sicily and the criminal culture of *Omertà* – but transferred to another continent. I travelled further back in time, researching and reading and arrived in Bangu 50 years ago. From the world of the *bicheiros* I travelled back to Europe and discovered secret suitcases of gold ingots collected in Zurich. Following them completed the circle back to Copacabana and the World Cup of 2014.

1

Welcome to Rio

Havelange's gangster friends cannot stop killing

April 8, 2010, Avenue of the Americas, Rio de Janeiro:
BOOM! The Toyota Corolla is armoured to repel bullets but the extra gauge steel in the doors doesn't protect the teenage driver from the bomb strapped under his seat. The armed bodyguards in the two cars behind can only mourn 17-year-old Diogo Andrade who was whacked. They may never find all of him.

His dad, Rogério, sitting in the passenger seat, escapes with a broken nose. Later, in a hospital bed in Barra D'Or, he begins plotting revenge. He knows who ordered the bomb. But how did his security team fail to spot it?

Shocked drivers, backed up behind the wreckage along the boulevard in Barra da Tijuca, running parallel to the glittering beaches, get out to watch police and paramedics in the bright morning sunshine wearing rubber gloves collect the body parts they can find in the gutter. They gawp at the tangle of smoking Corolla wreckage and another car destroyed – caught in the blast. It's those gang wars. Will they never stop?

It's the spring of 2010, the contractors and their powerful friends are shaking down the taxpayers with extravagant plans for remodelling the Maracanã, reducing the popular seating to make space for a necklace of hospitality boxes that only the international high-rollers can afford.

Welcome to Rio, where the white collar gangsters are battling, employing lawyers and politicians as their weapons, over the wealth the World Cup and the Olympics could provide. More visible – on the Avenue of the Americas – is another of Rio's turf battles, a divided mafia family snarling over the city's numbers rackets, the slots and the white powder trade.

Forget the small-time drug dealers in the hillside *favelas* with the best views over the ocean, exchanging bullets with the Federal police and the army, ethnic cleansers clearing the way for the arrival of the hotel chains. Land is one of the most precious commodities in town and if homes have to be bulldozed, that's what you do to build a first-world economy – the profits banked in the Caribbean.

These killers down on the boulevard are longtime members of another city elite, celebrated in the media and the sports world, protected by corrupt police and politicians.

THE ECHOES of the blast bounce back from the hills. Does the Redeemer shed a tear for the lost boy from the summit of Corcovado Mountain? João Havelange resting in his elegant apartment shudders. This vulgar violence is unnecessary.

Hadn't he done everything for the Andrade family? Put Rio's Godfather in charge of the national team? Given him football prestige? Tried to warn off the anti-mafia cops. When that damn woman judge refused to be intimidated, visited him in jail?

His old friend Castor, great-uncle to the dead boy, had kept the town tight. Minimal murdering. Paid for Carnival for the Rio masses. At the same time the patrician Havelange was learning how to create a global crime family without a death, even a broken leg. Money was the grease, supplied by the global brands and the world's TV networks, competing to get a slice of the commodity he controlled.

ELSEWHERE in the city Romário is talking with officials from the *Partido Socialista Brasileiro*. He wants to evict Ricardo Teixeira, longtime president of the Brazilian Football Confederation, and his corrupt cabal who have dominated and robbed the Brazilian game for decades. One way would be to run for Congress in six months' time. Politicians have power. And there's little Ivy, his darling five-year old Down's daughter. Romário has discovered first hand how little his country provides for the disabled. Some weekends he plays in benefits in small towns across the land raising funds for facilities.

Brazil's football bosses laugh behind their hands. Romário? He's another playboy star. He's hung up his boots. His striker days are over. What kind of threat can this child of the favelas be to them, men of power, wealth and with a squad of obedient politicians on their payroll?

In São Paulo José Maria Marin, once the darling of the military dictatorship along with his companion in crime, Paulo Maluf, perhaps the most gross thief of the Brazilian people's money, is now a vice-president of Brazilian football. All is well, the people have long forgotten how he helped set the scenario for courageous reporter Vladimir Herzog to be tortured to death. And if 'Tricky Ricky' Teixeira has to emigrate abruptly, in the familiar Latin American way, to one of his lovely homes in Florida, José Maria will replace him at the honeypot.

THE ROAR of the death blast on the Avenue of the Americas cannot be heard in faraway Johannesburg. With eight weeks to go to the opening game in Soccer City, Sepp Blatter and his South African capos have enough problems. Outraged by price gouging, fans are staying home. In the townships citizens protest every day; 'service riots' send messages to politicians that public money should be spent on homes, water, sewage plants and jobs, not stadiums that will become white elephants. Why should they listen? They have the police beat back the protestors.

The World Cup is good news for Danny Jordaan, leader of the bid and now chief executive for the tournament. Quietly, his brother Andrew has been given a well-paid job as hospitality liaison with MATCH Event Services at the Port Elizabeth stadium. A stakeholder in the MATCH company is Sepp Blatter's nephew Philippe Blatter. The majority owners are Mexican brothers Jamie and Enrique Byrom, based in Manchester, England, Zurich, Switzerland and with some of their bank accounts in Spain and the Isle of Man.

The Brothers are not happy. They won from FIFA in a tender the lucrative 2010 hospitality contract aimed at wealthy football patrons, mostly from abroad. If that wasn't enough, they also won the ticketing contract to manage and distribute the three million tickets. The brothers are charging top rates for hotels and internal flights and expected to make huge profits. Instead, they are on their way to losing $50 million. They plan to recoup these losses in Brazil in four years time.

THE ZURICH LAWYERS have earned their fees. In a few weeks it will be made public that the criminal investigation into the FIFA officials who took kickbacks on World Cup marketing contracts from the ISL company is closed. The lawyers have achieved a great deal; the names will be kept secret forever. A little money will be repaid. Case closed. Were Brazilians involved? No comment. And you, Herr Blatter? No comment.

The FIFA president had been worried that the cops would publish the evidence that back in March 1997 he knew about a $1 million bribe destined for Havelange. That bastard British reporter had been tipped off. But if the story surfaced again the president would hire his own investigators and have himself acquitted. Later in the year one of the Swiss detectives takes the British reporter for dinner at a restaurant overlooking a lake. 'Don't give up,' he says.

THE FIFA PRESIDENT is demonstrably depressed. Is his reign coming to an end? In February he grants an interview to a woman reporter from the Cairo paper *Al-Ahram*. Suddenly, he launches into a grandiose list of his achievements. Sounds like his obituary. Because she was a well-informed Arab, Blatter cannot hold back.

'With Mohamed, we had a wonderful time together as friends up to the last congress in May,' says Blatter. 'All of a sudden our friendship was broken. Ask him, why? I don't know.'

Not true. Blatter does know. Mohamed, the reporter knows, is Mohamed Bin Hammam from Qatar. For twelve years he has provided the cash to buy the votes to keep Blatter on the president's throne. Now he wants the job for himself. He can raise more cash than Blatter and will win. The election will be in a year's time and even as poor young Diogo is blown apart, Mohamed is assembling his bags of cash and brown envelopes. Yes, he really does put his bribes in brown paper envelopes. Next year somebody will photograph one.

THE GREEDY OLD MEN at FIFA don't hear the blast. They listen only for the rustle of greenbacks. This year, 2010, is going to be their richest. Four months after the World Cup they will decide which country gets to host the World Cup in 2018. Worried that they may not live to pocket more bribes in another four years, when they have to choose a host for 2022, they announce they will vote for both tournaments in December this year. Christmas presents, twice.

Look at the bidders! Putin wants it badly for Russia. The *jalabiyas* of Qatar want it. Two of the richest petro-dollar states in the world, begging. Wow! Bliss! Ricardo Teixeira has a smile on his face all year. Across the border, in Asunción, the president of Conmebol Nicolás Leoz smells money – and more. He co-existed easily with the vile Stroessner, he's been extracting bribes from football forever. He doesn't yet know that his thieving will feature on British TV in seven months.

The Nigerian vacuum cleaner Amos Adamu has been a member of FIFA's 24-man ruling executive for four years. He passed the test to join FIFA with ease; he stole every penny he could find in Nigerian sport. He still hasn't delivered the accounts for the All-Africa Games in Abuja in 2003. When the good times roll his son Samson will doubtless get a share.

Across the continent, in Cairo, Africa's football leader Issa Hayatou isn't getting any poorer. Later in the year one payment will be pinned on him by the BBC. There are so many of FIFA's leaders to wonder about but evidence is hard to get. Frequently under fire is Thailand's Worawi Makudi. The accusations roll in, Worawi rolls them away, his fellow leaders circle the wagons.

Six months ago João Havelange, the most senior member of the IOC, led the Rio delegation to Copenhagen to bid for the 2016 Olympics. They will not cost much because only two years ago the city staged the Pan American Games and the bidding team insist that venues need only a coat of paint to be ready for the Olympics.

Brazilian IOC member Carlos Nuzman was nominally the bid leader but Havelange was accompanied by Jean-Marie Weber, The Bagman, the marketing company manager who suitcased $100 million of bribes to sports officials – including

Havelange – in the last century. President Obama spoke up for Chicago. Weber talked to his old friends at the IOC – and that was that.

A VOLLEY of rifle shots dispatched Antônio Carlos Macedo as he rode his Harley-Davidson through Rio. He had been Rogério Andrade's head of security and was gunned down in late 2010, a month before the vote for the 2018 and 2022 World Cups. Rogério decided he had planted the bomb that detached his son's limbs. The Andrade family has been killing each other since Havelange's mentor, Castor, died of an apparent heart attack in 1997. His son Paulinho, who expected to inherit most of the crime empire, was executed, supposedly by Rogério, a year later. Several more gangsters have been eliminated but the city is unlikely to be as stable again as the years when Castor and João ruled.

2

Best of Friends

The crime boss and the boss of world football

It is Rio's wedding of the year. The father of the bride is Brazil's biggest gangster, racketeer and, they say, murderer of 50 rivals. He stays out of jail by paying off the city's politicians, judges and police. He owns a football club. The two most honoured guests sit at his table. I'm looking at a photograph taken at the wedding banquet. One guest, to the right of frame, is tall, avuncular with a Roman nose and has the hardest eyes in the room. It's João and he controls world football.

Between João and the gangster sits his son-in-law, the young man who in a few years time will become boss of Brazilian football. Young Ricardo is beaming, exuberant, confident in the company of the gangster. Behind them stand two men, watchful, protective, not smiling. This photograph reveals how world football came under the control of organised crime.

*

MY PEOPLE, WELCOME TO CARNIVAL! Dressed in shimmering white suit, shoes, socks – Castor Andrade goes down on one knee in the middle of the Sambódromo, raises his arms in triumphant salute and beams at the adoring crowds in the stands. His commanding presence says, 'I bring you Carnival.'

And he does. The gangster is patron of the samba school that won the Rio Carnival title in 1979, 1985, 1990, 1991, and again in 1996 when he was out of jail, the year before he died. He has taken control of the Carnival business in Rio, creating the *Liga Independente das Escolas de Samba do Rio de Janeiro*, publicly soaking up government grants and, privately, a vehicle for laundering dirty money.

Castor completed his legal examinations in the early 1960s but joined the rackets founded by his grandmother and his father and never practised law. He lets it be known that he is a good Catholic, making acts of devotion to Our Lady of Aparecida.

At the Carnival in 1993, he uses the occasion to shout an angry speech about what he called, 'the persecution of the *bicheiros*.' It was a mistake to flaunt his years of immunity. He was pushing his luck, taunting the special prosecutor investigating him.

That's how Castor Andrade, the host at the wedding party, makes his millions, so liberally dispensed across the city. He runs the numbers rackets and the slots. Rumour says he plays in the white powder trade, that he is linked to Colombian, Italian and Israeli gangsters.

In 1964 the generals roll their tanks onto the streets of Rio to govern Brazil for another 21 years. They leave Castor alone to operate his criminal networks. The General in charge of the Rio police is instructed to 'avoid problems with Castor de Andrade.'

He's big all over Brazil. His friendship with the Big Man at his table at the wedding banquet opens the door to high office in the nation's sport. Two years after the military coup Castor is bringing the dictatorship acclaim, leading the *seleção* to victory in the O'Higgins Cup in Chile and a year later at the Rio Branco Cup in Uruguay. He receives honours from the football federations of the states of Rio de Janeiro and Minas Gerais.

At the heart of football in Rio he is patron of the Bangu club, handing out bundles of cash to the team. Under his leadership, the club has a special asset, a man to be feared by referees. In a game against America at the Maracanã, he runs onto the pitch waving a revolver at the officials. Bangu are tying 2-2 but a surprise penalty decision gives them victory. Years later there is still a bronze bust of him in the Bangu lobby with the trophies he helped them win.

CASTOR IS PLAYING games again. He's accepted an invitation to be a guest on Jô Soares' top-rated TV chat show. It is 1991 and the investigators are getting nowhere. So let's give them the finger, on network television. His vanity can't resist the invitation to sit in the chair where we've seen the most important personalities, politicians, artists and celebrities. Soares doesn't shy away from the question viewers want asked.

'What is the connection between your family and the *Jogo do Bicho* business? How did it all get started?' Castor doesn't duck. Remember, he went to college, he is fluent when he lies, his Portuguese language is elegant, his voice soft and sweet.

'My grandmother, a widow, lived in Fonseca Street, in the Rio suburbs. To help run the house, she took bets from *Jogo do Bicho*. My father was a train driver. After he married my mother, her family influenced him to enter the *Jogo do Bicho* business.'

Castor continues. 'But this was in the past. Today, there is no connection.' The audience laughs. Jô Soares laughs. Castor laughs. Everybody knows Castor is boss of the *Jogo do Bicho*. Everybody knows that, behind his respectable performance, sits a murderer and lifelong criminal.

He spoke about soccer and then, another of his jokes, he was chilling. Apparently a robber had broken into Castor's home. 'He was in the right place for jewellery and money. But, once they realised I lived there, they decided to leave immediately, scared,' he laughed, calmly.

'PLEASE PROTECT ME. Andrade will kill me. I'll tell you everything.' The honest detectives have found an informant. One of Castor's gang has walked through the door. He has pocketed gambling bets he should have handed over to the Boss. He's in trouble and only they can help him.

He gives the cops a valuable insight into Castor Andrade's gambling empire. It's a variation of the numbers racket – and Castor controls the numbers. The *Jogo do Bicho*, the animal game, is illegal but it's a tradition and while it stayed small, it was tolerated. Just a part of Rio's vibrant street life.

His grandmother Iaiá ran the games with her son Euzébio de Andrade Silva. Their racket was one of many scattered across the city. Punters select from a sheet of animal images – dogs, deer, many more – and bet on their favourites. Birthdays, superstition, everybody believes that one animal is their lucky one. The *bicho* operator makes the draw, in private, and the results are pasted on trees and lamp posts. The cops look away.

The informant keeps talking, lifting the curtain. Castor inherited the family rackets and went to work with his uncles. Violently, they eliminate their rivals, taking over more and more *pontos* on the street corners where the bets are collected. Castor's son Paulo joined the gang and in time they controlled the gambling in nine of the city's suburbs. The streets echo with the roar of motorcycle couriers collecting the cash and the betting slips.

The money is pouring in. Castor expands. He invests in slot machines and video games. He trades guns. His metal workshop does favours for the generals when their military vehicles break down. He owns gas stations and a second-hand car business.

The informant knows that Castor has bought fishing boats. They must be for bringing in the white powder from the north. There's a Sicilian mobster hiding in Castor's textile factory in Bangu. The police are filling their notebooks.

Castor smokes the biggest cigars. In public he is the good family man, married and faithful to Wilma. But we all know, don't ever speak it, Castor has mistresses in apartments around the city.

The informant doesn't know how widely Castor spreads his money. But they never have any trouble from the police. And then he goes off, back to the streets. He has discovered that Castor didn't notice the missing money.

But he has said enough.

ALL SEEMS QUIET so the man with the Uzi who protects the piles of cash steps outside to take lunch. In the rundown suburb of Bangu, the streets are full of shoppers buying bread and coffee.

Discreetly, the cops, six teams of them, sweating and nervous, climb out of their unmarked cars, make their move to the target house in Fonseca street. It is late March 1994. Every day Castor pays off police officers to protect his motorcycle couriers collecting the bets of thousands of *Cariocas*, gambling on corners, avenues and meeting places all over the city. But these visitors are different.

Mrs Rosana, Castor's secretary, hears the knocking, looks through the spyhole. She doesn't recognize the officers waiting at the door. Somebody says, 'They are not our cops.'

Castor skips out of the back door. He's gone. But look what he's left behind. The rows of tables, lined by men and women counting the cash. And the books. Here's the gangster's secret world of power and influence.

An urgent call to headquarters to Marcos Paes, in charge of this Military Police Special Operations team. He is told, 'We've found two ledger books.' He orders, 'Nobody moves, nobody touches them but me.'

'I was shocked when I saw who was being paid off by

Andrade,' remembers Paes, now chief of security at Rio's Legislative House. 'There were police officers I knew and worked with, prosecutors, judges, and important politicians. We knew they corrupted people. But we could not have imagined how far Castor reached.'

There's one name on the lists that everybody knows. He's known worldwide. The generous Castor, king of the Carnival, has presented the boss of world football with a special box to view the Carnival. Cost: $17,640. It was becoming a way of life for João Havelange: taking secret payments from shady characters in return for favours.

'I HAD ARMED GUARDS for years. It was very dangerous to investigate the *Jogo do Bicho*. Death threats were common, to me, to my family,' says Antonio Biscaia, the prosecutor commanding the investigation. The Andrade family were Rio's first mafia gang, he says.

'One evening, as I was leaving a restaurant, a car with four men in it raced up and fired 15–20 shots. My guards threw me to the ground and I was unhurt. The gunmen got away.

'We had to do everything in secret because we knew about the involvement of the police and other levels of power with Castor. Not a lot of people were willing to arrest Andrade.'

The books are taken to Biscaia's office. He makes two copies, they are locked in a safe. In the middle of the night, Biscaia receives a phone call: some officers just tried to break in and steal the books. Immediately, he moves them.

Twenty years later we meet him at his office in downtown Rio. A serious man of average size, short grey hair, rimless glasses, he smiles at some of his memories. Sparingly, he tells what he found in the ledgers. Yes, of course there was Havelange. And endless names and deals.

Castor records the financial transactions of his mafia family and associates, name after name, deal after deal. And what an insight into how Rio really works! Castor's is a life of social and important connections. Politicians, police, prosecutors, judges, governors, football officials, everybody benefiting from his rackets.

Biscaia ponders every question, cautiously. 'It was scary, really,' he remembers. The prosecutor closes his eyes to recall the details from those days. He doesn't stretch to long phrases.

Investigating *Jogo do Bicho* at that time was 'difficult,' he puts it. 'There was always something to discourage you. Castor's reach extended throughout the power circles. He was dangerous. He had this image of the guy next door, but he was an assassin, he would do everything to expand and continue to lead the mafia.' Again, Biscaia closes his eyes. There's more to tell.

João Havelange didn't only take from Castor Andrade; as we will see, he gave back.

'AS FAR AS I KNOW, Castor's people tried to kill me three times. It was scary to know how close they got to me and my family.' Denise Frossard was the judge who could not be bought. In 1993, she jailed Castor.

At the end of a sunny winter day Denise, dressed in gym clothes, meets me at the door of her house. She leads me to her second-floor office. She offers water and coffee, and I take the blue coffee capsule of a Nespresso machine. Then we face each other across a glass table.

'This guy was seen with important officers, with personalities and even with politicians. This sends a clear message to everybody else: look, I'm powerful, I have connections.'

For her, Castor's *bon vivant* image was just another way of doing business. 'I studied his personality carefully. He wasn't a soccer lover, a Carnival lover. He was pragmatic. The connections to these cultural icons were useful for him – and that's it. It was just business, nothing else. He was a dangerous criminal.'

Denise, just over five feet tall, cannot sit still. She constantly moves her feet under the table and kneads a paper ball with her fingers. Sitting on a black leather sofa, she sways from side to side, front to back and speaks quickly, mixing languages and philosophy to make her point.

Her apartment, the last in a long, uphill, cobbled stone street in an upscale neighbourhood of Rio de Janeiro, seems to have been chosen as a hiding place. She is far from Bangu. Through her window she sees a breathtaking postcard of Rio. Mountains intertwined with the sea and the sunset at the famous Lagoa Rodrigo de Freitas. Her office is spacious and tastefully decorated, her books spread along the white walls, carefully cleaned by a lady who leaves shortly after my arrival.

Denise laughs constantly during our conversation. Her eyes and face are focused on me, but every now and then she turns her attention to something outside the window. The view is indeed mesmerising, but she doesn't pay attention to anything in particular. These are the only moments where Denise seems to lose herself in thought.

Remembering the attacks at the time of the investigation and conviction of Castor de Andrade doesn't seem easy for her, even 20 years later. 'It was hard, very difficult,' she breathes slowly and touches her forehead as if it was possible to erase the episode from her past. This is the only vulnerable moment of this 63-year-old Federal judge. Born in the state of Minas Gerais, she moved to Rio in 1970. 'You know, they, Castor and his colleagues, were not playing, they were not here for fun. Never have been. They were dangerous.'

Denise highlights that 'part of the respect he got from the other criminals was because of the image he had of acceptance by the powerful.' Accusations of homicide and torture against him are common, but never proved and, you may suspect, never investigated.

Before giving me a ride back home, she reinforces the image of Castor as a violent man. 'There was no passion, there was no compassion when we speak of the heads of *Jogo do Bicho*. It was all business: carnival, football, religion, everything was built; all of Castor's social relations in these environments were built with the goal of raising money, power and influence. Nothing was passion there. Castor was a cold, pragmatic and cruel person.'

THE DEFIANT SPEECH that Castor delivered at the Sambódromo in early 1993, attacking 'the persecution of the *bicheiros*' was a fatal mistake. He could not be allowed to get away with it any longer. His immunity must be ended. The investigations gained pace.

Later in 1993 Castor Andrade is brought before Judge

Denise Frossard. She jails him for six years along with two of his capos and his son-in-law Fernando Iggnácio.

Castor's account books and ledgers are made public. The list of pay-offs astounds. Among them, former president Fernando Collor de Mello, Rio governor Nilo Batista, Rio mayor Cesar Maia, seven businessmen, three judges, 12 congressmen and seven assemblymen, 25 police commissioners and 100 police officers.

Further afield there's São Paulo mayor and colossal thief of public money Paulo Maluf. His close associate fellow São Paulo politician, José Maria Marin of the pro-military Arena party, will one day replace the disgraced Teixeira at the top of Brazilian football. Nothing seems to change in Brazilian football.

'CASTOR DE ANDRADE is respected and admired by his friends, for his education, his politeness and his accomplishments. I also know that Castor de Andrade provides selfless services to many philanthropic entities protecting underprivileged children in Bangu and to organisations assisting paraplegics.'

This astonishing letter, 'To Whom it May Concern,' was found attached to Castor's criminal file, planted by corrupt policemen. It was written for him six years earlier by João Havelange, world-famous boss of FIFA, when Castor was coming under scrutiny by Rio prosecutors. It's a year after the wedding banquet, the cops are sniffing and Havelange's letter is his best attempt to protect his gangster associate.

'I authorise Castor de Andrade to use this declaration at his convenience. Castor de Andrade, controversial man of great character is a loveable person, who is pleasant to be around and who knows how to win over friends through one of his predominant personal qualities: his loyalty.

'This I have noted during more than 30 years, many times in the fierce competitive struggles in the sport governing bodies. Castor de Andrade is a good head of family, a dedicated friend, is admired as a sporting and "samba school" director. Furthermore he is a self-sacrificing protector of the associations of senior citizen homes and of under-age children in need.'

Havelange's begging letter lists Castor's achievements in football and his services to his country. Havelange stresses, 'I am president of FIFA and Castor is a recognisable figure of this sport in Rio.' The signal is clear; Havelange is a powerful world figure – don't mess with his friend.

He continues, 'Those who attack Castor are perhaps ignoring these positive traits of his personality.

'I've known Castor Gonçalves de Andrade Silva for more than 30 years. Before that, I knew and was a friend of his father, Euzébio de Andrade Silva. I can give a testament that portrays him in many aspects of his life. I know he is married to Mrs Wilma de Andrade Silva for almost 40 years and they have two children: Paulo Roberto, a 36-year-old civil engineer and Carmen Lucia, 21, in her third year studying Law at Estácio de Sá University. Castor and Mrs Wilma have three grandchildren.

'I authorise Castor de Andrade to use this declaration at his convenience.'

João Havelange, Rio de Janeiro, 2 October 1987

*

Did João Havelange forget his old friend and mentor Castor Andrade after he was jailed in 1993? Not at all. The President of FIFA continued to show solidarity: he visited this criminal scumbag in prison.

SINCE CASTOR'S DEATH, the fight for power and money within the clan has left a trail of blood from dozens of murders committed in the past decade in Rio. The dispute between Rogério Andrade and Fernando Iggnácio, involved at least 50 civilians and military officers. One of them was Rogério's son, 17-year-old Diogo, mistakenly killed in the bombing in 2010. Fernando Iggnácio and Rogério de Andrade are still the big chiefs of *Jogo do Bicho* all over the country. Another major mafia figure controls a large part of the Rio Carnival. Policemen again turn their eyes away from the gambling bets being collected on the street. Again, they and the politicians continue accepting bribes.

Some years before, Rogério Andrade had already ordered the assassination of his cousin, Paulinho (Castor's son), to take over his share of the *Jogo do Bicho*. 'You kill your family, friends, doesn't matter. Everything is acceptable for power. There's nothing romantic about the practice of *Jogo do Bicho*,' Denise says.

Additional research and interviews by Carolina Mazzi

3

Havelange's Golden Briefcase

Why is it so heavy when he leaves Zurich?

Zurich airport, anytime, 1974–1998. The easy thing for Rudi the chauffeur was meeting and greeting the FIFA president when his plane arrived from Paris. Havelange loved to stay a day or more in Paris on his way from Rio. Rudi packed his boss's luggage into the executive limousine, putting the small aluminium briefcase to one side. It was easy to carry. It would be different on the return journey. It would need both hands to swing it up into the car trunk.

When the president opens his case in FIFA's old offices at Sonnenberg out tumbles maybe 20 green, vacuum-sealed packs of powdered coffee, gifts for the staff. 'It tasted horrible,' recalls one FIFA official. 'It wasn't what you expected from Brazil.' Once the case was empty Havelange set off with Rudi to one of Zurich's best-known gold dealers. He was known there as 'a very good client' because every trip from

Rio to Zurich involved a trip with Rudi to fill the case with gold ingots.

'On average Havelange would spend up to $30,000 a time,' remembers a clerk. Where did the money come from? Nobody knew for sure – but Havelange was never short of big bundles of cash to hand over at the precious-metal dealers. Was he buying the gold on behalf of his gangster friends in Rio? Or was he laundering the kickbacks he extorted in Switzerland in return for handing lucrative World Cup contracts to his friends?

That little aluminium briefcase made at least five trips a year to Zurich with the FIFA President and returned home filled with ingots. How did Havelange smuggle several kilos of gold back into Brazil? Easy! He had a diplomatic passport and his luggage was never searched. His micro-managing subordinate, Sepp Blatter, must have seen everything, certainly said nothing, as he observed the criminal ways.

One of Havelange's great achievements was to conceal his criminal activities behind the aristocratic mask of a tough but benevolent gentleman. I discovered this at FIFA's congress in Seoul in 2002. By then Havelange was honorary president, replaced by his ambitious bag-carrier Sepp Blatter, a shabby bureaucrat who could never emulate Havelange's class.

I was trying to get a good photograph of Havelange as he mounted the stage from the congress floor. He saw me, stopped halfway up the steps, adopted his paternal pose and gazed down, the very figure of a charismatic captain of industry, giving me time to run off a few shots.

Havelange's tame reporters in Brazil and Europe created a legend that his extraordinary business skills made FIFA rich.

They got it totally wrong. He was lucky, arriving at the helm of international football as TV and sponsors were prepared to pay more and more money to officials like him who were happy to quietly privatise the People's Game.

The hard truth is that an honest FIFA president could have driven harder bargains with commerce. Havelange's priorities were his bribes and contract kickbacks, self-enrichment rather than the enrichment of the game. How Horst Dassler and his operatives at his International Sport and Leisure marketing company, midwives to global capital, must have laughed behind his back. Their clients would have paid more if Havelange was a true negotiator with a great product to sell. Instead, he gave it away for kickbacks.

EQUALLY DISHONEST was Havelange's public portrayal of himself as a good family man. 'I had the great fortune in 1946 to marry Anna Maria Hermanny-Havelange, and our marriage has lasted 52 years so far,' he announced in 1998. 'We had one daughter, Lúcia, and she has blessed us with three grandchildren, Ricardo, Joana and Roberto, who are our joy and our hopes for the future.'

This makes a reader uneasy. He cared so little for his daughter Lúcia that he allowed her to marry the slimy Teixeira who, in his middle years, dumped her for the much younger Anna.

Havelange proved himself world class in the pool and encouraged admiration of his Olympic exploits at swimming and water polo in 1936 and again in 1952. He was determined to be equally successful between the sheets. Havelange always honoured his dear wife, Anna Maria, at FIFA functions but every official present knew the secrets of his bed hopping.

One of his most memorable mistresses at FIFA was a beautiful tall woman, let us call her Ms Gorgeous.

In time she caught the eye of the president on one of his visits from Rio and they started an affair that would run for five years.

Ms Gorgeous was installed in a luxury apartment in Zürichberg, the most elegant suburb of Zurich, decorated with the most expensive furniture. Solid-gold gifts were showered upon her.

Havelange did not spend a lot of time in Zurich and Ms Gorgeous, bored, began entertaining a middle-ranking FIFA manager. They did little to hide their sporting activities and soon everybody in the building knew. Another of the president's functionaries became jealous and wrote an anonymous letter to the wife of the new lover of Ms Gorgeous. The decline into farce began.

In 1985 FIFA's top officials toured the Soviet Union, beginning in Moscow. Havelange took a Brazilian racehorse owner, an old friend and ally from Rio, and Abilio d'Almeida, a Brazilian member of FIFA's ruling Executive Committee – the 23-man ExCo – as guests. Briefed apparently by jealous Zurich officials, they told the president that he was not the only athlete presiding over Ms Gorgeous.

The tour took them to Azerbaijan and their hosts in Baku planned a spectacular night of food and entertainment. Havelange appeared depressed and after a few minutes he stood up, signalled to his Brazilian entourage to follow him and walked out. The evening was wrecked, the hosts were speechless and the show cancelled.

The FIFA staff soon learned that a day earlier in Minsk, Havelange had been tipped off that Ms Gorgeous was making the two-backed beast in her room with her other lover. Havelange phoned the man's room and asked if she was there. Instead of denying, he said to Havelange, 'Wait a moment, here she is.'

When the FIFA squad returned to Zurich, Havelange refused to see Ms Gorgeous and paid her off. Her lover was spared.

WRENCHING the leadership of FIFA from the ageing Englishman Sir Stanley Rous cost a lot of money. By the time Havelange had toured the world, often with the *seleção*, there was a big hole in the finances of the Brazilian Federation for Sport. He had been milking it since 1958 and by the time he left in 1974 for FIFA, the hole was reportedly $6.6 million deep.

The generals who had held power for two decades wanted to investigate Havelange for stealing the money from sport. Their dilemma was that from June 1974 he was a world figure, boss of the biggest sport. To accuse him of corruption could shame Brazil. He got away with it.

ANOTHER of Havelange's claims is that he has been an 'idealist and visionary.' He omits arms dealer from his personal and financial history. Following the collapse of the fascist Salazar dictatorship in Portugal from 1968 there was massive capital flight to Brazil. In 1994, in an extended profile of

Havelange in *Playboy*, Roberto Pereira de Souza investigated his involvement with Portuguese emigrés in shipping munitions to the brutal dictator Hugo Banzer in Bolivia. De Souza reported that the documentation had been destroyed on the order of former president Fernando Collor de Mello. In what was described as a 'shady' deal, 80,000 grenades were sold at a vastly inflated price.

Havelange skipped swiftly from one neighbouring dictator to another. The next World Cup was in the military prison that Argentina had become. Uruguayan writer Eduardo Galeano summed up, 'To the strains of a military march, General Videla pinned a medal on Havelange during the opening ceremonies in Buenos Aires's Monumental Stadium.

'A few steps away, Argentina's Auschwitz, the torture and extermination camp at the Navy School of Mechanics, was operating at full speed. A few miles beyond that, prisoners were being thrown alive from airplanes into the sea. "At last the world can see the true face of Argentina," crowed the president of FIFA to the TV cameras.'

Embracing the foul murderers in Argentina yielded Havelange more than a medal. FIFA got a new vice-president who helped drag the organisation's reputation into the gutter a generation before the latest gang of thieves. Admiral Carlos Lacoste gained notoriety over the allegation that he ordered the assassination in 1976 of his respected colleague General Carlos Omar Actis, appointed to organise the World Cup. Actis infuriated Havelange because he would not spend money on a new stadium or upgrading Argentine TV to show the tournament in colour.

Eduardo Galeano saw through Lacoste. 'The admiral, an illusionist skilled at making dollars evaporate and sudden fortunes appear, took the reins of the World Cup after the previous officer in charge was mysteriously assassinated. Lacoste managed immense sums of money without any oversight and, it seems, because he wasn't paying close attention, he ended up keeping some of the change.'

Lacoste passed all Havelange's tests and became a vice-president of FIFA in 1979. Fortunately he did not last long. When Argentina returned to democracy in 1983 President Raul Alfonsin objected to Lacoste representing the country abroad. Despite Havelange's best efforts, Lacoste was forced to step down in 1984. Havelange felt that Julio Grondona, who had taken over football in Argentina in 1978, could have fought harder for Lacoste and relationships were chilly for the next few years. But Grondona had seen the main chance and if Lacoste could be dumped, he would be prime candidate to fill the vacancy at FIFA.

Archive photographs show Grondona sucking up to General Jorge Videla, who led the military coup and was eventually convicted of every kind of vile human rights abuse and sentenced to life in jail. As well as arming dictator Banzer and helping dictator Videla win the World Cup, Havelange enjoyed his handshakes with a third Latin American mass-murderer, Chilean dictator Augusto Pinochet. The old men of FIFA, the CBF and Conmebol see no reason to apologise for how football has been manipulated and disgraced.

Grondona was promoted to head FIFA's finance committee; Jack Warner from Trinidad was appointed deputy – but his price for delivering votes to Havelange and Sepp Blatter was high. When Warner was steered to power at Concacaf in 1990 he made his pledge to Zurich in a confidential fax. 'I shall always remain eternally grateful and permanently indebted to you and I do wish to give the assurance that in all our deliberations and actions loyalty to you, to our president Dr Havelange and to the organisation of FIFA itself, shall always be paramount.' Grondona looked the other way as Warner looted football (see Chapter 8).

FIFA's limited financial reports conceal much of Havelange's exploitation of FIFA. Various big numbers have been suggested for his expenses and the high cost of his office in Rio. I managed to obtain his claim for his last year in 1998. The cost of his Rio office was 1.8 million Swiss francs. That's a lot of phone calls.

During his 24 years as FIFA president Havelange had an extraordinary, almost unbelievable privilege. He could sign checks without any additional signature from any other official. He had the sole authority to write cheques to his friends, to people he needed to bribe – and to himself. He handed this secret privilege to Blatter, later.

One special luxury Havelange indulged in was buying expensive watches to present to rich people, especially the rulers of the Gulf. Part of the gift culture of the billionaire sheikhs includes gold, platinum and heavily jewelled watches. The mantra at FIFA House in Zurich was: 'You have to give to receive.' FIFA paid for the gifts going to the Gulf – but the officials kept the gifts they collected on their visits. FIFA's favourite supplier was the Geneva branch of international jewellers Harry Winston's 'Rare Jewels of the World' boutique in Quai General-Guisan.

Even after he was replaced by Blatter, former president Havelange continued to spend FIFA's money with Harry Winston. I know because a friend in Switzerland gave me a copy of an order placed by Havelange's personal secretary. On June 11, 1999, on FIFA headed notepaper, she ordered five beautiful watches, one made of platinum. The total bill was for 97,000 Swiss francs.

In retirement Havelange went on spending like a drunken billionaire. He had the right to check – with a guest – into any luxury hotel in the world. And he could spend up to 30,000 Swiss francs anytime on his FIFA American Express card. When Honorary President Havelange paid 600 Euros for a bottle of wine in a Paris restaurant, there was muffled rage in the FIFA finance department.

Ricardo Teixeira shared his former father-in-law's expensive tastes – when FIFA was paying. Like every other member of the FIFA ExCo, Ricardo had his own account at FIFA's office in Zurich. It is where they hide money from the tax inspectors back home. They can charge outrageous expenses for travel and hotels because FIFA doesn't ask them to provide receipts, tickets, restaurant bills, evidence of spending. Blatter is happy to keep them happy so they are never asked to justify their claims. It is not his money they are pocketing!

The money is stashed in their FIFA accounts. If they are doing illicit rackets with World Cup tickets they can bank the profits safely here. They were also allowed to claim $200 a day in per diems for every day away from their home country and that goes into their Zurich account. President Blatter (Account Number 469) soon lifted the daily allowances to $500 a day and created a new allowance of $200 a day for partners.

Problem: how to get the money, in the currency of your choice but usually US dollars, back home? The clerks in the FIFA finance department hand over bundles of cash. On the way to the airport, stuff them down the front of your trousers and up under your armpits. It can help to have a girlfriend with very big knickers.

I have some of the secret documents from Ricardo's FIFA account in Zurich, number 1663. From 1994 when he was elevated to the ExCo until 2012 when he was forced out, this was his private goldmine, beyond the reach and knowledge of any Brazilian tax inspector. Here's one small example of how FIFA could be looted.

In the early summer of 1998 Ricardo had to return the World Cup trophy, won in 1994, to FIFA's office in Paris, ready for the upcoming World Cup. According to his expenses claim, it took 10 days to find somebody, anybody, to accept the trophy. He claimed $7,700 just for being there. There was another $11,550 in airfares. Did he also charge the CBF for his airfare?

4

At Last! The Secret Bribes List

How João and Ricardo got rich

Baur au Lac hotel, Zurich October 2010: 'Mr Teixeira, Mr Teixeira! Ricardo turns to look. It is a scruffy, grey-haired man in a Joe Colombo-style beige raincoat shouting at him from the hotel gateway. 'Mr Teixeira, did you take your bribes through the Sanud company?' Teixeira freezes. He stares. He can't think of anything to say.

The concierge in the car park of the Zurich 5-star hotel is blocking the noisy fellow, keeping him away. But he is a reporter, he has a TV cameraman at his shoulder and the camera is pointing at him, Ricardo, boss of Brazilian football, thief of thieves, visiting Zurich to continue looting the next World Cup.

Ricardo enjoyed his breakfast and is about to step into the black Merc at the hotel door taking him to FIFA's glass palace on the hill for today's meetings. The FIFA flunkies hold the car door open but Ricardo is numb. He can't move – and his tongue is glued. He stares at the reporter at the gateway, baffled. Sanud? He thought he had buried Sanud.

There had been two emails from those nosy bastards at the BBC in London, requesting an interview. Ricardo ignored them. What could they know?

That politician, Senator Álvaro Dias from Paraná, got close. His investigators discovered some strange 'loans' to Ricardo from a company called Sanud in Liechtenstein. But Ricardo and the guys buying his vote at FIFA had set Sanud up as a 'brass plate' company. There were thousands in the little city of Vaduz, capital of Liechtenstein, their owners hiding behind inscrutable local lawyers. Where Sanud's money came from would remain a secret – forever.

Ricardo had learned to ignore the bastards. Reporter Juca Kfouri and his exclusive 'revelations.' The hooligans on the terraces with their *'Fora Teixeira'* banners. Filth. Blatter protected him. Blatter hadn't got any choice. Ricardo knew too much. He had CBF under control. He had his own bench of sit-up-and-beg politicians in Brasília. Ricardo was untouchable.

The BBC bastards were only recycling the Dias Senate investigation report from 2001, nine years earlier. They couldn't have any new facts. They filmed him being driven away. Then they went away. That was the end of it. Pricks.

'I THINK THIS is what you want.' Ten weeks earlier, a warm evening in the late summer in 2010, at the agreed time, somewhere in middle-Europe, the source arrived, planted their briefcase on one of the beer garden tables, opened it and produced a file of four pages.

A list of 175 secret payments beginning in 1989 and running for the next 12 years. $100 million of kickbacks and bribes paid by the sports marketing company International Sports and Leisure – forever after known as ISL – to obtain multi-billion-dollar lucrative contracts for the World Cup.

I had known for nine years, within days of the collapse of ISL into bankruptcy in the spring of 2001, that this list existed. In bars around the world, where reporters drink late into the night with indiscreet sports officials, I had asked, who got the bribes from ISL? Everybody knew they had been paid and we were pretty sure who took the money. But no documentary proof.

I asked every policeman, every court official, every FIFA official who would meet me privately in bars in the Zurich suburbs, every manager who had worked at ISL. I flew tens of thousands of miles to find people who might be able to answer the question, 'Who got the bribes?' They knew names and suggested dates. Slowly, I built the case.

Now I had The List in my hands. The source beamed. Yes, we could buy them a drink, just one, a small one, before they left. I laid the file on the table and, with my BBC producer James Oliver, turned the pages, seeking the page for 1997. There it was. The evidence. The scoop of a lifetime. The name on a bribe of 1,500,000 Swiss francs, paid on March 3, 1997, was '*Garantie JH*.' (This figure would vary in years to come, in different official reports and in different currencies. But this was the number in the master Bribes List.)

At last! The proof that João Havelange, for 24 years the all-powerful, patrician president of FIFA had taken bribes.

I had been told it in TV interviews, had hinted it in newspaper articles, surprised Sepp Blatter with my television crew and the question – 'Was it Havelange that took that bribe?' – and Blatter had run away. Now I was holding a document that proved what I had long suspected; I was investigating an organised crime syndicate.

We turned the pages. Bribe after bribe after bribe. Some for millions of dollars. The source left and we called our editor at home in London. We had made the trip hoping for some good leads but now, unexpectedly, had in our hands the biggest corruption story, ever, in world sport. We told him we had the breakthrough but it would be a lot of work cracking some of the clues.

Then we laughed and laughed, stopped working and got drunk. For me it was nearly 20 years of feeling my way around the story, building contacts, sources. There was a lot of work to be done because straight away we saw that most of the bribes had been paid to anonymous companies registered in secretive Liechtenstein. We got to work busting them open.

AN ACCOUNTANT who had worked for ISL gave me the crucial breakthrough in the quest to name Havelange. I filmed an interview with him for the BBC in the summer of 2006. In a hotel room by Lake Lucerne, circled by mountains, he told me his accidental discovery. During a holiday period he was shifted to work in the ISL department that processed the bribes. He told me that, over a period of almost 20 years, ISL had paid out tens of millions of pounds to football officials for World Cup rights. And he had a name for me.

MAN: I became aware that ISL paid major amounts of money in order to get these rights.

AJ: How would you term this, these payments? What would you call them in common language?

MAN: Well, in common language, it's obviously corruption.

AJ: Bribes?

MAN: Yes.

AJ: So what sort of people were taking the money? I mean, was it very many people or is it just a handful of people?

MAN: On the top of FIFA there is just a handful of people in the position to make decisions as to who would get the commercial rights of FIFA.

AJ: And why did they pay the bribes?

MAN: They paid the bribes to get the best sports rights in the world.

AJ: From what you know about the bribes paid to football officials, was it just the occasional brown envelope in the back of a car park? Was it just – oh, we haven't looked after you for a bit. How was it done?

MAN: You can think of it as the same way as salary payments that are done out of a company.

AJ: So who was getting payments and kickbacks from ISL?

MAN: There were systematic payments out of ISL by bank remittances to key decision-makers. Mr Havelange, the then president of FIFA, was taking money. There were numerous payments and the magnitude was around 250,000 Swiss francs for at least one payment.

*

The BBC broadcast this interview on June 11, 2006. There was silence from FIFA headquarters. Havelange has never denied the allegation that he was systematically bribed over the years in return for World Cup contracts. Blatter never commented, we never heard from their lawyers.

The accountant had handled the payment slips as they went to an ISL bank for dispatch to Vaduz. What he didn't know was how the world's most popular – and valuable – sport had been hijacked.

MAKE ME FIFA PRESIDENT, said Big João to the German businessman, and we'll both get rich. The businessman Horst Dassler was also Big. His family created the Adidas brand in Bavaria and the dynamic Horst expanded the boots to shirts to balls enterprise into a global icon. That wasn't enough for the restless and ruthless genius. He spotted a huge business opportunity in world sport and created the ISL marketing company. To increase business for both companies he needed to get the officials of the international federations under control. They had their prices, Horst paid.

Tireless and determined, Horst became renowned in the 1970s for his gifts. Sports officials strapped beautiful Swiss watches on their wrists and signed their athletes to wear the Adidas three-stripes. An important European football official found a new Mercedes parked at his front door on his birthday.

His would be a short life but Horst's achievements were massive. He deployed bags of cash to lubricate FIFA's voting machine in 1974, and on the eve of that Germany World Cup Brazil's João Havelange became president of the world game. Elegant, charismatic and, like his mentor Castor back in Rio, a thief to his bone marrow.

Dassler created his own crime family, allying with the Brazilians' Rio-based crime operations. Havelange, with his connections to all that was shady in Latin America, made friends with the torturer General Jorge Videla and the Argentine junta for the 1978 World Cup. Were games fixed for Argentina to win?

Horst and his entourage were at the Montreal Olympics where many new officials were recruited, including a young German fencer and medal-winner, Thomas Bach. He went to work for Dassler's notorious 'international relations' team. He will be in Rio in 2016. He now has the top job.

Horst's influence grew. In 1980 he acquired IOC members' votes from the Soviet bloc and Africa. His well-timed article for the IOC's house magazine *Olympic Review* pledged that if members let business through their front door in Lausanne, their lifestyle would be greatly enhanced. Duly they installed Horst's choice for new IOC president, the Barcelona fascist Juan Antonio Samaranch, a man of great personal ambition and no noticeable morality.

A year later Horst fixed another vote. Primo Nebiolo, the Italian who never saw a bribe he didn't like, was imposed as president of the IAAF. Primo's deputy, later his successor, Lamine Diack, took money from Horst's boys and ISL now had control of football, track and field and the Olympics.

Positive drug tests were suppressed at the Games in Moscow

and again four years later in Los Angeles in 1984 to make the Olympic product clean and attractive to the global brands. Horst's business team achieved their dream. They privatised the Games. Then they took over football.

Sponsor money was diverted to grease FIFA's leaders and in turn, the World Cup was privatised. Sponsors, rebranded as 'partners,' paid huge bucks to exclude rivals, internationally and in the country hosting the tournament. A slice of those big bucks, that should have gone to develop football at grassroots, was re-routed by ISL into bribes for Havelange and his gang in return for the privileges the 'partners' required.

The system was in place – and then Horst Dassler died from a fast-devouring cancer in 1987. He was only 51. At the ISL head office, then in offices above the rail station in Lucerne, the only man who knew who was getting paid – and how much – was his adoring personal assistant Jean-Marie Weber. Weber became, as ISL's lightweight chief executive Christoph Malms admitted, the only man who could ensure ISL survived. Weber the Bagman became the channel for millions in illicit payments to criminals.

TWO YEARS BEFORE the meltdown ISL executives moved the company north from Lucerne to a sparkling white tower block in Zug. They got a better tax deal in Zug canton and were now only 30 kilometres from their FIFA 'partners' in Zurich if face-to-face cash handovers were required. They demanded too much and ISL crashed.

When the investigators, the detectives, the forensic accountants and the lawyers for the creditors, owed a stunning $300 million, all arrived at ISL's headquarters in the spring of 2001 they soon discovered the evidence of the vast bribes that the Bagman Weber had suitcased and wired to football's czars.

They dug through ISL's accounts, found some fascinating payments, assembled The List and locked it in a safe. What does it show? Columns of dollars and Swiss francs, currency conversion rates and dates. There were names of a few officials from football and other sports. And then the brass plate companies in Liechtenstein with names randomly selected to conceal who was getting the loot. Jumping off the page were Monard, Wando, Seprocom, Scienta, Beleza, Ovado and more.

The List began in 1989 and with it began the mysteries. That year, scattered among the payments to the Vaduz brass plates, were seven bearer cheques. These are the money launderer's dream, big corruption on a small sheet of paper. Bearer cheques do not name who is to get the money; they just say 'Pay the Bearer' and the bank, any bank, will. There will be no record revealing who got the money. Jean-Marie Weber knew how to look after those important men at the top of FIFA. They wanted money, lots of it, but no scandal.

There were seven bearer cheques in 1989. The first two, issued on 27 February, were each for $1 million! Whoever got that $2 million got another $1 million on 21 June. Ten weeks later they got another $1 million, In December (Happy Christmas!), there was another $1 million. It was a great, $5 million year for somebody. Was it João Havelange?

But it wasn't these bearer cheques that stood out for me. More significantly, in the long term, was the debut in the List on September 29, 1989 of a brass plate in Liechtenstein named Sicuretta. It got 1.5 million Swiss Francs – nearly one million dollars. Was the Sicuretta money going to the same official who was getting the bearer cheques? Or another official close to him? There were only two officials who needed bribing at FIFA. Plus a son-in-law to keep warm.

Another $3 million waltzed out in bearer cheques in 1990 but, more importantly, here was Sicuretta again. Two payments in the second half of the year, totalling more than $1.5 million. From here on, Sicuretta becomes the brass plate of ISL choice. Next year, 1991, Sicuretta's secretive owner pocketed $1.9 million. It had to be Havelange. He was the key decision maker, the only one who mattered, at FIFA and he was getting the biggest bribes.

Sicuretta's bribes were laundered to Liechtenstein by a Swiss lawyer with an office 10 minutes away from ISL's white palace in Zug. In mid-1991 ISL sent him a thank you - $1.25 million. It's in The List. In 1998, the Bagman Jean-Marie Weber took this lawyer to Paris during the World Cup where he was greeted by Sepp Blatter, about to take over from Havelange as FIFA president. That meeting is recorded in police files in Zug. What did they talk about? Did Sepp say 'Thank you'?

THEY WERE the best of times. Eight years of bliss. All Ricardo had to do was raise his hand a few times and grunt agreement when his father-in-law the president cast his hard-eyed, intimidating gaze around the FIFA boardroom table and announced, 'Now we vote to give the contract to our trusted friends at ISL.'

Havelange not only wanted money for himself, the greedy

fellow who married his daughter must be paid as well. He had learned much from Castor. Gangster families share what they steal.

Ricardo remembered, fondly, the first big lump of money, a million dollars, in August 1992. The next year was brilliant! In February, May and again in September of 1993, a million more dollars each time. It was the three million dollar year! It all went to his Sanud brass plate in Vaduz. And he wasn't yet a member of FIFA's Executive Committee!

In 1994 Sanud's contract kickbacks came three times, in February, May and November. One and a half million US dollars delivered to Vaduz to be laundered back into Ricardo's businesses in Rio as bogus 'loans.'

Then the best times got better. The FIFA World Cup contract had to be put out to tender. ISL had the 1998 France business but a host of rival marketing companies were getting ready to bid, and bid strongly, for the 2002 tournament. The bids would start coming in during 1995 and if ISL couldn't match them they would go bust. For the FIFA crooks, the Vaduz money tap would run dry. It was a time of two-way embraces and one love.

Ricardo felt ISL's warm embrace four times in the first few months of 1995. Twice in January, $250,000 was sent to Sanud's Vaduz account. In May ISL doubled the generosity with two more payments, each of $500,000. That was $1.5 million before the half year.

But the most powerful man in FIFA, milking the Sicuretta account, was bunged a stunning $3,650,000 at the end of March. As the long-expected huge rival bid loomed, Sicuretta was blessed in July with more; 2,100,000 Swiss francs – $1,826,000. That was $5,476,000 in 13 weeks to the one old man who controlled FIFA.

THE BIG BID arrived on the desk of General Secretary Sepp Blatter on August 18 1995. It came from Eric Drossart, the Belgian president in Europe of IMG, the American marketing company. Drossart, like everyone in the business knew about the backroom rackets between FIFA and ISL. How to break through the cosy conspiracy? Drossart bid a staggering $1 billion dollars for the rights to 2002.

Blatter was furious. The crafty Drossart had faxed his eye-watering bid to all 23 members of the FIFA Executive Committee. Many of them, especially the Europeans from UEFA opposed the contract remaining with ISL. In fact UEFA did business, apparently clean business, with ISL but the Europeans could smell the FIFA bribes and wanted to end them. One billion dollars would help a lot.

Blatter stalled IMG and the same day a grateful ISL paid $500,000 to Ricardo's Sanud account. Five weeks later ISL, clearly desperate to hang on to their FIFA contract into the next century paid Sicuretta another $1,900,000 bringing the FIFA boss's haul over five months to the enormous sum of $7,376,086.

In December, irritated by FIFA's delaying tactics, IMG's Eric Drossart wrote again to Blatter, promising to pay more than any rival bid. Blatter replied, wishing Drossart a Merry Christmas and promising nothing.

As the new year of 1996 began, ISL had six months left to fight to keep the FIFA contract. They started, again, by greasing Ricardo, sending $500,000 to his Sanud at the end of January. In February they stepped up the rate of bribes and $1,350,000 went to Sicuretta. Did Jean-Marie Weber have any money left? Weren't the Brazilians draining ISL dry?

There was still money left. In April ISL paid a further $1,350,000 to Sicuretta. On July 3, two days before Havelange was due to take the decision – ISL or IMG – Jean-Marie Weber reached deep into ISL's reserves and pulled out two payments to Sanud of $250,000. The same day he authorised $1,350,000 to Sicuretta.

Havelange defeated his UEFA enemies and on the morning of July 5, 1996 gave the World Cup to ISL. There was a twist. As the vote neared, Blatter had upset the IMG calculations by announcing that both the 2002 and the 2006 World Cups were on the table. ISL had been tipped off long before. IMG had to talk hurriedly to its bankers to raise the guarantees.

The shakedown on ISL wasn't over for 1996. Two months later the Brazilian greed roared back and on September 10, yet another $1,350,000 was sent to Sicuretta. The boy got more as well. On November 6 Sanud received $500,000.

Between them the two shadowy football officials behind Sanud and Sicuretta extorted more than $14,000,000 to guarantee that ISL kept the FIFA World Cup contract.

WAS SOMEBODY inside ISL trying to dump Havelange and his bag-carrier Blatter? In early February the first kickback of 1997, $1,600,000 to the senior Brazilian bloodsucker, went through to Sicuretta in the normal way. The machine seemed to be running smoothly.

Twenty-five days later ISL's dirty secrets exploded in Blatter's face. He could not pretend any more that he didn't know. On the morning of March 3, 1997 a document arrived at FIFA's finance department. It registered that ISL had paid 1.5 million francs – around $1 million – into a FIFA account at the UBS bank in Zurich. It didn't make sense. When legitimate ISL cheques arrived at FIFA they were for hundreds of millions in fees from sponsors and TV networks.

The covering note sent panic rippling through FIFA headquarters. Finance Director Erwin Schmid hurried to the office of then General Secretary Sepp Blatter.

Blatter read the note. *'Garantie JH.'*

FIFA's ruling executive wasn't told about the 'guarantee' to João Havelange. Blatter kept it secret. It took five more years for a brave source inside FIFA to tell me. I published the revelation in a London newspaper on the eve of the World Cup kick-off in Korea. My editor published the story big and although we didn't have independent proof that Havelange had taken the bribe, we used a very big picture of him!

How did it happen? It could not have been an accident – unless there were temporary staff working in the ISL finance department. My friend said that it wasn't him.

ONE WEEK later ISL sent a massive $1,900,000 to Sicuretta. João was still milking the system. Later in the year they sent Sicuretta another $2 million. A month later $500,000 went to Sanud and in November yet another $500,000. Then, suddenly, payments to Sanud stopped. Was it all over?

The good times couldn't continue much longer. Teixeira had embezzled at least $9.5 million dollars in six years from FIFA. The Brazilian greed was bleeding ISL to death. They hoped that Havelange's retirement in 1998 after the France World Cup might reduce his demands – but he didn't think so! A new brass plate called Renford Investments was registered in Vaduz. It was jointly owned by Teixeira and Havelange and in 1998 Renford scored three payments, totalling $3 million. Sicuretta continued to thrive collecting nearly $3 million in two payments.

ISL needed more money if the company was to survive. They prepared to issue shares and float the company. They wouldn't be able to hide the bribes from new investors with rights to inspect the books so $24 million was moved to a new Vaduz brass plate named Nunca – Spanish for 'never.' The plan was to pay FIFA officials bribes from Nunca – and hope that Havelange's demands would diminish as he aged.

They didn't. Did Teixeira and Havelange pick up the vibrations that ISL was in terminal trouble? Attempting to escape the grasping couple from Rio, ISL had diversified into other sports and spent a fortune buying international tennis. It was a disaster. The FIFA duo didn't care. They wanted 'their' money. Sicuretta extorted an astonishing $6 million in 1999 and Teixeira squeezed another $1 million for Renford.

Jean-Marie Weber and his ISL colleagues begged their associates at the huge Japanese media company Dentsu to lend them a few millions. They needed a recommendation from a senior Dentsu manager. He approved the loan and received what can only have been a kickback. The money was laundered through a Hong Kong company called Gilmark and in November 1999 banked 1 million Swiss francs – $638,000. Six weeks later another 1 million francs was sent his way.

As ISL sank through 2000, running up $300 million of debts, Renford sucked out another $500,000. Gilmark kept bleeding the ISL corpse until it expired in January 2001. I asked Dentsu about this manager who somehow ended up trousering $2,515,720. They said he was no longer with them. Havelange was remorseless, forcing the transfer of a final $1.3 million into Sicuretta. Over the years he stole more than $45 million. There will be more in the other rackets he ran at FIFA. But this much we know.

BRIBE NOTE: When Havelange was questioned by Congressional investigators in Brasília he declared that he was a poor man and what little wealth he had accumulated was in the name of his wife

5

Looting Brazilian Football

Ricardo's favourite shoemaker

If you believe Ricardo, he discovered the world's most generous bank. It was located in Vaduz, in Europe, it lent him millions and charged interest, in the words of the Senator Álvaro Dias investigation, 'absurdly below market rates.' In fact, he never paid any interest or the loan back. Yes, it was the Bank of Sanud and he was its only customer.

We may never know how Ricardo laundered all of Sanud's $9.5 million out of Vaduz and into his pocket. Maybe it helped buy luxury homes in Delray Beach and Miami, Florida. But some landed in his Rio business R L J Participações Ltda. Sanud, the anonymous brass plate, owned 50% of the shareholding. Former wife Lúcia Havelange Teixeira, had 24.99% and Ricardo had 25.01%.

But RLJ was a sham. According to the report from Senator Dias, it never generated a penny in earnings. It was a shell, stuffed only with what Ricardo embezzled from FIFA. In Ricardo's accounts, unearthed by the investigators in Brasília, he owned a series of interlocking bars and restaurants in Rio including the Chopp House, the El Turf and the Port City. The common thread was that they didn't make money, they borrowed it, sometimes through offshore banks in the Caribbean, and Ricardo's CBF paid them to cater for elaborate football functions.

IN 1989 RICARDO, backed by his mob-associated father-in-law, took control of the Brazilian football federation, the CBF. The national team were contracted to wear kit supplied by the Umbro company. After their 1994 World Cup victory in the USA, the value of the *seleção* soared. Secret meetings began soon after and in July 1996 Ricardo disappeared to New York. He took a business associate, who made good profits out of their friendship, but there's no record of any other officials from the CBF.

A bunch of American businessmen from Beaverton, Oregon, whose company was registered across the Atlantic in a European tax haven, were waiting for him with their lawyers and a document containing 11,500 words. Ricardo signed it and gave effective control of Brazilian football to a foreign shoemaker.

The Americans, via their tax haven, paid Ricardo $160 million – with the promise of more later – and bought the right to choose players for the *seleção* and tell the team who they could play and where and when. There would be 50 of these games. They could open their own shop inside the CBF offices in Rio.

61

The contract specified that the shop could only sell branded shirts produced by the Americans – and their branded pants, socks, knitted pullovers, shirts, jackets and sweater sets, hand-bags, backpacks, headbands, hats, gloves, wristbands, glasses, protectors, special glasses to improve performance, training vests, towels, umbrellas and scarves, all with the Swoosh logo of the shoemaker. There would also have to be footwear for running, basketball, tennis, training, golf, hiking, aerobics, baseball, American football, cycling, in-line skating and vol-leyball. And football. And footballs.

At home matches a circular banner, 25 metres in width and displaying their Swoosh logo, would be placed in the centre of the pitch. Any disputes over the contract could be resolved only in the courts of Zurich.

The foreign shoe company was paying lots of money and by the time the first tranche arrived in Ricardo's hands it had bounced around between Holland, three banks in America, one in the Bahamas and two more in Belo Horizonte and Rio. When big bucks travel these circuitous routes it is common-place that bits fall off.

Ricardo's travelling companion to New York, José Hawilla, who controlled the Traffic marketing company, was the only other Brazilian to sign. José had acquired rights to use the CBF to his own advantage soon after Ricardo took power at the CBF, the contract would give him $8 million over the next ten years.

Senator Dias denounced what he called the 'spectacular profits' that Hawilla made out of his dealings with the CBF. Dias added that it was yet another example of ruinous administration by Teixeira. It was alleged that between 1995 and 1999 Hawilla's tax filings revealed that his personal wealth had increased 20 times.

In the same year, 1996, the price of Ricardo's co-operation with ISL was $1.5 million. You cannot help but wonder, how did he approach Nike? Did he try his normal tricks on them? Did he try and shake them down, telling them of his account in Vaduz? Could he have been a tougher negotiator? Could he have got more money for Brazilian football?

What really happened to Ronaldo in Paris in the hours before the World Cup Final against France? Sometimes the simple answer may be the true one. The expectations of Brazil, of the world, put impossible pressure on a 21-year-old athlete, his nervous system rebelled and his mouth frothed. Did the pressure of being Nike's poster boy make him wander the field?

But reactions at home to this debacle and the way Ricardo manipulated the CBF stirred enough rage to ensure that the elected politicians must ask questions.

NIKE'S MONEY began pouring into Ricardo's open hands on the first day of January 1997. Four years later the CBF was insolvent. If it were a business, it would be bust, broken up, sold for scrap. Senator Dias's investigators estimated that by the end of 2000 the CBF was in debt to the tune of $31 million.

How did that happen? There were some extraordinary secret financial deals done at Ricardo's private empire but the shoemaker's fabulous windfall money wasn't enough for

Ricardo's manipulations, bribes and payoffs to keep control of Brazilian football. Something very smelly was happening. He went abroad and borrowed money in a way that may never have happened ever before.

In October 1998, the year after the Nike tap began to flow, Ricardo decided that the CBF needed to borrow $7 million from the Delta National Bank of New York. Dias's investigators discovered that at the time Delta were charging Brazilians – companies and individuals – between 9% and 10% interest.

Ricardo agreed to pay an astonishing 43.57% rate. And . . . sit down for this . . . he paid the interest before it was due. That boosted the final rate up to an unbelievable 52%! As with the Nike money, the Delta loan had to travel. It was routed to another New York bank, then to the tax haven of Nassau, Bahamas and then to the CBF account with the Rural Bank in Belo Horizonte. As with most CBF money transfers, large amounts fell off en route. Ricardo could not give any explanation for any of this when questioned in Brasília.

Ricardo seemed addicted to Delta, agreeing to a series of loans with high interest rates the money slimming down as it travelled through the international banking system on its way to the CBF. Two months after that first Delta loan Ricardo signed up for another $4.5 million, this time at a 25% rate of interest. Again, the loan was repaid early, boosting the true rate to more than 30% and again, it travelled from New York through the Caribbean, losing hundreds of thousands of dollars on the way.

Both loans seemed hard to justify because within two

months a fat $15 million was due to arrive in Brazil from the shoemaker.

But Ricardo couldn't kick the Delta habit. Thirty-five days after the last loan, he signed up for another U$10 millions agreeing to pay 25% interest. Days later he was borrowing again from Delta, but this time for his own El Turf bar. Ricardo declined to explain why the cost suddenly plunged and he paid the same rate that other Delta clients in Brazil were paying – 12%.

The CBF was back with Delta in September 1999 borrowing $3.7 million at 21%, double the current market rate. Into 2000 Ricardo still could not shake the Delta habit, borrowing another $10 million at 16%. Finally, in September 2000, there was a sixth loan of $4.5 million at 14.5%.

In April 2001 Ricardo claimed to the Congressional investigation that there was nothing unusual about the rates he paid Delta. He named eight Brazilian companies and institutions, claiming they paid similar rates. Within days every one of them replied, 'Not True!' The CPI (*Comissão Parlamentar de Inquérito*) final report stated, coldly, 'The president of the CBF submitted false information.'

THE HONEST POLITICIANS in Brasília soon learned that Ricardo's relationships with banks never ceased to amaze. In July 1996 he opened a personal account with the Banco Vega, depositing $190,000. The next day he opened an account for the CBF giving Vega $1,027,940. A key executive at Banco Vega arranged for Ricardo to receive a rate of interest nearly double what was paid to the CBF. Lots more CBF money was entrusted to Vega. Many mysterious things happened and in May 1997 Brazil's central bank closed Banco Vega down.

There were more mysteries about the way Ricardo did business with the CBF's money. They frequently needed to engage in currency exchange and a company was contracted to get them the best rates in the market. All seemed well when the agents got a rate of 0.19% above the Central Bank rate for that day to buy a mere $185 for the CBF. Then Ricardo authorised the agent to buy $700,000. The charge to CBF? It was 15.44% above the Central Bank rate. The Dias investigation called it 'looting.'

As the shoemaker's money boosted the CBF's income to unparalleled heights, Ricardo continued getting bad deals in the money markets and pushing Brazilian football deeper into debt. He went outside the banks and borrowed money from private, unregulated lenders, sometimes paying up to 100% interest. In 1998 alone Ricardo authorised paying $178,918 interest on two of these loans. The investigators discovered more and their comments were scathing.

Sometimes the CBF chequebook needed a tourist passport. Its money just loved to travel. Sometimes, like unfortunate travellers, it disappeared. When Brazil competed in the Gold Cup in America in 1998 the CBF sent $400,000 to a bank in Miami. The money didn't gather dust. Swiftly, it was travelling again, this time back south to a bank in Montevideo. The CPI investigators could not find out what happened to the money or why it was sent to Uruguay. They did discover that a close friend and business associate of Ricardo handled the transfer. Brazil were knocked out by the USA and in the general mourning, nobody noticed the disappearance of $400,000.

THERE WAS SOMETHING puzzling about Ricardo's psychological makeup. The Congress investigators discovered there were two Ricardos. One was the incompetent administrator, the naïf in the financial markets who innocently agreed deals with predators who drained the CBF's wealth and drove it almost to bankruptcy, despite the huge income from the shoemakers.

The other Ricardo was a different man; the smartest operator in the financial markets. The Congressional investigators analysed Ricardo's private dealings in the Commodities and Futures Exchange. Every year between 1995 and 2001 he made profits. They calculated he had made 1,409 deals in that time – that's a deal every 36 hours! Many of his deals were gambling on future prices for US dollars. He was very good at it, very successful and made lots of money for himself. It seems he forgot all these skills when it came to managing the affairs of the CBF.

Was it the idiot Ricardo or the smart Ricardo who forgot to hire an independent auditor at the CBF? Senator Dias pointed out that this meant stakeholders in Brazilian football didn't know what was happening to the windfall from the American shoemakers in Oregon.

THE WINDFALL soon found its way into the pockets of Ricardo and his tight little team controlling Brazilian football. They began paying themselves well but it never seemed enough and between 1998 and 2000 they increased their salaries by 300%. Ricardo's soared to $239,267 although there was no evidence that he worked any harder. But the biggest winner was Ricardo's uncle Marco Antonio, the CBF secretary general, who by 2000 discovered he couldn't feed his kids on less than $286,000 a year. To help with new shoes for the little ones Marco and the rest of the gang paid themselves 13th and 14th monthly salaries.

The CBF's board of directors were not cheap to employ. The income of the Confederation quadrupled – from $18 million in 1997 to $79 million in 2000. The CBF's expenses rose even faster with increased salaries, bonuses, interest and debt charges and by 2000 they were in debt! Ricardo found a quick answer. Reduce the amount spent on football from 55% to 35%!

There was no choice if Ricardo was to lead the imperial life that he demanded. In October 1997 he spent four days in New York and couldn't bear to take taxis like everybody else. So he hired a limousine on permanent standby for any little trip around town and that drained $1,185 out of the CBF. And he wasn't cheap to feed! The Congressional investigators analysed his dining bill for three months in 1998. They looked at 18 meals costing a total of $12,594.40 and pointed out that when the CBF president ate it cost an average of $700.00 per meal.

The CBF gave Ricardo a credit card and it never stayed in the dark long enough to gain cobwebs. The card became well-known at the Lidador shop, famous for their fine champagnes.

RICARDO ENJOYED CHAMPAGNE by the bucket at his own El Turf restaurant in February 1996. As well as the Dom

Perignon and many bottles of aged whisky, there was fillet steak and juicy chicken, washed down with 1,300 litres of beer, all paid for by the CBF. He and his friends were celebrating the launch of the IAFB – *Institute Assistance Futebol Brasileiro.*

It sounded wonderful. Ricardo said the purpose of this non-profit association was to improve the lives of 60,000 players, past and present. It would help them find jobs, vocational courses, five hospitals would be built for injured players, there would be free life insurance and legal assistance for former athletes and their dependants.

The Congressional investigators could not find any hospitals. They couldn't find any benefits to any players. But they found a lot of benefits for the friends of Ricardo. He personally appointed the staff of 17 – three were sisters and two were also paid salaries by the CBF – and 95% of the grant to the IAFB went into their pockets. The rest went on stationery and utilities bills. Senator Dias commented, drily, 'very little is left to carry out concrete actions.'

Another concern to Dias was that one of the members of the IAFB supervisory board was a close friend of Ricardo who had substantial business deals with the CBF. The CPI report asked, was it likely that he would criticise anything at the IAFB?

AFTER THE WORLD CUP there were some funny things happening at FIFA's finance office. In 1999 Ricardo sent the enormous amount of $2,989,593 from the CBF to FIFA. Asked why, Ricardo was at his most obscure. It was 'a settling of accounts to offset receivables and payables between two entities' – whatever that meant. Where did the money really go? Where did it go after landing at FIFA? Neither Blatter nor Teixeira will answer.

The saga of Brazil's money from the French World Cup and FIFA continued into 2000. One day Ricardo walked into FIFA's Finance Department in Zurich. He was carrying a bulging bag. 'How can we help you, Sir?' he was asked. He opened the bag and out tumbled $400,000 in cash.

Straight-faced, Ricardo claimed the money was an advance payment due to the Brazilian federation for the costs of their appearance at the 1998 World Cup in France, twenty months earlier. He didn't explain where he had acquired so much cash – and from whom.

Ricardo told them to transfer the money to the CBF account. The Finance clerks were puzzled – they thought that this sum of money had already been paid to the federation. But when they checked, there was no record of the money arriving at the CBF. Ricardo's story was mystifying from beginning to end.

The clerks agreed to transfer the money to the CBF – but insisted it went to the federation's current account, marked as a payment from him. Oh no, said Ricardo, that isn't what I want.

Instead he asked for the money to be returned to him – but this time in a cheque. Amazingly, he got it. In that moment, FIFA House changed from being the home of football into a one-stop, criminal, money-laundering shop.

A couple of days later Ricardo went back to the FIFA office, returned the cheque and asked for his cash back. Astonishingly,

FIFA's finance department agreed – and gave him the $400,000 back in a bag. It's likely that he took a taxi to his favourite Zurich bank with a document saying that FIFA had paid him the money.

I found this story buried on page 19 of the confidential annual Management Letter for the year 2000, sent by FIFA's auditors, the Zurich branch of KPMG to Blatter. KPMG were politely horrified, recommending that in future cheques or cash should only be made to 'authorised people.'

I emailed Ricardo, KPMG and FIFA, asking about the source and destination of this money. None replied.

REPORTERS INVESTIGATED CBF and wrote stories revealing Ricardo's mismanagement and the money mysteries. The fans hated him. Why didn't the judges, the politicians, the lawyers and other football officials blow the whistle, wave red cards, get him jailed? How did Ricardo get away with it?

Answer: they were being paid off. The shoemaker's flood of money was diverted away from football to fund political campaigns, creating a network of politicians who would protect Ricardo's rackets in Brasília and state governments.

Cash was 'donated' to state football federations who then passed it to politicians to fight elections. CPI investigators discovered that CBF donations to improve football would rest only 24 hours in the accounts of some state federations before being shifted sideways to the politicians.

Dias described the stealing as a triangular relationship between the CBF, federations and election campaigns. It was a fraud, vote-buying in a country that was struggling to learn again to be a democracy following two decades of military dictatorship. By 2000 the 'donations' had soared to more than $7 million. That was the price of protection – but the money was being 'donated' by the generous folks in Oregon: without their knowledge, of course.

The CBF did not ask for accountability from federations on how they spent the money – and there was another give-away. They did not have to pay their annual subscriptions to the CBF. Dias said that Teixeira letting them keep the money created ties of dependence and subordination. He described the federations as distributors of perks and strongholds of nepotism, their primary purpose to support politicians who are elected indefinitely.

The politicians who made it to the Congress in Brasília found that Ricardo looked after their every need. A mansion valued at $1 million was rented on a farm on South Lake for their exclusive use.

Ricardo never forgot what his partner Sepp calls 'the Family of Football.' In the year 2000 $8,000 was sent to a community north-east of Rio. In the CBF accounts it was recorded as 'Help to City of Piraí.' The money was moved immediately to the account of a cousin of Ricardo who was hoping to be elected for the local council. Dias also noted that Ricardo owned three farms in Piraí. Shamelessly, he sold milk from them to the CBF.

Dias concluded that while the politicians in Ricardo's net-work did very well out of the shoemaker's money, there were no systematic donations to former players or their associations.

Ricardo purchased his politicians. Many people thought he

also purchased his judges. Several enjoyed all-expenses-paid trips to the World Cup in America in 1994 and again in France in 1998. They enjoyed business-class travel and fine hotels and their wives went with them. Some had sat in judgement over cases involving Ricardo or the CBF. When questioned, one judge explained that he accepted the trips because he thought it important to understand popular culture.

Several of Rio's lawyers were also keen to take CBF money, even if the litigation was about Ricardo's private affairs. Whether it was suing reporter Juca Kfouri or defending dirty dealings at the El Turf restaurant, Ricardo could always steal the shoemaker's money.

Senator Dias's investigation into CBF corruption in 2001 succeeded despite the best efforts of Ricardo's team of paid-for politicians. Dias told me, 'Football had become a huge and profitable business in Brazil, but attempts to investigate were unsuccessful because the CBF kept a close relationship with governments, the Congress and the judicial system. In the Congress Teixeira created what we call his *bancada da bola*, a group of deputies to protect the CBF.

'I decided to take responsibility, as a senator, to investigate the huge number of complaints of corruption that the government authorities ignored for so many years. Silently, I worked to get enough senators' signatures needed to install an Investigation Committee in the Senate. My strategy, to overcome CBF's lobbyists and watchmen, was to work to create the investigation committee on Fridays when not so many senators are in Brasília.

'After we started the investigations in the Senate, the

members of the *"bancada da bola"*, for long working under the influence of CBF and Ricardo Teixeira, realised that it was impossible to fight against the Senate committee.'

The CBF's strategy was to create another investigation committee in the Congress. This was led by Congressman Aldo Rebelo – and he did a good job. But the CBF's placemen had planned their sabotage: the final report didn't get enough votes to be approved.

Dias added, 'CBF and Ricardo Teixeira also tried to compromise the investigations in the Senate. Many senators abandoned the committee, and others were against the final report that indicted 17 *cartolas* – top officials in Brazilian football – including Ricardo Teixeira. So I went to the tribune on a day when the Congress was full and the press were present, and denounced CBF's attempt to corrupt the committee. The press gave big coverage of my speech and none of the senators wanted to be under suspicion. My Final Report was approved.'

Ricardo Teixeira's tame politicians had done their best to block the CPI. When that failed, Sepp Blatter stepped in, warning that 'We won't tolerate investigations that put at risk the rules of soccer.' If the senators called referees and CBF officials to testify, Brazil would be banished from the world game. 'Brazil will not take part in the 2002 World Cup, the World Youth Cup,' said Blatter, 'and the Under-17 World Cup, the Women's World Cup and the Futsal indoor tournament in Guatemala.'

This did not impress Senate President Antônio Carlos Magalhes. 'The Congress won't let itself be intimidated,' he said. 'We need to bring morals to this country and that has to involve soccer. If the price to pay for this is not participating in a World Cup, then let the price be paid.'

No more was heard from Blatter but this wouldn't be the last time that he completely misjudged popular feeling in Brazil. The *Seleção* went on to defeat Germany in the 2002 World Cup final in Japan. What would the sponsors and the world's TV networks have said if Brazil had been banned?

But even Dias couldn't get the full truth. Early in the morning of June 27 1999 a fire was discovered at the CBF training centre in Teresópolis. A storage facility containing important documents relating to CBF financial history, including the accounts from 1985 to 1994, was destroyed. The senators asked for an investigation into whether the fire was lit deliberately. Nothing happened.

Dias recommended criminal indictments for Teixeira. The CBF boss should have been jailed many times over. For reasons we can only speculate about, the police, the prosecutors and judges failed to deliver the investigations and penalties the people deserved.

6

Knifing Mandela
in the back

Bribes took the World Cup to Germany

A Rio racehorse owner was paid $1 million to strangle Brazil's faint hopes of hosting the World Cup. The dark campaign to give the 2006 tournament to Germany involved the humiliation of Brazil and the shafting of South Africa, wrapped up in a strategy designed to retain the FIFA presidency for Sepp Blatter.

As the age of hyperinflation ended in Brazil, Ricardo Teixeira and João Havelange wanted the World Cup tournament and access to the vast amounts of money involved. They had wanted to host in 1994 but the collapsing economy inherited from the generals made a bid impossible and victory went to America.

Now, in 2000, Blatter was fighting to survive at the next presidential election due in 2002. Europe was still angry at the way he and Havelange had manipulated and bribed voters in Paris in 1998. The only hope of retaining power was to divert the 2006 World Cup to Germany. That should satisfy the UEFA countries; their officials would get jobs and tickets out of the tournament. This would be the deal. Meanwhile, Africa had been assured by Blatter it could expect to win. That was a problem – Mandela would get the shaft but hey! no worries, the old man didn't have a vote at FIFA.

Brazil did launch a bid but Conmebol's 10 votes would be insignificant at the presidential election and Blatter did not need to include them in his cold-blooded calculations. Blatter's German associates ensured that the CBF boss was compensated and the bid evaporated three days before the vote.

THE THREE CRUCIAL PLAYERS in 2000 in the campaign to win 2006 were a German billionaire TV mogul, one of Germany's most respected former footballers, and a German bagman who had learned his trade at the knee of the great puppet master, Horst Dassler.

Fronting Germany's bid was Franz Beckenbauer, winner of the World Cup as player and later as coach. In the shadows was Beckenbauer's less well-known deputy, Fedor Radmann, with his short white hair and unremarkable suits. Their careers had entwined for decades. Beckenbauer had helped Dassler in the 1980s. As the ISL company acquired FIFA, Olympic and athletics TV and marketing rights, they were parked in a shell company named Rofa, co-owned by Beckenbauer and his manager Robert Schwan, in the Swiss town of Sarnen where they could not be reached by creditors.

Radmann was employed by Dassler from the earliest days – he was made head of the then under different ownership Adidas

International Relations Team – aka the Department of Dirty Tricks & Vote Fixing. After Dassler's death several of the team reinvented themselves as individual 'consultants' to cities and countries bidding for the Olympics and the World Cup, offering their inside knowledge on the peccadilloes of international sports leaders.

In past years, reporting that murky world and Dassler's team, I found the most entertaining was the devious Anwar Chowdhry from Sunnyside Villas in Karachi. Dassler gave him the job of fixing elections in Asia and paying bribes to make sure that national teams in every sport wore Adidas kit. Chowdhry's reward was a rigged election in Bangkok lubricated with curious, personal inducements for the voters that made him president of world amateur boxing

In 1999 I went to the World Amateur Boxing championships in Houston, tipped off that the Cubans, who were expected to win most of the Gold medals, would be cheated by bent judges. They were, they staged a ringside demonstration and went home early. I despised Chowdhry so much that I declined to request an interview with this liar. He was so annoyed that he sent his son-in-law to summon me to his tenth-floor hotel suite. Curious, I went and was harangued by Chowdhry, lounging in his unbuttoned pyjamas and showing rolls of bypass scars. All his judges were, he assured me, 'Bastards.' After stealing millions of dollars, Chowdhry was ousted in 2006.

This was Fedor's world. He knew everything about greasing the sports machine. Cancer destroyed Dassler in the late 1980s and Fedor moved away from his beloved Berchtesgaden where he was born in 1944 to work for Leo Kirch, the half-blind, reticent, German TV mogul and third player in the Great 2006 Conspiracy.

Sepp Blatter, Leo Kirch, Franz Beckenbauer, Fedor Radmann, ISL boss Jean-Marie Weber, another former German football star Gunter Netzer and later Blatter's nephew Philippe were the ultimate insiders in the world of football power. One sub-group, known as the 'Munich Mafia,' circulated around Bayern Munich. Fedor and Jean-Marie and other members of Dassler's old fixit team were tight with the IOC in Lausanne in South Switzerland. Another Dassler protégé from the 1980s Thomas Bach, once a member of the Adidas International Relations Team, became president of the IOC in 2013 and will be in charge of the Rio Olympics. It was always, and remains, a private world of businessmen and sports officials. Leo Kirch died in 2011.

GERMANY'S BID was in trouble. By early 2000 South Africa seemed to be leading Germany in the scramble for the votes at FIFA's ExCo. This was no good to Leo and his Munich-based pay-TV channels. 'Kirch knew a vote for Germany would be worth gold,' reported Munich's *Süeddeutsche Zeitung*. But Germany, with its tight financial regulation, experienced anti-fraud detectives and determination to control ticket allocations was not first choice for some ExCo members. South Africa offered lax supervision, a growing post-apartheid culture of public corruption – and photos with Nelson Mandela to show off to friends, family and neighbours.

Fedor had the skills to fix this problem. Leo had the money and Beckenbauer was, helpfully, president of Bayern Munich. They came up with a plan. It remained secret until unearthed three years later in May 2003 by Jörg Schmitt at Germany's *Manager Magazin* and Thomas Kistner in the *Süeddeutsche Zeitung*.

Six weeks before the vote, scheduled for July 6, 2000, Kirch turned on the money tap. That day one of Leo's lawyers sent a confidential letter to Dieter Hahn, the KirchMedia executive closest to Leo Kirch. It was a report on the arrangements made by Fedor Radmann and Gunter Netzer. Now Fedor needed the money!

They had been busy negotiating rights to some surprising football matches for a team of Bayern's immense status. They would play Malta's national team and there would be an extraordinary fee of $300,000 for the TV rights, to be paid by KirchMedia into an undisclosed bank account in Malta. The president of Malta football, Joe Mifsud, was a member of FIFA's ExCo.

Another big fee would be paid in Bangkok for Bayern to play Thailand's national team. Another big fee would be paid for Bayern to play Trinidad's national team. The president of Trinidad football, Jack Warner, was a member of FIFA's ExCo – and known as a man who even holds his hand out in his sleep. The match never took place – but a year later Warner was given Caribbean TV rights to the 2002 and 2006 World Cups. The price was 4.8 million Swiss francs but it is unlikely Warner ever paid.

Another big fee would be paid for Bayern to travel to Tunis and play top team Espérance. Its president was Slim Chiboub, married to a daughter of Tunisian State President Ben Ali and who may have been able to put pressure on Tunisia's ExCo member Slim Aloulou who was known to favour South Africa. Slim Chiboub made it to the FIFA ExCo in 2004 but was voted off in 2009. He departed Tunis swiftly when his father-in-law was ousted in the Arab Spring.

A bonus for the foreign teams was that Bayern would pay all their own expenses. In total KirchMedia was prepared to spend a budget of 3.5 million Euros to win it for Germany. Why spend this money? German analysts estimated that in 2006 KirchMerdia could make an additional profit of 500 million Swiss francs if the tournament was played in Germany.

THE RACEHORSE OWNER from Rio had a long history with Havelange, Teixeira and Blatter. He had toured the world with Brazilian teams, taking Pele to Zaire where they were photographed with President Mobutu. It was unlikely he knew Leo Kirch and at this stage is it important to know that over the years Leo Kirch had created the largest movie archive outside Hollywood. He was a shrewd and knowledgeable operator, distributing movies to TV stations. He was the best.

Nonetheless, Fedor Radmann created what reads like a three-page fantasy, a contract in which the Brazilian racehorse owner would be a 'Consultant' to advise Leo Kirch on 'film exploitation, film licensing, merchandising.' It was stated that the 'Consultant has longstanding experience and contacts' in the business.

What was all this sudden and unexpected expertise worth? The contract spelled it out: There would be 'a lump-sum compensation of $1 million . . . in four instalments. First instalment of $250,000 will be due five days after the conclusion of this agreement.' The money would be paid to the 'Consultant's account at BEMO Luxembourg with Société Générale New York.' KirchMedia would pay $250,000 every year for four years.

The memo to KirchMedia manager Dieter Hahn continued, 'Herr Radmann asks that the consultancy agreement is signed today so that he can give it [to the Brazilian racehorse owner] in Munich. Herr Radmann also asks that the first instalment of $250,000 be transferred.' Raising the money would not be difficult. Leo Kirch at that time had a big stake in F1 motor racing and KirchMedia was valued at $5 billion.

What did the Brazilian racehorse owner do with this first instalment? He already lived in a posh apartment block at one end of Copacabana beach and was rich enough to race his horses in Brazil, the Gulf and France. Was the money channelled to Ricardo Teixeira, to encourage him to vote for Germany and compensate him for Brazil's failure?

He signed the contract on May 31, 2000. Kirch signed on June 6, a month before the FIFA vote. It is unlikely that the racehorse owner's Luxembourg bank saw the rest of the money. KirchMedia collapsed with massive debts in April 2002.

*

AS THE DAY OF THE VOTE approached the lobbying, sleeve-tugging and whispers intensified. The danger for Germany was a 12-12 draw. Blatter would have to make a casting vote and he had announced that if this happened, it would go to South Africa. It was essential to say this if he was to keep the African vote behind him for the 2002 presidential Election.

But his old friends Radmann and the Brazilian racehorse owner would have told him about the money flying around and that Germany was likely to win. Terrific! That was Zurich's strategy; Blatter would be the ultimate winner, winning the UEFA votes, sympathising with the African losers and making them promises for the future.

The voting began. In the first round England got five votes. In the second Germany and South Africa tied with 11 votes each. England got two and was eliminated. One of England's votes was cast by New Zealand's Charlie Dempsey. He had been mandated by his regional confederation in Oceania to vote for England and when they dropped out, to back South Africa. Even if Germany picked up the other floating vote, the result would still be a draw, Blatter had to back the Africans. The result was now obvious. See you in Cape Town in 2006.

They voted for a final time: Germany 12 votes, South Africa 11 votes! See you in Munich in 2006. But that was only 23 votes. Somebody had not voted. Who was it? It was Charlie Dempsey. He had walked out between rounds. He was at Zurich airport, catching a plane home.

Charlie dodged reporters as best he could but when cornered, babbled about 'intolerable pressure' on the eve of the vote. This must have been intense. Charlie was now an old man but he emigrated from a tough area of Glasgow at the age of 30 and built a successful construction business in New Zealand. What had intimidated this bare-knuckle, in your face, old-fashioned street fighter?

An early morning call to his room from Nelson Mandela? Then a fax from an anonymous source in Germany offering a bribe of a bundle of good German sausages and a Swiss Cuckoo clock in return for his vote? Apparently this was enough to shatter Charlie and he slithered out of FIFA's back door, a broken man, unable to cast his vote.

Later that day it was revealed that the fax – which went to other ExCo members – was from a German satirical magazine. German tabloid *Bild* attacked the hoax as a 'Bad joke against Franz Beckenbauer.' A major shareholder in *Bild* was Leo Kirch – and Beckenbauer wrote a regular column for the paper.

IT WAS A MASSIVE scandal; nobody outside FIFA believed Dempsey. He had only one function at the FIFA meeting: to cast a vote. Now he was sure to be thrown out of the Oceania presidency along with his daughter Josephine King, who he had appointed his general secretary in 1988. Because he was terrified by a cuckoo clock, a parcel of sausages and a call from Mandela? There was something deep and dirty going on here. The suspicions were huge, especially after the voting scandals two years earlier when Blatter was elected FIFA president in Paris. The rumour soon spread that Radmann had 'fixed' Charlie.

Anticipating the possibility of a 12-12 draw, the arrangement was that Charlie would leave the vote, go back to the Dolder Grand hotel and collect a briefcase left for him in the cloakroom. It contained $250,000. A cab would rush him to the airport for the flight home. Charlie died in 2008, aged 86, and we may never know what spurred him to throw away his career in football in Oceania.

Fourteen years later we are still waiting for Blatter or any member of the ExCo to publicly criticise Dempsey, if only for walking out of the crucial vote. The rest of the world did; why not them? It's tempting to think this is another manifestation of the criminal enterprise created by Havelange and maintained by Blatter. The crooks do crooked things; the others, well-rewarded to leave Blatter to run FIFA any way he chooses, avert their eyes and seal their lips.

Actually, it's worse. They are shameless! Three weeks after the vote, in August 2000, the ExCo met again in Zurich for normal business. I have a copy of the confidential minutes. Blatter told his colleagues that 'the controversy surrounding this election showed how vital it was for the Executive Committee to abide by the principles of solidarity and unity.' When Blatter is in trouble he lurches into this meaningless corporate-speak.

The minutes continue, 'The FIFA President expressed regret that the outcry in the wake of the election had forced Charles Dempsey to hand in his resignation from the FIFA Executive Committee and the OFC Presidency and that he had answered Charles Dempsey's letter of resignation on 15 July by assuring him that the Executive Committee would in due course seek a way to recompense him for his long and loyal services to FIFA.'

Blatter, who would have doubtless been told everything by Radmann and Weber, kept his word and in 2004 Charlie got his FIFA Order of Merit. He got another cloying tribute later, during the World Cup in Germany and it came from another ExCo member, the lowlife Chuck Blazer.

It began sanctimoniously, 'On the opening day of the World Cup, the Germans should dedicate the games to Charlie Dempsey of New Zealand. More than any other man, Charlie assured the hosts that this day would finally come.

'Interestingly enough, Charlie didn't do it by casting his vote for Germany six years ago; rather he succeeded by not voting at all. Following his support of the English bid, Charlie couldn't bring himself to vote outside of Europe. Even though the Oceania Confederation, in its Congress just months before the vote in Zurich, had directed their delegate to the FIFA Executive Committee to vote for South Africa following his support for England, he just couldn't do it.

'For Charlie that would be like breaking marriage vows. After all, Europe did support Oceania becoming a Confederation and Charlie wasn't one who forgot his friends. Charlie told his associates that he had been getting calls through the night from Nelson Mandela and Gerhard Schröder [the German Chancellor] and he was a nervous wreck.'

EUROPE WAS HAPPY. Now Blatter had to comfort Africa. The South African Football Association was so angry that there was talk of taking the obviously crooked decision to arbitration. Blatter talked them out of it and promised that in future the World Cup would be rotated through the continents – and Africa would stage the 2010 tournament. That was OK with Teixeira. He needed Blatter to survive and it was certain that rotation in 2014 would take the World Cup to Latin America. He could fix the final stage of bringing it home to Brazil.

The Brazilian racehorse owner may have been the other big loser – apart from Nelson Mandela and FIFA's shrinking credibility – in the KirchMedia conspiracy. When the liquidators arrived in the spring of 2002, ousted Leo and his managers from the company and began checking through the archives, they would have found the contract and realised that it was an improper payment, that looked like some kind of bribe and was not in the interests of creditors. The Brazilian racehorse owner is likely to have received a demand for the $250,000, with the threat of legal action if he did not pay up.

That contact payment in the summer of 2000 was a wire transaction; the money went direct from KirchMedia to the racehorse owner's Luxembourg bank. Separately, what was the source of the $250,000 paid to Charlie Dempsey? It looks like Jean-Marie Weber and ISL footed that bill. Years later we discovered in the secret ISL archives a payment to an unknown company for exactly $250,000 . . . the day before the vote.

'WE COMPLEMENT each other ideally. That was the case during the successful bid,' said Franz Beckenbauer in the autumn of 2000, announcing that the Berchtesgaden Bagman would be one of his vice-presidents on the Local Organising Committee for the 2006 tournament. Fedor Radmann would be entrusted with marketing, tourism . . . and protocol. It was that last bit Radmann never quite understood, despite giving an assurance that he had terminated all his 'consultancies' and had no conflicts of interest.

Then one morning the *Süddeutsche* informed them – and the rest of the world – that forgetful Fedor still had a 'consultancy' with Leo. Whoops. The public was assured that the relationship would be terminated.

A few months passed and here was Thomas Kistner writing in the *Südeutsche* again with another example of Radmann's forgetfulness. He was still in bed with his longtime chums at Adidas, a major FIFA sponsor. The organising committee was having its differences with FIFA and here was Fedor up to his tricks again, playing for both teams. For the last time, the committee members demanded, is there anything you think you ought to tell us? Fedor told them to relax. No more conflicts of interest. Definitely.

In his next disclosure Kistner christened Fedor 'the Relationship Artist.' He had a serious angle on a story that was convulsing Germany. Radmann had forgotten to disclose that he had a business partner, graphic artist Andreas Abold, who had been paid big euros to design the theme logo for the 2006 tournament. Yet another conflict of interest. The images of happy smiling kids were dismissed by Brazil's *O Globo* as 'laughing, bloated faces.'

Enough was enough. Interior Minister Otto Schily put his foot in Beckenbauer's door and booted Fedor out. No more a Veep. But if you only got your news from FIFA's press releases, you wouldn't know any of this. Blatter's retelling of this poison in the Germany organisation was even more disgraceful than his praise for Charlie Dempsey.

'Vice President Fedor H. Radmann has asked the chairmanship and the advisory board to be granted the right to leave the daily operational business,' said Blatter. 'A wholly independent non-profit-making limited liability company is to be founded on 1 July 2003, to handle all 2006 FIFA World Cup cultural activities.' This was Fedor's new home. Not sacked – reassigned!

The press release quoted the Relationship Artist: 'Personally speaking, and with our common goal at heart, I believe everyone would benefit if I were able to work for the 2006 FIFA

World Cup without being a regular employee.' Franz Beckenbauer added, 'Fedor Radmann has requested to continue to support us in an advisory capacity. Our trust and belief in him is unshaken.'

That was one Radmann out – but one remained. His wife Michaela was still on board, her job was liaising with FIFA in the Accommodation Department. A couple of doors down the corridor was another wife to chat with. That was Sonja Såttele – who everybody else knew as Sonja Abold – in the Marketing Department.

The following year it was the turn of the German edition of the *Financial Times* to take an interest in the Radmann –Abold partnership. Under the headline 'Award among friends,' it revealed that the German government had held a competition to select an agency to create a campaign to encourage Germans to be friendly to foreign football fans. The budget was three million Euros and Andreas had won! What made lots of folks unhappy was that among the members of the jury that were so enthused by the Andreas Abold presentation were ... Fedor and Michaela Radmann.

(Fast forward to 2009 and Andreas Abold was hired at vast expense to work on Australia's World Cup bid. It was a big fee because it concealed payments to Funny Fedor – who managed to secure only one vote.)

THE CONTINUING RADMANN scandals in Germany would not have bothered Blatter. Quite the contrary. That was Radmann's duty in the private FIFA world; having the determination to do what others dare not – and rewarding himself at the same time. Fedor was a 'Made Man' in FIFA's crime family.

The World Cup tournaments of 2006 and 2010 were now sorted and the votes of two continents secured. Rebellion was still to be expected but the dissidents in UEFA could be divided and the generous Mohamed Bin Hammam would look after any problems remaining in Africa. Issa Hayatou would be pushed by an ungrateful UEFA to run against Blatter but they didn't have any money – Bin Hammam did and he would spend it where needed.

Another member of the FIFA family was emerging as a world-class football entrepreneur. A man accused of every kind of financial crime – and getting away with it! The politicians tried and failed to catch him. Prosecutors and judges were denied support to convict him – or bribed to ignore his wrongdoing.

A warm feeling must have come over President Blatter as he read reports of the investigation by Senator Álvaro Dias in Brazil. Ricardo Teixeira was a really bad man! Where had all that Nike money gone? Paying to take judges to the 1998 World Cup in France! Looting the CBF with huge salaries and expenses for himself and his associates! Diverting money to buy votes to keep himself in power! Secretly moving money through the Caribbean! Embezzlement! The CBF sounded like a mini-FIFA!

And of course Blatter knew all about the ISL bribes. Over coffee and cakes during his regular visits to FIFA House, Jean-Marie Weber would have told him every payment from the 1980s, first to Havelange and then when Teixeira was admitted to privileges on the kickback list.

Schooled by Andrade and his corrupt father-in-law, Teixeira was a fraudster-in-waiting when he took the helm at Brazilian football in 1989. Since then he had passed all the tests. Looting the CBF was a rite of passage. He was ready to be given his own World Cup.

I WROTE to Fedor Radmann about the 2006 bidding scandals. He replied that he doesn't know *anything* about persuading Charlie Dempsey to walk out. And he insists that he is not the Fedor Radmann named in the secret memo arranging to pay the Brazilian racehorse owner $1 million and the fees to foreign teams to play Bayern Munich. It must be somebody else with the same name. He'd like me to make that clear. That's what he says and I'm very happy to get it on the record.

We finally met in Paris on March 22, 2011. I was filming at the UEFA Congress for a BBC *Panorama* film and during the lunch break I spotted Beckenbauer and Radmann standing on the left side of the conference platform, deep in conversation. With my camera crew at my shoulder I headed towards them. 'Hello, gentleman, please can we talk?' They looked at me, startled, and then like racehorses out of the stalls, they were gone! Walking very fast they moved along the front of the stage and then shot off up the centre aisle. We followed for a while but, as UEFA officials frowned at me, it was time to stop. So I never did get the chance to talk about Leo, his money, the racehorse owner from Rio and how Germany won the vote to stage the 2006 World Cup.

7

You Want
World Cup Tickets?

The Brothers have plenty

Imagine the three million tickets for the World Cup piled up in a mountain of cardboard. You love football? You want a tiny part of that mountain? You can try through FIFA's lotteries or buying through national associations.

All fans are equal in the competition for precious tickets. You lose . . . but FIFA says it was a fair contest. The mountain has vanished. Never mind, next time perhaps, in four years in another country, you might get lucky.

FIFA warns, don't buy from 'unauthorised' dealers. Herr Blatter's enforcers have the power to impose tough penalties on what he calls 'illegal' activities. Your tickets might be torn up at the stadium door because you didn't buy through his selected agents.

Sepp asks you to believe that when they are not selling you tickets with their markups and cover charges, they are out there, policing and suffocating what he calls 'the Black Market.' He will not permit a parallel, open, competitive market, as you find in any other kind of business. Football's World Cup tickets industry must remain an unregulated monopoly.

Look at that mountain again but this time, imagine it is an iceberg floating on the ocean. Suddenly the quantity of tickets available to fans has shrunk. Where have they gone? Peer beneath the surface and you can glimpse another world where the tickets you dreamed of float tantalising out of reach.

There may be only three fishermen in the world who really know what is happening in those dark depths. Sepp – and Jaime and Enrique Byrom. Sepp has known the Byrom brothers since 1986 when the World Cup was in Mexico, the land of their birth. In those days Sepp was FIFA's general secretary, carrying out every wish of his boss, João Havelange.

Herr Blatter knew the Byroms were close to Mexican soccer boss and TV mogul Guillermo Cañedo, a vice-president of FIFA. Cañedo was close to João Havelange, the FIFA president. Sepp worked for Havelange. Any friend of the president was to be looked after. The Byrom brothers, in their early thirties, were organising tours to the World Cup and, well-connected, had a great future doing business with FIFA.

They prospered, moved to England and now run a huge share of FIFA's World Cup operations from a modern two-storey building in a business park in the green, southern suburbs of Manchester, close to the international airport. One of their companies is Byrom Holdings and it has its home in the Isle of Man where they don't have to publish accounts. One of their bank accounts is in Sotogrande in

Spain. The brothers have acquired pleasant homes in upscale villages in the Cheshire countryside, rubbing shoulders with the star footballers of Manchester's two great clubs.

Every ticket for every World Cup game goes through Jaime and Enrique's computers. Whatever Sepp tells you, some end up in the hands of the dealers. Over the years tickets have passed through the varied hands of a Polish martial arts expert, Caribbean hustlers, a very fat man in Trump Tower, fixers in Eastern Europe, indeed all over the world, all doing secret business in the vast underside of the iceberg with the blessing of senior FIFA officials. One ticket dealer told me that 'Up to 40% of tickets come out of FIFA's back door.' That staggered me. I had thought maybe 10%.

A decade ago, in 2003, the executive committee in Zurich awarded Jaime and Enrique – he's the one with the beard – the contract through a tendering process to sell tickets for the Brazil World Cup. Later they awarded them another plum tender; 450,000 of the best tickets to sell in hospitality pack-ages to the high-rollers you can spot in the luxury boxes necklacing each modern stadium. Among them is a special plum; 12,000 of the best tickets for the final on July 13, only for those boxes. It is appropriate that Taittinger champagne have the exclusive refreshment contract.

Renting these VIP skyboxes with their chefs and waitresses to entertain your business associates can cost more than $2 million. Jaime and Enrique hoped that every one of them ringing the Maracanã and every other stadium would be packed full. After the losses they made in South Africa, it was vital to the future of their business.

*

IT IS CHRISTMAS DAY 2005 in Trinidad. The national team has qualified for the next World Cup in Germany and fans dream of acquiring tickets. The *Express* newspaper publishes every day through the holiday period from its offices in Port of Spain and reporter Lasana Liburd has an unexpected front-page present for FIFA vice-president Jack Warner. Spread over three days, an exclusive investigation features Jack's dealings with Jaime and Enrique.

Warner, as he always does for any football competition, is running his ticket rackets. Liburd reveals that Warner's family-owned business, Simpaul Travel Services Limited, is acquiring tickets from the Brothers and reselling them in packages. This breaches FIFA's ticket rules. The story goes global; a FIFA boss profiteering from World Cup tickets angers fans everywhere.

Brother Enrique is dispatched to Trinidad. He produces a report for FIFA claiming that Trinidad has been supplied with 10,749 tickets. Jack's story is that some are going to his local sponsors, and others are scattered through the island to caring people in local football. Simpaul, Warner claims, are only getting a miserly 1,774 to sell onwards, packaged with rooms booked through the Brothers.

These, it will turn out, are only the visible tip of Warner's 2006 iceberg. Deep in the dark, subterranean world of FIFA, Blatter, Warner, the Brothers and tickets is another operation involving thousands more pieces of cardboard. It will take several more months to discover.

But the current fire cannot be doused swiftly, so, to change the media's agenda, Jack announces, desperately, that he is out of his depth, ignorant and in need of advice on FIFA's ticket rules. He reports himself to FIFA's rubbery Ethics Committee.

Advice? Jack joined FIFA's ruling Executive Committee more than two decades earlier and would have sat through hundreds of meetings discussing ticketing rules. He knows more than most about them. Blatter condones this deceit. We are all insulted.

Jack and his wife Maureen hurriedly transfer their Simpaul directorships to two local stooges, a housewife and a woman veterinarian. That is enough for FIFA and, in their kindly way, they mildly reprimand Jack for his forgetfulness. At one bound, Jack is free, cleared to steal again!

Three years pass and Jack and Maureen quietly resume their positions as directors of Simpaul. Their son Daryan has stayed at the helm of Simpaul, running the rackets. There is more and bigger business to be done with the Byroms for the 2006 World Cup.

A MONTH LATER, in the spring of 2006, two auditors from the Ernst & Young company knock at the Brothers' company's door in England. Dealers around the globe, the Americas, England and Japan, are tipped off that they are in trouble. This triggers all-night sessions, hurriedly rewriting invoices, ticket and room orders. It can get very busy underneath an iceberg showing cracks.

But it isn't enough. Jaime, Enrique, Jack and Daryan have problems. The auditors are peering into the dark water. Soon they can discern that the previous year, in June 2005, the Warners had placed orders, huge orders, with the Brothers' company for more than 5,000 tickets for the World Cup in Germany.

They have been ordered on behalf of travel trade businesses that will package them with rooms and flights and resell. Again, the Warners are using their Simpaul company to camouflage the deal. It is a clear breach of FIFA's rules and should unleash draconian penalties. More importantly for the Brothers, if authorised agents discover their legitimate business is being undermined by what smell as if they could be insider deals, they could be firing off massive compensation claims.

The auditors from Ernst & Young are hired by FIFA's General Secretary Urs Linsi to watch for ticket rackets. This is the first time Linsi has been in charge of a World Cup. He's not spent a lifetime at FIFA and he is taking a risk, going after the Brothers' company and Jack; they've been around longer and Sepp needs them more than he does this accountant, hired from a Zurich bank. Eighteen months later, Linsi is gone, with a gagging agreement as part of the huge severance deal.

The E&Y suits are digging in. Are they finding documents that compromise the Brothers' business? Have dealers in the subterranean secondary market – the 'Black Market' – been favoured over authorised resellers? If they find out, would these companies sue FIFA for breach of contract? It could be devastating.

Angry letters and emails swirl around the planet. By early

April there's a secret deal on the table. A 'settlement letter' is drafted and the scandal stays submerged.

Some tickets reach fans. Others do not. Most importantly, the scandal is suppressed. The World Cup can proceed without any nasty smells. Italy beats France in the final, Sepp stays in the shadows to avoid being booed by fans.

The scandal cannot be suppressed forever and it explodes in September 2006 when I disclose in a London newspaper two secret reports the E&Y suits had sent earlier in the year to FIFA's Urs Linsi. I acquired them from a reliable source inside FIFA. Again, a journalist is exposing the rackets, not FIFA, not the Brothers' own company. Sepp protects the people in his private world.

The first report is delivered to FIFA on April 11, 2006 and there is sufficient evidence to expel Jack Warner. He had ordered 5,400 tickets to resell, breaking FIFA's rules. But a public punishment will spotlight the Byroms' company, who supplied them. The scandal is hidden.

Not so lucky, in the first week of the World Cup, is fellow FIFA Executive Committee member Ismail Bhamjee from Botswana, forced to resign for selling 12 tickets at three times face value to undercover reporters. Unlike Warner, Mr Bhamjee doesn't have a sack full of votes to lend to Sepp at every Presidential Election. Disposing of him gets FIFA good headlines. It's another eight weeks before Warner's bubble bursts.

The Warner problem must be kept under control. Sepp selects a reliable Swiss lawyer to 'examine the circumstances surrounding Simpaul's sale of World Cup tickets.' He is not pointed at the cause of the scandal, the Brothers' company's sales to Simpaul.

The reliable lawyer interviews Jack, Urs, the auditors and the Brothers' company. Jack is cleared, as you would expect of a man whose 35 votes from the Caribbean region keep Sepp in power. The reliable lawyer decides that Jack had no idea that his son Daryan, chief executive of the Simpaul company who shares the same roof and breakfast table, was bumping up the price of tickets as they were resold. The naughty boy did not tell his daddy!

The Brothers' company had to be mentioned but it was too precious to Blatter's operation to be dumped. The harsh verdict on their organisation? 'Their conduct has not been error free,' says the reliable lawyer. Wow. That's it. Game over. Back to business as usual.

Simpaul are denied tickets for future World Cups. Daryan is ordered to pay a 'fine' of 754,375 Euros to a charity 'to compensate for the profits he had made through the resale of World Cup tickets.' Daryan pays a little – almost certainly plundering a FIFA grant to Trinidad – and then stops. The word among the traders in the parallel market is that Daryan's profits from his dealing with the black market are nearer $3 million.

This scandal surely means the end of Jack Warner's nearly two decades of illicit ticket rackets. The Brothers' organisation will never dream of dealing with him again . . . will they?

ANOTHER WORLD CUP, it's in South Africa and the gang's all here – with a new team player. Sepp's nephew Philippe has joined; his day job is chief executive at the Infront sports marketing company, based in Zug. Infront is in the same suite of offices where Jean-Marie once organised the bribes from ISL to Sanud and Sicuretta, kickbacks for the boys from Brazil. Infront has been awarded tasty FIFA marketing and TV contracts by Uncle Sepp.

Now nephew Philippe's Infront has acquired five % of MATCH – the company predominantly owned by Jaime and Enrique Byrom that has the exclusive World Cup hospitality contracts aimed at the big wallets of the corporate world. You can see them high up in every stadium, enjoying the best views, champagne and fine catering in those VIP boxes. After winning the tender, the FIFA ExCo has granted them 380,000 tickets to sell in their upmarket packages.

The Brothers' company has appointed agents around the world to sell their luxury packages and they seem to have kept the business in the family of football. In Nigeria the man with the wad of expensive tickets is Samson, son of ExCo member Amos Adamu. Some doubt Amos's integrity. When he presides over major sports events in Nigeria, money can evaporate. It's against the law for civil servants to have foreign bank accounts but Amos has one, Swift number AEIBUS33, with the American Express bank in New York. He once tried to steer a grant from the IOC to it but was blocked by another official. Amos is a nasty piece of work. When a Nigerian journalist went digging into Adamu's rackets, siphoning off public funds, he was hit with a stupendous damages claim for £2.3 million. When I published this in the international media, Adamu dropped the action and crept back under his stone – but went on enjoying the fruits of being a member of Sepp's ExCo.

Delivering the PR patter is Andreas Herren who, after half a lifetime blocking the media for Sepp at FIFA House, up on the hill above Zurich, now speaks soothing words to reporters on behalf of the Brothers' company – and Philippe – from his new office in Zollikerstrasse, a few blocks back from the lakeside.

There's lots of juicy contracts to be won for supplying services to the World Cup and the Brothers' company is doing well. Following Mexico in 1986, it operated tours for sponsors in Italy in 1990 and had a narrow escape when tickets were hard to come by for the final in Rome.

In the USA in 1994 the Brothers' company became 'Official' supplier of accommodation for fans and the FIFA Congress. They've kept that business, doing it in Brazil in 2014 and are set to do it again in Russia in 2018. In 2002 they tendered and were awarded the World Cup ticketing business. On the way they picked up the Ryder Cup in golf, European rugby and French tennis.

In 2003, after winning another tender, FIFA's ExCo awarded the Brothers' company the contract for handling the millions of World Cup tickets at the South African 2010 World Cup. There was more; after winning yet another tender, the ExCo also gave them the tickets business for the next World Cup, 11 years later in Brazil in 2014.

They operate under the business name of the FIFA Ticket Office – the FTO. FIFA assures us that the Brothers' company will police the parallel market, down in the dark, icy waters, preventing the seepage of tickets to the secondary market to be repackaged with rooms and flights.

It is important because that illicit activity would undercut the authorised agents, travel firms who have paid a $30,000 premium for access to tickets and then had to buy a bundle with a face value of $80,000.

That's the theory. But it won't work this year. There's a glut of tickets. As the tournament nears, they are stacked up in inventory with few customers. Soon they will be dumped on the market.

FIFA talks tough about penalties and sanctions and says the Byroms' company will develop 'legal and operational strategies to address the harm caused to fans by the parallel market.' This is puzzling. That's exactly what the Brothers' company were doing with the Warners in 2006. They would not dream of doing it again in 2010, would they?

THE BROTHERS have their FIFA Ticketing Office in Cresta, a suburb to the west of downtown Johannesburg. Mid-afternoon on March 19, 2010 an accounts manager sends an email to two customers who are working together. One is a woman in the Caribbean, the personal assistant to a Very Important Member of FIFA's Executive Committee. The other is a man in Oslo, a well-known ticket dealer in the illicit, parallel market.

The message is devastating: 'If we have not received the Bank Payment Authorisation Slip of the outstanding payment by Tuesday 23rd March 2010, you have to consider that your ticket order will be cancelled.'

Is the Brothers' company still feeding the parallel market, breaking all the rules they are legally contracted to uphold? It appears that they have agreed to supply tickets to a dodgy FIFA vice-president who is reselling them into the black market.

But these clients no longer want the tickets they had ordered months previously for the 2010 World Cup. It is the beginning of the South African ticketing disaster. Fans are walking away in increasing numbers. The dealers already have tickets they can't sell. They don't want any more.

This alarming message from the Brothers' FTO in Cresta is confidential, but is circulated among their friends. It is copied to two women employees of Philippe Blatter's Infront company in Switzerland. Will they tell Uncle what is going on? Also on the copying list is a senior manager from FIFA and his assistant, also in Switzerland. Finally, it is copied to a top man with Jaime and Enrique in Manchester. He is ticketing operations manager with another of the brothers' companies, MATCH Event Services. Let's call him *Mister Tix*. We will meet him again.

So the Brothers' company, the Nephew's company and Sepp's FIFA itself seem to be complicit in this secret racket to trade in tickets beyond the reach of ordinary fans.

The saga began in December the previous year. The Caribbean woman emailed to the man in Oslo who wanted to buy tickets; 'It was definitely nice talking to you,' she wrote. 'Thanks for the list, I will see what can be done. Can you give me an idea of the financial remuneration? Also, would you be in a position to advance the funds required to pay to FIFA/

LOC for the tickets being ordered? With regards to the numbers we will try our best.'

They do. From an office in Trinidad an order is filed with the Byroms' FTO for 310 tickets at a face value of $84,240. They are mostly Category 1 tickets, priced from $160 to $600. The order was topped off with a demand for 38 final tickets. Those should bring in a lot of profit from fans desperate to see the biggest match in the biggest tournament. The money had to be sent to a bank in Sotogrande in southern Spain.

On January 20, 2010, the Caribbean woman emailed Oslo, 'Important. Here's the first bunch of tickets, you have to pay by tomorrow! I got them 2 hours ago. There will be a 10 percent fee on top of the price.' There were problems obtaining the full order but she assured the clients, 'We have other options for tickets purchases, and have already set about speaking to the relevant persons.'

BUT IT WASN'T TO BE. Within weeks the ticket traders knew that World Cup 2010 was a bust. Fans were not spending their savings on tickets; they were buying big-screen televisions and staying home.

Sepp and Jérôme Valcke were claiming big ticket sales. This was not true. These were unsold inventory held by travel agents who were now dropping prices just to get some money, any money, back on their ill-advised investment. Blatter told Reuters that all tickets for the World Cup semi-finals and final were sold out. It wasn't true and discounted final tickets were available the day before the game.

On March 1 the woman personal assistant in the Caribbean

emailed their partners in Oslo. Where was the money promised for the tickets? She added, 'I hope it was paid, as Mr Warner would be quite upset as he would look as if he ordered and could not pay.'

So it *was* Jack Warner, swimming in the underwater market again, feeding off the invisible part of the iceberg. Eighteen days later, on March 19, when Warner and his Oslo associates still had not paid, the widely circulated 'pay-or-get-lost' ultimatum was sent from the Byrom–FIFA Ticket Office in Cresta to Trinidad and Oslo.

Who had placed this order? It was not the Simpaul company. They were banned from dealing in World Cup tickets. It wasn't Warner personally, nor his assistant. It was an organisation based on the opposite side of Edwards Street in Port of Spain, Trinidad, from Simpaul. It was the Caribbean Football Union: president, Jack Warner.

Journalists at the daily *Dagbladet* in Oslo, Torgeir Krokfjord and Espen Sandi, who unearthed these documents proving that Warner was involved again in the tickets rackets and again with the Brothers' company, obtained another scoop. One of the Oslo dealers feeding them information secretly aimed the video camera on his smartphone at two other FIFA ExCo members discussing ticket business with him; they were Nicolás Leoz and Ricardo Teixeira.

'I WAS STAGGERED when I saw the ticket prices for South Africa,' one fan told me. 'The cheapest seat for the group stage in Germany was $49 – but had been jacked up to $88 for 2010. This was unacceptable to most fans. Then we discovered that the cheapest final ticket had risen from $168 to $440.' It got worse. In their hospitality packages the Byroms' company was charging $755 for internal flights between World Cup cities. Local no-frills airlines were only asking between $140 and $196.

From February 2010 Jaime and Enrique's company began dumping many of the 1.9 million bed nights they had reserved in hotels, splendid and modest alike. As ticket sales slowed, public bodies like city councils and utility companies began buying tickets and distributing them to employees. School children were drafted to fill seats when the tournament began. South African politicians could not be embarrassed after all their speeches claiming that the country welcomed the event. The TV networks that paid millions wouldn't be happy screening half-empty stadiums.

Two weeks before the tournament the press was reporting that more than 160,000 World Cup tickets were still unsold. On the eve of the football the ticket dealers in the Johannesburg hotel bars estimated that only 60% of tickets had been sold at full price. After the World Cup it was reported that 1.2 million tickets were never sold but on their website the Byroms' company claimed 97.5% of the tickets – 2,967,349 of them – had been sold.

A year later, in June 2011, the Brothers' company conceded it had missed its hospitality sales target by a massive $50 million. Their spokesman denied vigorously this was any kind of disaster for the company because they had 'made a long term financial investment into its 2010 and 2014 project.' So they would start their Brazil business $50 million out of pocket.

Those VIP boxes at the Maracanã had better be full!

Jaime and Enrique's Brazil operations are getting some help from Sepp's ExCo. On page 19 of the Byroms accounts for the year ending March 2012 they reveal a loan of £6,210,128 from FIFA 'to fund the obligation for MATCH Services AG to provide accommodation services for the 2014 FIFA World Cup Brazil.' It's not just a £6 million leg-up; the loan is interest-free! This apparently sweetheart deal is not reported in FIFA's accounts.

How did they get the Brazil hospitality contract? There was a tender process and it was awarded to the Brothers in 2007 by FIFA's Executive Committee. Vice-President Jack Warner controlled three of the 23 votes. After his dealings with the Brothers' company in 2006 – and his secret plans to do business with their organization again in 2010 – they would surely have appeared the best candidates to him. The icing on the Brothers' cake was that they also got awarded the contract after winning the tender for 2018.

For the Brothers' company, FIFA is the gift that keeps on giving. In November 2011 the MATCH Hospitality deal was extended to 2023, 'Following an industry evaluation conducted by FIFA.' This time they didn't bother to call for tenders.

The formal announcement may have surprised some. It continued, 'The agreement also further strengthens FIFA's fight against ticket touts. Thanks to their expertise and monitoring facilities, MATCH Hospitality will be in a position to assist FIFA in enforcing the provisions governing the sale of hospitality packages, effectively preventing unauthorised dealers from luring corporate clients and individuals into buying such packages from them.'

By this time Jack Warner had been forced out of FIFA. One less racketeer wanting dirty World Cup business.

THE ÁLVARO DIAS investigation report into how Ricardo Teixeira ran the CBF totals 951 pages. It's not all long-buried history. Many of Teixeira's decisions when in power were having a massive impact on the World Cup and its many contracts. Start reading at page 21 of Volume 2 and savour the relationship between Teixeira and the Stella Barros travel company. The headline is 'A True Partnership of Profits for a Company and Losses for CBF' (*Uma Fiel Parceria de Lucros para a Empresa e Prejuízos para a CBF*) In the three years between 1998 and 2000 Teixeira's CBF spent a staggering $12 million with the company.

Senator Dias was unhappy about some of the information that his investigators discovered in the CBF archives. It seemed to him that the CBF was not getting all the benefits it should when so much money was going from Teixeira's CBF in the direction of Stella Barros. Dias wanted to know why the company did not appear to give any discounts to the CBF, despite the huge volume of business. He believed that airlines offered average discounts of 15% and the CBF should have been saved $982,000.

Dias wondered if money was being pocketed by someone at Stella Barros – or perhaps somebody at the CBF. All very puzzling but there was no proof. Unfortunately, the CBF accounts were a mess and Dias simply could not discover all he wanted to know about the Stella Barros–CBF relationship.

Another CBF business relationship worried Senator Dias. He noticed that one company boomed after it began doing business with Teixeira. Again, Volume 2, from page 174, is an educative read. Dias reveals the lucrative deals where the CBF sold exclusive marketing and worldwide television rights to the Brazilian national team to the Traffic company, owned by José Hawilla. Then Traffic acquired a slice of the famed Nike contract and made what Dias described as 'spectacular' profits. By 2000 Traffic was the fifth biggest sports marketing company in the world with revenues of $111 million.

THE WORLD CUP brings old friends together. In October 2011 the Byrom Brothers' MATCH company announced their partners for selling hospitality packages in 2014. Firstly, step forward, Grupo Traffic. In what seemed like an attempt to send reporters to sleep, the press release from the Brothers claimed the deal 'represents by far the largest commitment in the hospitality industry in sports for a single territory and is a major milestone for the success of the 2014 FIFA World Cup™ Hospitality Programme.'

'The 2014 World Cup is the ultimate proof of the evolution and professionalization of Brazilian football,' says José Hawilla. Some people think the performance on the pitch says more about Brazil. But he has excellent references; the former FIFA ExCo member from New York, Chuck Blazer, says he had two decades of working with José and 'he is a man of extraordinary character. I would say that his hand-shake was better than most written contracts.'

The second partner in the stadium necklace business was Top Service Turismo, part of the Grupo Águia, owned by the Abrahão family. It had absorbed Stella Barros in 2004. Reporter Rodrigo Mattos revealed that Claudio Abrahão shared the family fondness for Ricardo Teixeira so much that he sold him a wonderful beach front penthouse apartment in Barra da Tijuca, in Rio, for $300,000. This was especially generous because, according to the transfer duty paid, the apartment was actually worth three times as much, valued at $843,000. Lucky Ricardo!

8

How Blatter Keeps Power at FIFA

Sepp buys votes with FIFA's money

Jack steals. He is a career thief and it has made him a multi-millionaire. To hide his stealing, he lies. He lies to his colleagues in football, he employs a bookkeeper in his homeland to pose as an auditor and lie for him. For more than 30 years Jack Warner stole tens of millions of dollars from FIFA. Sepp Blatter must have always known but would pay any price – and it wasn't his own money – to bribe Warner into delivering 35 crucial votes at presidential Elections.

Most of those votes came from compliant officials in Caribbean islands without professional football and dependent on FIFA handouts in public and World Cup tickets in private. Their region is known as Concacaf, the continental confederation controlling football in the Caribbean and Central and North America. It is insignificant in the global game – only two nations made it to the second round in 2010 in South Africa and then went out – but hugely powerful in the politics and corruption. Concacaf became Warner's powerbase.

Those 35 votes, alongside the 50-plus from Europe, and as many again from Africa and nearly that total from Asia, are pivotal when the 209 national football associations are called to vote on FIFA's presidency. So, any demand by Warner had to be conceded.

João Havelange helped set up Warner's rackets in the 1990s but when investigators asked him for assistance in March 2013, to verify some of Warner's wilder claims, Havelange claimed he was too ill. Two months later Havelange was forced to quit his FIFA honorary presidency as the ISL bribes scandal finally caught up with him.

Fast forward six weeks from his humiliating exit from world football, Havelange was miraculously recovered and in good enough health to enjoy a splendid lunch and two bottles of wine with Sepp Blatter in a Rio restaurant, guarded by 16 policemen, even as the tear gas was swirling around Brazil's stadiums.

I told the story of Warner's rise through Caribbean football in *Foul!* but, restrained by London lawyers, had to give generous credit to the defences and explanations of Chuck Blazer, Warner's American partner in crime. In Chapter 9 I'll reveal the truth about Blazer's stealing, hand in hand with Warner and, again, with the knowledge of Blatter.

Warner, a history teacher in Trinidad, manipulated himself to the top of Caribbean football and in 1983 that won him a seat on FIFA's Executive Committee – the ExCo.

Havelange, tutored by Rio's organised crime boss Castor Andrade, spotted and nurtured this new and malleable talent. Warner would deliver whatever Havelange and Blatter needed. A crucial need for them in 1989 was that the USA must qualify for the 1990 World Cup in Italy. The next tournament, in 1994, would be in the USA and it was essential to build media interest in a country where football was low on the sports agenda.

Warner held the key. He controlled Trinidad football. To the delight of the entire country the national team was one game away from qualifying for Italy the next year. All they had to accomplish was a draw with the USA at Trinidad's national stadium on 19 November 1989. Trinidad had a skilful team and were tipped to win, even more than the required draw.

Warner saw his chance for eternal gratitude from Zurich. He did everything possible to make life difficult for his team, providing them with the worst training facilities he could get away with. There was a curious change of match officials shortly before the game. Warner needed chaos at the stadium – and saw a chance to enrich himself illicitly at the same time. He printed 45,000 tickets for a stadium that could only hold 28,500 fans.

On match day the Trinidad team had to be lifted over the heads of the angry thousands who had tickets but were locked out of the stadium. Trinidad fans have forever contested the referee's decisions but all that mattered was that the Americans scored one goal, Trinidad didn't score any, and the marketing of 1994 was secure.

Chuck Blazer from New York, already a football official, was as keen as Warner to climb the FIFA tree. Ignoring the defeat and misery in Trinidad they conspired in 1990 to seize control of Concacaf. Warner became president and immediately appointed Blazer as general secretary. Two decades of robbery began.

HOW COULD he steal millions of dollars from FIFA and Concacaf and be sure that Zurich would look the other way? Warner pondered how to pull off the big heist and made his first move in March 1995, paying $1 million for a plot of land in Tunapuna, on the road to Piarco airport. He was not out of pocket for long. Three months later he announced that Concacaf needed a Centre of Excellence – known as the CoE – for training the region's players and FIFA would pay for everything.

Quietly, in February 1996, his family-owned company Renraw (Warner spelled backwards) was incorporated. The following month Renraw spent $314,460 acquiring a second plot at Tunapuna. Warner was building a property empire – and it didn't cost him a cent. A month later Concacaf held its congress and Warner told delegates that the purpose of the CoE was to 'help raise the quality of Concacaf soccer.' FIFA President Havelange was present and the minutes record that he congratulated Warner 'for his vision in building the Concacaf Centre of Excellence in Trinidad.'

Havelange's enthusiasm was understandable. He would be leaving FIFA's presidency in two years time' and he needed Warner to swing his 35 votes behind Blatter at their congress in Paris. They dare not lose control of world football or allow anybody not in their corrupt gang to get access to FIFA's archives and discover the truth about Havelange's looting. It would be a tough fight – the worryingly honest challenger, Sweden's Lennart Johansson, would be backed by UEFA. The money poured in to Warner's new businesses. He was a man who could be bought – if the price was right.

It was a high price for the global game but Havelange happily turned on Zurich's money tap. In January 1996 FIFA sent $250,000 to Trinidad. Two weeks later FIFA sent another $1,700,000. The money was gushing and in April FIFA sent $500,000 and another $500,000 in May. Yet another $500,000 followed in June and the same amount again August. 1996 was a great year!

In September Warner registered a new, private business in Trinidad – the 'C.O.N.C.A.C.A.F. Centre of Excellence.' He could then set up bank accounts in a name suspiciously similar to the real thing. He did and they sucked in money intended for the development of the CoE. But he wanted more.

Warner told Havelange that Concacaf needed a bank loan for the construction and in 1997 FIFA guaranteed a $6 million loan from the Swiss bank UBS. In April UBS, which held FIFA's accounts, handed over the first $2 million, another $2 million followed in August and yet another $2 million in November. How was this money to be repaid to FIFA? It wasn't. In May 2003 FIFA's finance committee – Warner was deputy chairman – agreed to write off the loan. Football paid, again.

At the end of the first round of construction Warner held a ribbon-cutting ceremony and gave the Centre a new name.

It became the Dr João Havelange Centre of Excellence. This kept up the lie that it belonged to football – not secretly to the Warner family.

In the forecourt Warner erected a circular structure modelled on a Greek temple and between the pillars was a bust of Havelange. It was topped off with a globe and a huge Concacaf banner. As more money was hijacked over the years the Centre grew. Today it is fronted by a glass-walled fitness centre where the island's middle classes pay to use exercise bikes, weights and all the apparatus of an expensive leisure centre – the Warner family-owned, FIFA-funded health club.

Behind it in the FIFA-funded but Warner-owned complex is Le Sportel Inn with 44 rooms and two penthouses. The Nelson Mandela Room is for business seminars. Next to it are a series of large halls rented out by the Warners for conventions, wedding parties and industrial shows, a swimming pool rented out to schools and clubs – and the Marvin Lee Stadium, named after a local player who died after an horrific injury in an international game.

FIFA's regional development officer ordered that an artificial surface was laid on the pitch at a cost of $800,000. It was perfect for all-weather football and became the home of the Warner family-owned Joe Public professional team. The FIFA official was Warner's second son, Daryll.

The Centre's website continues the lie that this private facility is associated with Concacaf.

Warner took money with both hands from every possible source. Even as he was building up the CoE he made sure that his Concacaf office in Trinidad was sucking in more cash.

Between 1996 and 2003, monthly payments to run the president's office ranged from $10,000 to $25,000. From 2004 to 2011, the payments increased and ranged from $25,000 to $45,000 per month. Over those 15 years Warner scored more than $5.3 million to run an office that also handled his political and business activities.

THEN WARNER WAS off to France for the coronation of Sepp Blatter and the 1998 World Cup – and more crude thieving. Warner wanted to be as far away from his FIFA colleagues as possible and he arranged to be based in Marseilles. With his wife Maureen he checked into the Sofitel hotel. The police discovered later that on the morning of June 23 Warner went to a post office and dispatched a parcel for him to collect later in Paris. That evening they watched Norway beat Brazil 2-1.

When they returned to the Sofitel they had a shock for the management. A burglar had broken into their room! $35,000 worth of Maureen's jewels had been stolen! $30,000 in cash belonging to Jack had been taken from his locked case! Call the police!

The police did their best but it was the perfect crime. There was no forensic evidence, no forced door or luggage locks, no strange fingerprints. Warner had the only key to his case. The only member of staff who had a copy of the electronic door key was a reliable under-manager of 20 years' standing. The police talked to him for a few hours – and let him go.

Local reporters say that the police realised the truth of this bogus robbery but decided, for political reasons during the World Cup, to drop the investigation and not prosecute Jack.

I heard the story and emailed Warner with some questions. Why had he and Maureen not asked the hotel management to put the cash and jewels in their safe? Why was he carrying so much cash? How did he acquire it? (If he ever did have so much money, he would have got it from black market ticket sales.) Did he have any idea how his case of money was opened? Why was his wife travelling to a soccer tournament with such a quantity of jewellery?

Warner did not reply.

It was unlikely that the Sofitel's insurers would have paid a customer who had left $65,000 of cash and jewels lying around his room. But Warner knew that there was somebody who would pay. Six weeks after the 'robbery', FIFA's insurers paid up. The German company got huge business from FIFA and it was sensible to pay off such a powerful member of the ExCo.

WARNER returned from France and helped himself to more of FIFA's money. His Renraw company purchased the third and final plot of land for the CoE for $392,775. He wrote to FIFA saying that it had cost $640,000. They sent the money. A quarter of a million dollars profit for one simple, lying email!

In regular reports to FIFA Warner listed the CoE as a Concacaf asset. Warner reported to the Concacaf executive committee that this latest land acquisition was 'recently acquired' for them. It was a lie. A simple check in public land records would have revealed the truth.

From the beginnings of this vast crime Warner assured both FIFA and Concacaf that they owned the land. All the millions of dollars supposedly invested in regional football were in truth building a huge leisure empire on land owned by the Warners for the family to operate, profitably, for themselves.

FIFA had paid for the land and the construction. They had given Warner an asset he could use as security for borrowing money. In September 1998 he approached Trinidad's First Citizens Bank and borrowed $475,000. He got his accountant Kenny Rampersad to co-sign the loan deed. In Trinidad Rampersad had to tell the truth to the bank; that the property belonged to Renraw and another Warner company. Rampersad was also employed by Warner to prepare financial reports for Concacaf. He told a different story in his report for the same period – that the property was a Concacaf asset.

Warner told the same lie, repeatedly, to Zurich. When FIFA asked where they should send money to, Warner said, send it to an account named 'C.O.N.C.A.C.A.F. Centre of Excellence.' This was one of his private accounts.

WARNER WAS OFFERED every opportunity to steal and he took every one, year after year. Nearly $5.6 million was provided to the CoE by Concacaf's New York office between 2000 and 2011. How was it done? From 2000 to 2003, Concacaf sent $1,260,000 in 23 separate wire transfers to a bank account at First Citizens controlled by Warner and named the 'Dr João Havelange Centre of Excellence.' Typical payments were of $50,000. Beginning in April 2004, Concacaf wired $50,000 to this account every month. In 2011, the last period of his gross embezzling, the amount increased to $75,000 per month.

FIFA played its part. On top of the $15,950,000 already paid, Zurich threw in an additional $10 million for further development of the Centre. This had to be repaid so for four years Warner declined the $2.5 million that FIFA donated every year for regional football development between 2003 and 2006. The money should have been distributed around the region.

Warner sent FIFA's head of finance a letter, dated December 20, 2001, 'authorizing' FIFA to transfer the first two instalments of $2.5 million in 'assistance to this Confederation for each of the years 2003 and 2004 . . . for the operations and development of our Centre of Excellence.' He instructed Zurich to send the money to an account at the First Citizens bank. That account is a personal one in the full name of 'Austin Jack Warner.' This stealing was rubberstamped by the Finance Committee, the members of the ExCo, the Internal Audit Committee and auditors KPMG.

SEPP BLATTER was worried at the 2002 World Cup. If he was going to continue charging the world's television networks vast amounts to screen the tournament he had to have full stadiums. The problem was the Korean people. They patriotically attended every match played by the Korean team. But would they be interested in buying tickets once their team was eliminated? Baseball and basketball were as popular as football. Blatter turned to his match officials to help keep the stadiums full.

In the second round Korea faced Italy, always formidable opponents. Even more formidable, for the Italians, was referee Byron Moreno, from Ecuador. He awarded a strange penalty to Korea after only four minutes – but it was saved. Then the game went well for Italy with a goal from Christian Vieri after 18 minutes. Apparent victory was stalled at 89 minutes when Korea levelled.

Just before half-time in extra time Francesco Totti was brought down in Korea's penalty box. Replays showed that Italy should have been awarded a penalty. Instead Moreno sent off Totti for diving. In the second half Damiano Tommasi's golden goal was disallowed, again to the incredulity of fans worldwide. Three minutes before the end of extra time, Ahn Jung-hwan leapt above the Italian defence to head in the golden goal. Korea went through to meet Spain in the quarter-finals. Their luck couldn't hold, could it?

Spain found themselves playing against Korea, referee Gamal Ghandour and linesman Michael Ragoonath from Trinidad, nominated for the tournament by the reliable Jack Warner. Spain scored in the second half; the referee disallowed it. The match went to extra time. Spain's Fernando Morientes scored but up went Ragoonath's flag. A goal kick was awarded. Replays proved him wrong.

Spain won a corner in the last minute of extra time but the referee blew for full time a minute early, before they had a chance to take it. Korea won the penalty shoot out and went through to the semi-finals.

Edgardo Codesal, who refereed the final of World Cup 1990, resigned in disgust from the referees' committee. Codesal alleged in the Mexican press later that pressure was exerted to appoint Ragoonath for the Spain vs Korea game.

Codesal also criticised Warner for hugging Kim Dae-jung, the Korean president, directly after their victory over Spain. Warner later said that he was 'glad that Korea won,' and in a rare moment of truth, admitted the result was 'better for TV.' Ragoonath had to know that if he displeased Warner, his career was over. He would never travel again out of Trinidad on football business. Germany knocked out Korea in the semis. These days Blatter says FIFA is cracking down on match-fixing.

WARNER USED HIS STOLEN MILLIONS to fund one of Trinidad's two main political parties, the United National Congress – the UNC. It gave him huge power in a small island. But he hated belonging to a party in opposition. Elections were due in early November 2007 and Warner came up with a master stroke to win popular approval.

He would fly to South Africa with UNC party leader Basdeo Panday, demand an audience with Nelson Mandela and extract from the great man his blessing for the UNC in the election. That would stun his opponents in Trinidad. Surely Mandela would agree after Warner insisted that he had delivered crucial votes at FIFA's ExCo to give South Africa the 2010 World Cup. Mandela owed him.

Blatter thought so too and FIFA issued a confident press statement that 'Jack Warner paid a whistle-stop visit to South Africa today to meet with Nelson Mandela as well as executives of the country's Premier Soccer League.' The impression was given that Warner was leading a FIFA delegation.

Mandela, now aged 86, was protected by his bodyguards from scavengers like Warner. When Warner arrived he was told that he would have to sign an agreement that he would not ask Mandela for anything and the meeting could not be political. He hesitated – how could Mandela say 'No' to him, the great Jack Warner? It was fatal arrogance. He was not allowed anywhere near Mandela.

Mandela's spokeswoman told reporters, 'We assumed that the delegation was part of a FIFA working group. Mr Warner did not see Mr Mandela, as he was not in agreement that Mr Mandela could not be approached to endorse an election campaign or a candidacy.' Panday did sign and got a few moments of courtesy and some photos with Mandela. Then he was out too, without a blessing for the UNC.

Under the headline 'FIFA official "makes up" visit to Mandela' South Africa's *Sunday Times* reported that Warner 'was left red-faced . . . after being shown the door' by Mandela. Back home in Trinidad the press were also amused at the arrogant Warner's discomfiture. 'This is the last week before the election, and I do not want to be sidetracked by anything,' he said abruptly in a brief telephone interview. The UNC lost the election.

In 2013, when Mandela died, Warner would have been expected to rush to South Africa to be seen rubbing shoulders with world leaders at the funeral. Instead, he stayed home in Trinidad. The widespread belief was that if he left the island he might be arrested abroad for involvement in fraud, money laundering and bribery.

WARNER NEVER MISSED an opportunity to use his power at FIFA to make countries racked by cultures of corruption and bribery crawl to him. It also helped if they were rich in oil.

Blatter gave him the potentially lucrative position of chair of the FIFA committee that allocated the Under-17 FIFA World Cup. Warner knew Nigeria's incredibly corrupt Amos Adamu, director general of the Nigerian National Sports Commission. (Adamu later joined FIFA's ExCo and was kicked out in 2010.)

Not surprisingly, Warner selected Nigeria to host the 2009 Under-17 championship. Adamu's Local Organising Committee presented the Government with a bloated budget of 35.5 billion Nairas. This was greed too far and, under threat of withdrawal, the budget was slashed by three-quarters to 9 billion Nairas.

Warner was soon playing FIFA's usual racket. They wait a while and then attack the host country for being too slow, hoping to force the government to put more fat into the budget, to be shared out between contractors and FIFA officials.

The pressure was ratcheted up in early 2009. Firstly, Warner was his brutal self. 'I have always had faith in Nigeria but at the moment that faith is not there,' he told Nigerian reporters. 'I cannot go back to FIFA and say, yes, Nigeria is ready, because plenty still has to be done before we get to that stage. If Nigeria doesn't get its act together, Nigeria won't host it.'

That didn't impress the locals and one day later Warner tried an emotional outburst. 'I love Nigeria more than even some Nigerians . . . I'm appealing to all Nigerians to match the facilities with the faith I have in the country. I believe you can do it; please don't let me down.'

One of Nigeria's leading newspapers, the *Guardian*, was

not prepared to tolerate this whining greed from Warner. A few days later it published a scathing editorial.

'It is absurd that this FIFA Vice President Mr Jack Warner is so passionate about Nigeria hosting this FIFA event and that he speaks to Nigeria in patronisingly gratuitous terms that suggest his organisation is unaware that this tournament ought not to be the priority of Nigeria at this stage of our political and social economy.

'Apart from the forbidding cost, he must be aware that this event was foisted on Nigeria through very mischievous means and, for that matter, the objectives of this cadet championship are so spurious and irrelevant to Nigeria now and in the near future.

'Nigeria was presented a dodgy *fait accompli* after it was brazenly blackmailed by self-serving civil servants in contravention of every civil service guideline, and in connivance with FIFA that it must host this tournament willy-nilly.'

The *Guardian* continued that there were better ways of spending the budget. It could instead go towards 'rehabilitating the gas supply pipeline to assure Nigerians of better energy delivery . . . or the computerisation of 200 secondary schools in Nigeria.

'The stark truth is that Nigeria should steer away from the FIFA Under-17 tournament. Mr Warner should not deceive Nigeria to spend her very scarce resources to suit his organisation's priorities and save FIFA the disingenuous task of blackmailing Nigeria in these very difficult times.'

June 4, 2009: Nassau, Bahamas: Warner erupted. His ironclad fiefdom, the Caribbean Football Union, part of Concacaf, was under challenge. Peter Jenkins, a football official from the islands of St Kitts and Nevis, population 53,584, had the audacity to stand for election as a delegate from the CFU to Concacaf against the incumbent, 'Captain' Horace Burrell from Jamaica.

Burrell's most noticeable contribution to world football up until then had come in 1996 at the FIFA congress in Zurich. When the delegate from Haiti had been prevented from attending, Burrell, with the complicity of Warner and his entourage from the Concacaf region, had broken all FIFA's voting rules and put his partner Vincy Jalal in the empty seat, to vote as Warner instructed.

Peter Jenkins argued that small nations like his should have a voice at Concacaf. Warner said this opinion was 'divisive and unacceptable.' Of course his power at FIFA was based on his collection of small island federations, most without professional football, but whose votes counted equally with the big footballing nations of Latin America, Europe and Africa.

Warner would not tolerate elections at Concacaf. He urged delegates not to support Jenkins. Channelling his inner Joe Stalin, Warner said, 'I am very critical of the fact that Caribbean football is split over a candidate, which is unprecedented, and this is what we have fought against over the years.' Jenkins was contravening their 'political conventions.'

Burrell was one of Warner's closest associates in the Caribbean, frequently nominated for prestigious positions in FIFA. If he could be challenged, cracks might be seen in

Warner's absolute power. Warner's response was ruthless. He ordered that Jenkins should be expelled from all football positions in his homeland. It was the same for the regional bodies. 'I have instructed the general secretaries of both the CFU and Concacaf to remove you forthwith,' he wrote to Jenkins.

Burrell added that he felt 'disrespected' by Jenkins. Another of Warner's sycophants, Colin Klass from Guyana, said he too questioned Jenkins' intentions. 'I had serious concerns as I am sure that Peter is aware of the system that we have and he has chosen to ignore it for apparently personal reasons and I must say that what he is experiencing is the price one pays for their actions.' Klass was ejected from football in the Concacaf scandals that began in May 2011.

Warner's iron fist slammed down on two national associations, Antigua and Grenada, who initially gave Peter Jenkins their support. 'They will be written to and be asked to submit reasons why disciplinary action should not be taken against them for their attempts to destabilise Caribbean football and Caribbean solidarity within the CFU,' said Warner. 'If their explanations are not satisfactory, disciplinary proceedings shall be instituted against both countries.'

One of Jenkins' supporters pointed out that FIFA donated $10 million every four years to develop football in the Caribbean but 'the Leeward Islands, Windward Islands and Netherland Antilles received none of it.' Jenkins had the courage, if fatal, to ask about the FIFA grants disappearing into the belly of the CoE. The Concacaf leaders were silent.

It would be another four years before independent investigators confirmed that all the money, year after year, had been siphoned off by Warner through his false Centre of Excellence bank accounts.

THE WORLD CUP was the most exciting time for some members of FIFA's ExCo. Not the football; it was the competition every four years between well-funded bidding countries that could be induced to pay bribes. The evidence is that bribes were paid every time during the campaigns going back to the bitter battle between Japan and Korea to acquire 2002. It is more complicated than simply figuring out who sold their vote to the winner. Many losers have been stung. Several contestants for the 2010 African World Cup paid bribes. Every few months more evidence slithers out.

If Qatar did pay bribes to host 2022 – and there is no solid proof yet – a smart operator like Warner, who had to be seen to vote for the USA, a member of Concacaf, would still have seen an opportunity. It is to be expected that he floated the idea in Doha that the last thing Qatar needed was enemies at FIFA. Warner, controlling three vital votes, could make big problems behind closed doors. Pay me, he would have demanded.

Both Warner and Blazer found it essential to meet President Putin in Moscow before the vote in December 2010. Putin wanted the prestige of hosting 2018 and, as importantly, the construction industry wanted more contracts. The Sochi Olympics had been a bonanza for corruption. Now the Oligarchs wanted the rich banquet of new football stadiums. My own sources in the Russian construction industry tell me that the big companies would pay what was required to win the vote. A few million dollars upfront would soon be absorbed when the contracts were skimmed.

THE ONLY bidder to allege corrupt demands in the contest to host 2018 and 2022 was England's David Triesman, who headed their bid. Triesman gave evidence to a Parliamentary committee of MPs in London. It was a great show! (Triesman was not born an aristocrat. A former communist, he was elevated to the House of Lords by Tony Blair to be a Labour Party spokesman.)

In return for his vote, Jack Warner wanted a personal cheque for £2.5 million 'to build an education centre in Trinidad.' Warner never stopped stealing. Later he asked Triesman for the astonishing and unbelievable amount of £500,000 to buy Haiti's World Cup TV rights for the earthquake-hit nation, again to be channelled through him. Warner responded that the allegations were 'a piece of nonsense' and added, 'I have been in FIFA for 29 years and this will astound many, I'm sure.'

Triesman continued; Paraguay's Nicolás Leoz wanted a British knighthood – 'Sir Nicolás.' Later, one of his Asunción bagmen whispered it would be helpful to win his vote if the English FA Cup tournament was renamed 'The Sir Nicolás Leoz Cup.' Teixeira, the Brazilian vacuum cleaner, told Triesman to 'come and tell me what you have got for me.' Thailand's FIFA member Worawi Makudi wanted to be given the TV rights to a friendly between England and the Thai national team. Makudi has denied the allegation.

There was a dark entertainment that day. London PR man

Mike Lee, who counted among his successes winning the summer Olympics for Rio in 2016 and London in 2012 and winter games for PyeongChang 2018, testified about the kind of 'narrative' needed to win votes. His latest success had been winning the 2022 World Cup for Qatar.

Lee's self-congratulatory speech was interrupted by Conservative politician Damian Collins, who informed Mr Lee that the previous day the *Sunday Times* had filed a memo with the Parliamentary committee containing stunning allegations about how Qatar really won.

The reporters had spoken at length (as had I and several other reporters) with a whistleblower from the Qatar bid team. She claimed to have been in a hotel room in Luanda in early 2010 when the Qatar bidders negotiated bribes of $1.5 million each for the votes of Issa Hayatou, Amos Adamu and Jacques Anouma from Ivory Coast. The Qatar team issued a statement denying the 'serious and baseless' allegations that will 'remain unproven because they are false.' Hayatou and Anouma also rejected the allegations. Adamu had been expelled from FIFA months earlier.

WARNER'S STEALING from the Australian World Cup bid was in a class of its own. If investigators half a world away hadn't stumbled over a half-million-dollar fraud, it would have remained a dirty secret known only to Jack Warner, his sleazy middleman, a few redfaced Aussies and their billionaire boss.

In August 2010 a delegation from Australia arrived in Trinidad, desperately seeking the votes of Warner and the two other Concacaf delegates he controlled at FIFA. Warner took them to see a complex of buildings and sports facilities at Macoya, on the road between Port of Spain and the airport. It was his Centre of Excellence but the Australians were fooled by the fiction that it belonged to Concacaf. To one side was the Marvin Lee Stadium. Warner told the visitors that it needed an 'upgrade.'

A month later the gullible Australians sent Warner a cheque for the astonishing amount of $462,200. By the time the costs of travelling and entertaining were bolted on, the bill could have been a little short of half a million American dollars. What happened to the 'upgrade' money? Warner diverted it to one of his phoney 'Concacaf' accounts at the Republic National Bank in Trinidad. Checks by investigators could find no record of the $462,200 in the real Concacaf accounts. The investigators concluded Warner was guilty of 'fraud and misappropriation.'

The Australian football federation – the FFA – seemed embarrassed by the $462,200 payment. They never issued a press release boasting of the help they had donated to Caribbean football and it did not appear in the FFA report to the government on how they spent a grant of $40 million to fund the bid. There was no mention in the FFA financial report for that year. A spokesman claimed that the money sent to Warner was allocated from FFA's international football development budget at the time and was not part of government funds provided to the World Cup bid.

WHO GOT AUSTRALIA into this mess? The links in FIFA's grimy world were extraordinary. At the heart of the manipulations was Swiss-Hungarian Peter Hargitay. The Australians hired him to win their bid because he claimed to be close to Blatter, working as his 'crisis manager.' Hargitay had never worked for a bid and had no track record of success. But he was backed by Australian billionaire Frank Lowy, chairman of the FFA, on the recommendation of FIFA Ethics Committee member and Sydney television personality, Les Murray. All three men were Hungarian refugees.

It didn't seem to matter that Hargitay was also a paid propagandist and adviser for Qatar's now discredited Mohamed Bin Hammam who campaigned successfully against Australia for the 2022 tournament. Hargitay persuaded his Australian clients to pay for a Trinidad Under-20 team to attend a training camp in Cyprus. But, crucially, he was also a paid adviser to Jack Warner at the time the $462,200 payment was extracted from the FFA.

9

The Belly Eats FIFA

Blazer's Michelin Guide to the world

Chuck stuffed his face in the world's most expensive restaurants. Football paid. When, at the end of 2012, the new people at Concacaf sacked him, they forbade him to pay himself any more money. The money tap was being turned off. But they forgot to tell the bank in time. Quickly, Chuck instructed the bank to pay him $1.4 million from football's cashbox. A few days later Chuck checked with his bank in Cayman. Had the transfer gone through? When he received a reply reporting that the money was safe in his account he responded, 'Yippee.'

See Charles Gordon Blazer once and you never forget him. Absorb the monstrosity. His arms and legs are no more than plump, his head is only slightly larger than average. Of recent years he has sprouted a dense bubbly white beard of the Santa Claus variety.

Look again. It's The Belly that stops pedestrians in the street, casts long shadows at dusk, causes private jets to lurch down the runway. He cannot ride in cars; FIFA had to hire a van with wide sliding doors. How many decades since sunlight caught a glimpse of his testicles? How did The Belly get to be so huge, you wonder? Why doesn't he stop eating so much?

Why does he blog non-stop, with photographs, about all the things ordinary people like you and I will never do? Chuck is meeting prime ministers and presidents, beauty queens, billionaires and football stars. Why the endless name dropping? Why his need to tell us about him guzzling in the world's most expensive restaurants, lubricated with fine wines? Why does he desperately beg the world to take notice of him? What is the secret of his neediness?

I've watched him for more than a decade, sensing early that he was corrupt, gradually picking up tips about his thieving and eventually discovering how he did it. One request to a trusted source in 2011 and I was given the evidence that he helped himself to at least $20 million from football, and probably a great deal more.

Now I think that I understand the reason for The Belly. Chuck Blazer always knew that one day the Internal Revenue Service and the FBI would corner him. Every day was a potential last meal before the executioners came for him. So make it expensive, make it vast, make it the best the world's top kitchens could deliver. And maybe, just maybe, if they put him on the scaffold his weight might snap the rope and he would escape. His parallel partner in crime, Jack Warner, was a permanent escape artist, why shouldn't Chuck get away with it?

*

BY THE MID-1990s Concacaf had moved into offices on the 17th floor of Trump Tower on New York's Fifth Avenue. Chuck went with them, nesting higher up on the 49th floor. He had an office built into his luxury apartment. Who was paying was not discovered for many years.

'Everybody in the office was instructed by Chuck to keep instant messaging on permanently. That way he could issue orders to the worker bees without having to talk to them,' recalls Mel Brennan, who took a job at Concacaf because he loved football.

Mel remembers the first time he was summoned upwards. He expected to find his boss wearing high-quality tailored clothes as he did at the World Cup and other tournaments, at business meetings, and committee meetings.

'This morning Chuck stepped out of his office dressed only in boxers and an undershirt. He issued his orders and returned to the darkness of his office, sitting on his chair, his prodigious stomach seemingly sitting on him, legs splayed alongside his desk, his multicoloured drawers illuminated by stark light from his computer screens.'

Mel Brennan discovered more. 'Oddly, the first thing this man told me about himself was that he wanted to write a book called "40 Years of Women with Cold Feet," an exposé of four decades of female efforts to snuggle cold toes under the enticingly warm folds of his enormous gut.'

Nine days into Mel's tenure as head of special projects for Concacaf his boss invited him to dinner. 'Know where we're headed?' Chuck asked me conspiratorially. 'Scores. Could be a long night.'

Scores? The famous upmarket strip club?

Mel grabbed his phone and called home. 'You need to check with your wife?' Chuck bellowed, bemused. 'I need to let her know it could be a long night, like you said,' Mel replied cautiously.

'Welcome back ,Mr Blazer,' announced the doorman. A special section of Scores was reserved that night for a group from Concacaf. They were served filet mignon and shoulder massages and there was a small TV in a corner, showing a football game.

When it was time to go, Blazer paid. How he did this was another shock for Mel Brennan. Blazer's American Express card was black! Mel had never seen one, few people have. They are known as the Amex Centurion Card; don't bother to apply. They are available by invitation only. The average Centurion cardholder has $16.3 million in assets and an annual income of $1.3 million.

Blazer had set up a chain of credit cards at Concacaf which all fed back into his Centurion Card, accumulating massive Amex membership reward points for him. Between 2004 and 2011 Concacaf paid nearly $30 million to Blazer's card account. Blazer claimed that only $3 million was his personal spending but external investigators could not agree because of the absence of documentary proof. And even this $3 million was paid by football through another of Blazer's clever devices.

CHUCK BLAZER SECRETLY diverted more than $20 million to his offshore bank accounts in Cayman and the

Bahamas between 1990 and his sacking in 2012. When Jack Warner became Concacaf president in 1990 he chose Blazer to be his general secretary. The first clue to the rip-offs they were planning came when, in defiance of all standards of good governance, Blazer was also appointed treasurer. He reported to himself and no other official was allowed to know the truth about Concacaf's finances.

Blazer wrote a contract arranging for a private company he owned to supply him as general secretary. The key points were a monthly fee and a quaintly named 10% 'override' commission fee on income from sale of sponsorships and TV rights.

Blazer's 'commissions' payments and 'monthly fees' were sent offshore to accounts at Barclays Bank, Grand Cayman, and the First Caribbean International Bank, Bahamas. These accounts supposedly belonged to companies owed money by Concacaf. In fact they were shells that never provided any services to Concacaf. Their function was to launder money to Blazer and evade taxes in the USA.

Blazer's initial contract expired in 1998 and was never renewed. That suited Blazer because Warner didn't stop him paying colossal amounts to his offshore bank accounts. It reduced the likelihood of American tax officials discovering that this American citizen running a business out of New York was secretly paying himself offshore.

Blazer also had an account with a Merrill Lynch bank branch in Cayman. He used this one for banking his profits from illicit World Cup ticket sales.

With no other Concacaf official to scrutinise him, Blazer

quietly expanded his 10% of sponsorships and TV rights to cover sale of match tickets, luxury suite rentals, parking, and venue concessions. Eventually he was taking more than $2 million some years. But if you looked in Concacaf's accounts – and very few were allowed to see them – you would not find any mention of compensation to the General Secretary. Only a line for 'Commissions' – but no explanation of who got them.

Sometimes, to escape attention, Blazer would break down the sums he was taking. In October 2008 he cut up a $150,000 payment to one of his shell companies and paid three cheques, each of $50,000, the same day. Another time he made two $500,000 payments on the same day to a shell.

Each year he built up his 'commissions payable' and 'fees payable' in Concacaf accounts and deducted payment for rent in Trump Tower and living and any other expenses. The large balances then went to his offshore shells. There is no evidence that he ever paid for anything out of his own pocket.

In recent years the monthly rent for Blazer's luxury apartment in Trump Tower was $18,000. One third was paid directly by Concacaf and the remaining two-thirds deducted from Blazer's 'fees-payable' account. He lived rent-free.

BLAZER SAW A CHANCE to copy Warner and steal a FIFA grant. In December 2005 FIFA's Finance Committee, deputy chairman Jack Warner, authorised a $3 million payment to Concacaf for the construction of a TV studio. It was then approved and paid through FIFA's marketing and TV company, controlled by Jérôme Valcke. Later the payment was scrutinised and approved by Cayman Islands football boss Jeffrey Webb, a member of FIFA's Internal Audit Committee.

Blazer scrutinised it for a moment and then skimmed 10% – $300,000 commission! He got away with this – and you may wonder what other rackets he worked on his FIFA expenses and per diems over his 17 years on the FIFA ExCo.

BLAZER AND WARNER nearly came unstuck in the spring of 2002 when they held their Concacaf conference in the Loews Miami Beach Hotel. I turned up but was denied admission. Unlike all other regional and FIFA conferences, the press was barred. Accidentally, I found myself sharing a busy elevator with Warner and, as we travelled slowly up several floors, I asked him in front of 20 American tourists to explain why he opposed freedom of the press. He glowed with silent rage.

His big problem that weekend was a challenge from the Mexican Federation. They wanted to replace him with 1990 World Cup referee Edgardo Codesal. And they wanted Blazer to explain some strange items in his financial report. A Mexican delegate stood up and read out seven questions. One asked for clarification about $1,195,000 in 'Commissions' listed under 'Marketing' expenses in the financial report.

Blazer replied that it 'corresponds to a decision of the Executive Committee taken in 1990 to provide compensation for the general secretary through commissions on revenue and for marketing and sponsorship,' and that this and other expenditures were 'consistent with budgets approved by this congress.'

His answer was expunged from the minutes of the meeting. All Concacaf meetings were recorded on audio tape.

Investigators discovered the labelled cassette case from 2002. It was empty.

THE BELLY. Blazer cannot let you get away from it. He used it as a barricade, preventing victims from escaping being photographed by his girlfriend Mary Lynn. Worse still, he created a blog in 2006 to show off his trophies. It was headlined 'Travels with Chuck Blazer and his Friends' and featured Nelson Mandela trapped inside a small charter jet by The Belly and Mary Lynn's toothsome grin, both always pointed at the camera lens. Even worse in December 2013, from the depths of his disgrace, The Belly cheapened Mandela's death by adding his own, tasteless tribute.

Hundreds more victims had to embrace Chuck or Mary Lynn, or both. The professionals – like Bill and Hillary Clinton – knew how to display their frozen 'I don't know who this person is but I'm so pleased to see them' face. To show his importance Chuck scanned and uploaded a copy of his credentials for the Republican convention in Minneapolis in 2008 with the inscription 'McCain - Friends & Family Guest.'

Mary Lynn's camera must have overheated sometimes. Former footballer Bobby Charlton was caught twice by her. She was official photographer when Chuck forced himself into the clouded world of Muhammad Ali and misspelled his name on the blog. The camera vultures swooped on Desmond Tutu, sitting in a low armchair, and nearly obliterated him with The Belly while Mary Lynn lit up the scene with her teeth. Chuck blogged him as a 'bishop' unaware the great man had been an archbishop since 1986. Along with The Belly's grandson, they captured British Prime Minister Gordon Brown, who clearly had no idea who was hijacking him.

Age and infirmity was no barrier to the vultures. Fay Wray, the star of the 1933 *King Kong* movie scowls at the camera appearing to say, 'Who is this fat bastard looming over me – and who is this woman kneeling at my feet and clutching my hand so I cannot take it away?' Chuck couldn't spell her name either.

Putin was more than a match for The Belly, manipulating him into changing the 'Friends' blog into a showcase for Putin's macho holiday snaps and advertising the joy of Aeroflot. 'I don't comment too much about airlines these days. There isn't much good to say about most of them. I learned a couple of years ago while commuting to Moscow in preparation for the FIFA Women's U20 World Championship, that the best food was surprisingly found on the Russian national airline,' enthused The Belly. 'I am happy to report that I wasn't disappointed and everything from the appetizers, the soup, the salad, the choices of main courses and dessert rivalled any of the better known airlines and surpassed most of them.'

When The Belly landed in Moscow, 'Mary Lynn and I snuck away to the Vogue Café, another one of Moscow's stylish posh places to be seen with an equally exquisite menu. Despite the distraction of the model types at the adjacent table, we really liked revisiting this discovery from 2006. GQ was also the chic club at late night and restaurant through the day and evening.'

The pope was privileged to be photographed with Chuck at a late 2000 audience with the ExCo. Blazer bowed his head to Pope John Paul in exchange for a handshake. The pontiff urged Blatter to use his 'immense power' to promote moral values and solidarity. Blatter solemnly nodded his head.

The good times always rolled for The Belly, however much the outside world suffered. 'I got a call from my friend and colleague Ricardo Teixeira in town with his wife Anna and daughters Antonia and Joanna. It was hard to tell on Spring Street in the midst of Soho that the US stock markets and the world banking economy were brought to their knees with losses of 20% in recent days,' blogged Chuck.

It got worse. 'Ricardo is the hardest working President of any National Association I have seen . . . He is tremendously dedicated to his Federation . . . he has a lot to be proud of and justifiably so.'

No need to buy the *Michelin Guide* to eating in New York. The Belly has tested and reported on all of them. Best for Porterhouse steaks is Wolfgang's. You get 'a great dinner at The Dutch, a hot New York Eatery at 131 Sullivan Street in Soho.'

'At Elaine's on 2nd Avenue between 88th & 89th Street there were some new appetizers like meatballs of veal and pistachio nuts. For me, a full Veal Chop was pounded and turned into a great veal chop parmigiana. Delicious.' The Belly is a frequent glutton at Terrase and Scarlattis. 'Most every football official from Dr Havelange to George Weah has been with me to dinner at Campagnola's Restaurant on First Avenue between 73rd and 74th Street on New York's Upper East Side'.

Fancy a snack? The Belly's been there already. 'Barney

Greengrass serves the best Nova, Eggs and Onions with Herring in Cream Sauce and Potato Pancakes. It was yummy.' Jack Warner's in town; 'a great dinner last night at BLT Market.' Russia's Bidding Committee for the World Cups 2018/2022 is in town to court The Belly. 'Their choice was outstanding, the top shelf restaurant L'Atelier de Joël Robuchon at the Four Season's Hotel. Simply superb.'

A visiting English delegation provides more football excuses to get fatter. Lord David Triesman and David Dein feed him at the Oak Room in the Plaza Hotel on Central Park South.

The Belly rolls on. 'A day after our Executive Committee meeting, as peace and tranquillity returned to New York City, the one remaining member Guillermo Canedo and his wife Adriana, joined us for a special meal at Eleven Madison Park.

'We had been trying to get a reservation there for weeks, but luckily we managed to swing one for their last seating at 9:45pm. What followed will be remembered for a long time as one of the best culinary experiences of a decade. It was great to establish a new relationship with a very special American restaurant to enlarge the choices of exceptional places to bring guests when visiting New York.'

The Belly doesn't wash his mountains of food down with water. 'Michel Platini knows that one of my favorite wines is Chateau Figeac, a rich St. Emilion from the Bordeaux region of France. He and I once sat in a lovely New York French bistro, Le Charlot (69th Street between Madison and Park Avenues), and uncorked a vintage bottle which I saved for special times.

'On the other hand, there is my long time relationship with Tuscan wines from Italy and in particular Masseto Ornellaia. Between the Figeac and the Masseto I am truly torn to pick a favorite.'

The Belly gives us insights into the private lifestyle he shared with other members of the FIFA ExCo. At the 2006 World Cup, 'We were served a very nice dinner following the cocktails in the Bayerischer Hof in Munich. The dinner was in a lovely private dining room on the second floor with a very talented Harpist playing soothing dinner music. Having rung the bell for cocktails at 1900 hours, and with the honor of having Dr. João Havelange, the Honorary FIFA President and his wife Anna Maria for dinner, we recognized his 90th birthday by all singing the traditional Happy Birthday song.'

The Belly proceeded to eat Germany. 'The good restaurants around the city had been booked for weeks but we were lucky that they made a place for us in the Lorenz Adlon, an incredible French restaurant on the second floor of the Premier Kempinski hotel. The view from the window was a panoramic view of the Brandenberg Gate.

'I must admit that the food offerings exceeded the view. First were two tasting menus. The seasonal of five courses; the other with seven. If that didn't ring your bell there were two full pages of a la carte dishes. We didn't opt for the tasting menus but decided to do a traditional appetizer dish and a main entree. The wine choice was tough, since there were so many to choose from, but I managed to find one that everyone liked and we polished off three bottles while digesting a really great meal. Mary Lynn and I devoured chocolate soufflé.'

Then The Belly was off to Cologne. 'The dinner was extraordinary with a choice of fish in a delicate cream sauce or veal on a ragout with a dark wine sauce.' In Munich The Belly began with stretching exercises in a beerhall. 'There is something about drinking beer in Munich that makes it magical even for a non-beer drinker like me. Oh, the sausages were pretty good too . . . and soft pretzels . . . even a spiral cut white radish that you put a dash of salt on . . . hmmmmm . . . salty pretzels, salty radishes, salty sausages.'

Then it was off to 'a lovely country inn at Starnberg located at the side of a lake of the same name. The food was great. Bavarian, full of taste and calories. Really delicious. It should tell you something when appetizers we ordered are called "*forespeis*," which literally translates as foreplay.'

The Belly remembers fondly, 'the groans of satisfaction following the four dishes including *Nürnberger* Sausages and sauerkraut; a noodle dish I can describe as a cross between Fettucine Alfredo and Kraft macaroni & cheese; also a regional dish of the most delicious and enormous "ravioli" type pocket pasta.

'Finally some local fish served with potato pancakes didn't stop Norbert (The Belly's host) from returning to the menu to order main courses. I wasn't sure where it would fit . . . but as you can see, with the consultation of our waitress Norbert found a few more dishes to let us know that you can't eat Bavarian food every day . . . well, at least I can't. But, it was great.

'Mary Lynn was too polite to refuse, so Norbert ordered her a delicious freshly cooked fish with almonds liberally sprinkled on top which came served with 3 large boiled potatoes garnished with cut chives and a side of steamed vegetables. Naturally, Mary Lynn who can still wear dresses that would fit a teenager, eats healthy food.

'Norbert, following my protests, said he would only order some little "sides" of *Brotzeit*. I should have been suspicious of the sparkle of glee in Norbert's eyes as a platter of cold cuts, cheeses and spreads landed on the table accompanied by slices of dark German bread.

'Finally, Norbert announces, "No German meal is complete without the desserts!!!" Mary Lynn raises her arm in protest, but to no avail as Norbert orders her a Bavarian Cream. Blazer knows that Norbert is right, so quickly says, "I will have the plum strudle with vanilla sauce."

'I know Norbert ordered something for himself, but once my dessert came I was into some state of sugar shock and have no memory of what he ordered. The coffee, I thought would keep me awake on the way back to Munich, but alas, gluttony and satisfaction overtook my body as I slipped into a blissful rest until we pulled up at the Bayerischer Hof.'

FOOTBALL did not need to spend its money on luxury apartments on Paradise Island in the Bahamas. It did, because Chuck wanted a Caribbean holiday home plus the rental income from holidaymakers. Nobody was checking what he did with Concacaf money. So Concacaf paid the $910,000 deposit on two apartments. The paperwork gets tangled at this point but Blazer ended up owning three units on the third floor at the towering blocks of The Reef – one of the ugliest constructions in the Caribbean. Once they were acquired he transferred ownership to another of his shell companies, in turn owned by two other shell companies in Nassau.

A holiday home in the Bahamas wasn't enough. Blazer wanted more homes in the sun and more Concacaf funds were used to purchase two apartments at the Mondrian South Beach hotel in Miami. The Mondrian is a waterfront luxury hotel and residence with a high-end restaurant. The apartments – a one-bedroom apartment and an adjoining studio – were purchased for $810,000.

It was a problem transporting The Belly around New York. Taxis were too small and it took time to rent vans. Blazer ordered a top-of-the-range Hummer costing $48,554 and it cost a further $600 a month to garage the beast near Trump Tower. The Belly and Mary Lynn were the insured drivers but it was rarely used and later driven down to Miami and again, parked most of the time.

THEN THERE WAS the country estate. The Belly wanted to show off his wealth. Mary Lynn's home state was North Carolina and her grandparents had left an elegant but deteriorating farmhouse on Route 64 out of the small city of Lenoir in the foothills of the Appalachian mountains. Chuck was keen to fund renovation of the tumbling down building. It was to be a grand affair.

There would be a magnificent sprawling façade with double doors leading into rooms for dining, living, TV and movies, breakfast and a kitchen. Up the broad staircase were six bedrooms, all with their own bathrooms. On the deck at the back was an outdoor pool with a Jacuzzi. One neighbour, pleased to see Lone Oak Farm being restored, was astonished to discover that Chuck wanted a secret panic room and extensive security precautions. Chuck purchased hiz 'n' hers quadbikes and careered around the area being photographed with puzzled local farmers and foresters.

Chuck looked after his children. Jason, a physical therapist, was paid $7,000 a month as director of the Concacaf Medical Department. Daddy arranged important foreign trips for Jason, representing Concacaf in Zurich at FIFA functions and presenting trophies in the Concacaf region and Latin America. Daughter Marci Blazer, a corporate lawyer, was nominated to sit on FIFA's legal committee.

10

How The Belly Flattened Warner

Then was caught by a 'Useless' journalist

'Congratulations Jack, Maureen, all of my Trinidadian family that I love for these many years.' Chuck was blogging after Trinidad held Sweden to a 0-0 draw in Dortmund in June 2006. The love for Warner and his wife lasted another five years. Then The Belly launched himself from a great height onto Jack and with one horrible, squelching noise, blew him out of football.

Warner had become too confident. He knew that Blatter hated the endless scandals involving him and World Cup tickets and would love to evict him from FIFA but, surely, he wouldn't dare. And Blatter had left it too late. Jack was changing sides. The man from Qatar wanted the 35 votes Jack controlled and he had unbelievable quantities of cash to buy them. Jack had stolen all he could using the Centre of Excellence pretence and it was time to find a new source of endless riches.

Mohamed Bin Hammam had provided the money to buy votes to elect Blatter in 1998 and again in 2002. Mo believed they had an understanding that after one more term Blatter would stand down and hand over football's imperial throne. But Blatter refused to depart – so he had to be pushed. Mo manipulated Blatter to make him head of FIFA's Goal Bureau, distributing huge grants to national associations. Mo had spent years buying support in Asia and Africa. If Concacaf's votes could be acquired, Blatter would not risk a fight and the humiliation of losing. A doctor's certificate would be produced, Blatter would retire to the Swiss Alps and, without the need of an election, Mo would be crowned at another FIFA coronation.

Warner summoned a meeting of the 25 members of his Caribbean Football Union members. They would obey Warner's orders in the Presidential Election and the other nine members in Concacaf – including USA and Canada – would have to follow. Mo paid Jack's family travel firm Simpaul to ship the officials in from their islands for a meeting in the Hyatt Regency hotel in Port of Spain on May 10, 2011. After Mo spoke, each delegation was given a big brown envelope containing $40,000 in cash, 'to spend any way they wanted.'

Jack and Chuck had stood back to back against the world for more than 20 years, both stealing, both protecting each other. Not any more. Chuck guessed why Mo was visiting Trinidad and that well stuffed envelopes would be on offer. He talked with his closest associates who would be at the meeting. A plan was made. Photographs of the bags of money were sent to Trump Tower. A video was shot surreptitiously on a cell phone. When The Belly had gathered enough evidence, he turned it over to a lawyer with the instruction to obtain testimony and draft a report. Before the end of May, Blazer had filed a complaint to FIFA accusing Warner of corruption.

A few weeks earlier I had encountered Mohamed Bin Hammam, a guest at the UEFA congress in Paris. I was filming for the BBC and asked him about FIFA corruption allegations. Mo replied, 'We are not transparent enough,' as if that was the answer. I asked him about Warner, notorious for his corruption. Mo answered, 'Your cause is not my cause. Your information is not my information. We are having different sources of—'

I interrupted, 'So Jack is alright?'

That was a question that Mo was not going to answer. 'As far as I am concerned all the people in the Executive Committee did a very good job, we have to support them until we put in rules and regulations, tell the people clearly what is the black and what is the white and then we have to make them accountable to this.'

June 20, 2011; Zurich. Jack has gone! He made a noise for a few weeks but the proof was enormous. Having won what he wanted, Blatter was too smart to put the boot in. His 'regret' statement at Warner's departure was calculated not to inflame Warner into disclosing his vast knowledge of Blatter's awareness of corruption. Jack, deputy chair of the Finance Committee, was one of the few in the world who knew how much Blatter paid himself in salary, expenses and bonuses.

Blatter's farewell kisses began, 'Mr Warner is leaving FIFA by his own volition after nearly 30 years of service, having chosen to focus on his important work on behalf of the people and government of Trinidad and Tobago as a Cabinet Minister and as the Chairman of the United National Congress, the major party in his country's coalition government.'

This slimy press release maintained the fiction that Warner had 'served' football. Blatter knew about the vast World Cup tickets rackets and Havelange would have told him that the Centre of Excellence was a multi-million theft by Warner that should deliver vital votes for both of them, forever. This embarrassing tribute from Blatter to Warner continued:

'The FIFA Executive Committee, the FIFA President and the FIFA management thank Mr Warner for his services to Caribbean, CONCACAF and international football over his many years devoted to football at both regional and international level, and wish him well for the future.'

And then Blatter went too far.

'As a consequence of Mr Warner's self-determined resignation, all Ethics Committee procedures against him have been closed and the presumption of innocence is maintained.'

Innocence? The world laughed – and raged – at Blatter for letting Warner go free. But why should he care? The embarrassing Warner was dumped. More importantly for Sepp's survival, the man from Qatar who was almost certainly going to beat him for the FIFA presidency was also gone, banished.

The Belly had won.

AMERICA HAD A NEW HERO! 'Chuck Blazer is witty, gregarious and a whistleblower' said the Associated Press. He was a White Knight! 'Blazer's personality and accessibility make him one of FIFA's more popular members,' gurgled the AP writer. There was more; 'The only American on FIFA's powerful executive committee has spent 30 years promoting football and has shown before that he will step in when he feels the game is being shortchanged.'

This AP suckjob noted that Blazer lived in Trump Tower but did not ask how he could afford the high rent. Unchallenged, Blazer was allowed to praise himself, 'If you look at the accomplishments of FIFA, I'm very satisfied when I look back at the 16 years that I've been there, our accomplishments have been very positive.'

There was no reference to the embarrassing Belly. Much of the AP homage had been lifted from a profile of Blazer in an American sports business magazine the previous year. At that stage Chuck and Jack were still a double act. Chuck had dismissed allegations against Warner. The thousands of extra tickets sold in 1989 for the USA–Trinidad game? The Belly rejected the allegation with, 'It made for a lot of noise and press but it had very little credibility.'

Chuck rearranged the truth about the 2006 scandal when Warner was caught selling thousands of tickets to the black market. There was no scandal. It was 'the result of changes to FIFA's ticketing policies. The whole nature of ticketing was in flux around that time,' Blazer said. 'He addressed it and made corrections to the business practice. It sounds worse than it was. It was a censure and not an expulsion.'

The American press had a new hero and facts were not going to get in the way of their good-news story. The *New York Times* looked at The Belly's blog and announced, 'Chuck

Blazer takes fans with him on his many travels in the service of soccer.' Service? Oh dear.

America's football officials were no better. 'We lead by example at U.S. Soccer, and most people say we are a very moral, ethical organization', said Dr Robert Contiguglia, US Soccer Federation President, before the new scandal. 'We did support Jack Warner and Chuck Blazer for Jack's election and we supported [Sepp] Blatter for the contributions he made to the game. We have a very good working relationship with them.' He added, 'Blatter is an icon of humanitarianism.'

Nastier was Concacaf Vice-President Alan Rothenberg, famous for paying himself a $7 million bonus for helping organise the 1994 World Cup in America. Back in 2002, when I first smelled corruption in Concacaf, I emailed Rothenberg, hoping to talk. He responded, 'I have no interest in talking to a biased hatchet man. If you had a shred of impartiality you would recognize the incredible contribution made to the enormous growth of soccer on and off the field that has been made worldwide by Sepp Blatter, both as President and before that General Secretary, and regionally by Concacaf's President Jack Warner and General Secretary Chuck Blazer.'

His rude response demonstrated the power of Warner, Blazer and Blatter over this multi-millionaire American lawyer and banker. Rothenberg had hoped to join the FIFA ExCo in 1995 but Warner kicked him aside and installed his crooked partner Blazer. Did Rothenberg scream 'stinking fish'? No, he dropped to his knees.

*

'YOU ARE USELESS as a journalist,' Chuck Blazer howled at me in an email a month after Warner's hurried resignation from FIFA. Two months later – in October 2011 – Blazer announced that he was resigning as Concacaf general secretary. He was following Warner out of football's door.

This is how it happened. I had been astonished by his uncritical press in America. Why had these dimwit reporters not realised that, if Jack was a crook, The Belly must be one as well? For two decades they were inseparable brothers in looting football.

It was time to dig. I had been aware for years of rumours that The Belly helped himself to 10% of Concacaf TV and marketing revenues but there were so many other corruption stories to investigate. Now it was time to find out how all that fat got inside The Belly. I knew that Chuck and Jack kept Concacaf's financial reports secret. Only a small circle of deferential officials saw copies.

I emailed a contact. Could they help? A few days later I had a bundle of confidential Concacaf reports on my screen. The Belly was greedier – and more slippery – than I had guessed. I began looking at the most recent, for 2010.

I read that the accounts had been audited. Chuck said so on page 38. On page 41 Trinidad accountant Kenny Rampersad presented what he claimed was an 'Independent Auditor's Report.' This was not true. Rampersad was not an auditor and should not have claimed the title. The Belly and Warner knew he wasn't. But none of the deferential elected officers of Concacaf would ever dare check that Kenny was no more than a simple accountant.

The thieving was on page 50. The top half of the page was headed 'Administrative & General.' In the list of Stationery and Supplies, Automobile Expenses and Property Maintenance were Salaries and Employees benefits, totalling $1,077,944. You might presume that Chuck's pay packet was in there. You would be wrong. But you would not know.

The lower half of the page was headed '*Marketing, Sales and Public Relations.*' Buried in the midst of *Printing* ($21,373) *Gifts and Awards* ($21,670) was *Commissions and Fees.* That was it. No indication who got them. For 2010 it totalled an amazing $1,919,671. For the previous year it was even better, $2,622,714. Over the period of the previous five years the anonymous Blazer paid himself $9.6 million in commissions on top of his 'fee' as general secretary.

Another source gave me documents showing that Blazer arranged to have his commissions paid to his offshore accounts in Cayman and the Bahamas. It was unlikely the IRS knew he was being paid this money. I emailed Blazer, asking him to explain this novel way of being paid and asked him to respond by the reasonable newspaper deadline I gave him. His reply came late and I knew immediately that he knew he was in trouble. Why? It was too long. Two pages of polite and convoluted sentences.

Blazer had no choice but to confirm the 10%. But he claimed that this is 'consistent with industry standards.' He did not disclose what these standards were. It was bullshit. There was more of this smelly stuff. How would he answer my question about his failure to reveal that it was him who was getting these commissions?

Blazer uses language as a weapon to confuse and obfuscate. You have met this kind of crook before. They gamble that if they deploy words you have never heard of, they will intimidate you. So here, now, deep from The Belly was 'everything has been reported fully to Concacaf's members consistent with the level of granularity of other items in the financial reports.'

'Level of granularity'? Granular, granulated, granules – what the (*Expletive deleted!*) was The Belly gibbering about? Translated into normal language he was saying that it is not important to tell his employers that he was ripping them off for millions of dollars a year.

Blazer confirmed that he employed his son Jason as Concacaf's $7,000 a month medical officer. But now The Belly was starting to quiver. He was getting rattled and stooped to insults. 'Your question about my son is completely inappropriate,' he wrote. 'I am a public person and recognize that harassment from people like yourself with agendas to sell books and papers and who have little regard for the truth, comes with the territory.'

I published the story on my blog under the headline '*Lucky Chuckie! Blazer takes secret 10% on sponsor deals.*'

There was another story screaming to be investigated. On his blog The Belly had published a sequence of photos of an antique Mercedes car he owned that was being renovated in Zurich. The Belly posed in Zurich with this lovely car and painted out the number plate before uploading.

He forgot that it could be seen in another shot of Mary Lynn with the car by Lake Zurich. I checked that number plate – ZH 627 187 – with the Canton of Zurich registration office and discovered the registered owner was FIFA and that the car was stored in FIFA's underground garage! It was obvious that Blazer was hiding this asset offshore from America's tax authorities. A FIFA spokesman told me, through tight lips, that FIFA charged Blazer fees to park his car on their property.

The last Big Belch from The Belly, 'You are useless as a journalist' was fired off from Trump Tower at 16:57:21 on July 17, 2011. The clock was ticking down on the Blazer family exploiting football.

WARNER AND THE BELLY were dumped in the dustbin of football history. Blatter promised there would be a new clean leadership in the Caribbean. Then he selected reliable members of the old Warner–Blazer group to be put in place. It seemed the quality he most desired was an inability to look back and see who allowed the Deadly Duo to get away with two decades of thieving. His choice for president of Concacaf was Cayman Islands football boss Jeffrey Webb, who had proved his reliability in the ten years he was a member of FIFA's Internal Audit Committee.

Webb was elected by Concacaf at FIFA's congress in Budapest in May 2012, all paid for by FIFA. Alongside as a vice-president was longtime Warner ally 'Captain' Horace Burrell from Jamaica. There were two free FIFA ExCo seats to fill. Webb took one and New York's Sunil Gulati, a longtime ally of Blazer, took the other.

Digging into my archives I have found a private email in

2002 from Jeffrey Webb to Warner, copied to Blatter. At the time, Blatter was facing a challenge from African football boss, Issa Hayatou, backed by some of UEFA's members. Hayatou's election team toured the Caribbean, looking for votes. They went to Cayman.

On April 4, 2002 Webb reported on his visitors. He was very proud of his interrogation of the delegation. Webb was enthusiastically supporting Warner's demand for a reduction in European places in the World Cup finals. This was television suicide for FIFA and marketing the tournament but if Warner could extract another place for Concacaf, there would be more money to steal.

Webb, like Warner, was keen to find any way possible to extract more cash from FIFA. Why couldn't the grants from the FIFA Goal Project be $1 million a time instead of the current level of a maximum of $400,000? How did Webb intend to spend this money on some of the smaller Caribbean islands? Gold-plated goal posts on Anguilla, population 16,000? What did Montserrat, population 5,000, need? Or Webb's homeland of Cayman, population 53,000?

Under the headline, *'Issa Team in Cayman Islands'* Webb emailed to Jack Warner, 'Dear President . . . After realizing that the meeting was not going the way they had hoped, the amount of knowledge that I possessed on certain topics, and my unwavering loyalty to Jack, certain allegations were made about the President of FIFA and the President of Concacaf,' reported Webb. 'I then said to them that unless someone has been convicted of something, I am not interested in hearing it, and the meeting ended.'

Warner was ecstatic. The next day he emailed back to Webb, 'You did great, Jeff, simply great, and I'm proud of you. Keep the faith.'

The same year, 2002, Jeffrey Webb went into business with 'Captain' Burrell. The Jamaican operated a chain of 'Captain's Bakery and Grill' restaurants and wanted to expand into Cayman. It was a marriage of two football bosses on Cayman's famous seven-mile beach. Then they went off to the FIFA congress in Seoul, where Jeff postured in the Blatter chorus line. 'My tiny country is not known for football but is known for finances,' he announced. 'The Cayman Islands have over $600 billion on deposit. We are ranked as the fifth financial centre in the world.' It was hard to see the relevance to football and Webb seemed to be the only person in the hall unaware that a large chunk of the money was dirty or dodging tax.

There had to be a delay in announcing the new Concacaf line-up, following the departure of Warner and The Belly. In the punishments handed out by FIFA's Ethics Committee after the Trinidad cash bribes the 'Captain' was suspended for six months for lack of co-operation with outside investigators. Burrell said the punishment was 'harsh and painful for me personally, but I will not appeal the decision.' Unfortunately, Burrell had to give up his position on FIFA's Disciplinary Committee, which he had retained despite the scandalous action of putting his Jamaican partner in Haiti's empty seat at the 1998 FIFA congress. He was allowed back after three months and his suspension was instantly forgotten. Three weeks later, in February 2012, Blatter appointed

Burrell to FIFA's committee organising Olympic soccer tournaments; more luxury hotels, more per diems, more tickets.

In June 2012 the new-look Concacaf set up an Integrity Committee to investigate the depredations of Warner and Blazer. It was chaired by former chief justice of Barbados, Sir David Simmons. He was joined by American judge Ricardo Urbina and a retired partner from Price Waterhouse, Ernesto Hempe. They hired a New York law firm to conduct investigations and interrogate witnesses. Warner and Blazer refused to co-operate. Warner claimed he destroyed all his paperwork the day he quit FIFA.

The 144-page report was revealed at the Concacaf conference in Panama City on April 18, 2013. One paragraph summarises the findings: 'It is apparent that Warner and Blazer each was aware of the risk of potential misconduct posed by the other and was most capable of holding the other accountable; but neither did so . . . to preserve the unfettered freedom to act in his own self-interest.'

Warner had committed fraud against FIFA and Concacaf in the funding of the Centre of Excellence. He had stolen nearly $30 million. He had committed fraud and misappropriated the money the Australians had donated to 'upgrade' the CoE stadium. Warner and Blazer had violated FIFA's ethics code.

Blazer had misappropriated Concacaf funds to finance his lifestyle and failed to manage the confederation's resources. He had failed to file tax returns in America and Concacaf faced civil, or even criminal, penalties. Simmons hinted that Blazer had avoided contact with the American tax authorities to stay off their radar and avoid being required to pay income tax. In the same way he had not tried to renegotiate his contract with Concacaf because once members discovered how much was going to his offshore accounts, his 10% would have been slashed.

Year after year Blazer had claimed Concacaf's accounts were 'audited' by Kenny Rampersad of Trinidad. The Simmons investigators soon discovered this was a lie. There was no testing or sampling of transactions, no collection of contracts, no review of bank reconciliations or wire transfer records and no risk assessment procedures. Rampersad was not a trained or chartered auditor. That made him an imposter.

Rampersad was far from independent – as auditors must be. He was Warner's accountant and involved in his acquisitions of land that became the CoE. Then he signed off Warner's and Blazer's claims that it belonged to Concacaf. He had hopeless conflicts of interest as 'auditor' of Concacaf, the CFU, the CoE and Warner's private companies in Trinidad. He also acted as Blazer's accountant when he was purchasing – with Concacaf money – apartments at The Reef on Paradise Island.

Blazer's claims at the Concacaf congress in Germany on the eve of the 2006 World Cup were exceptionally nauseous. He reported on his blog: 'Our Confederation now boasts an almost perfect record in completing its audit requirements to FIFA . . . this demonstrated the commitment by Warner to the standard of transparency and compliance in responsibly handling the funds granted to it by FIFA.'

SO FAR SO BAD. Missing from the Simmons report is any finger pointing at Concacaf itself. You might think that over the years some elected officials at the top of the organisation, with responsibility for protecting the members and the finances, would ask questions like, who was getting the vast commissions?

Jeffrey Webb was a manager at a big Cayman bank. Could he not have spotted the questions that had to be asked? His partner in the restaurant business, 'Captain' Burrell, claims to be a clever businessman. Did he not see anything wrong? Then there is Sunil Gulati, an economics teacher at Columbia University in New York. Why didn't he ask about the Commissions? The same week that Simmons published his report Sunil claimed that 'at the highest level [in FIFA] there is a sincere effort to try to reform and change the organization.'

I emailed Webb and Gulati asking how a banker and an economics lecturer didn't spot the commissions? Did they ever wonder what The Belly was paid? How could he afford Trump Tower, the Hummer, the grotesque feasting? They have never replied.

Blatter turned up in Panama City in April 2013 for the Concacaf congress and did his best to divert attention from FIFA's failure to notice the vast amounts of money being stolen over a 20-year period. If the finance department had done a quick land registry check in Trinidad they would have discovered that the CoE belonged to Warner, not football. Perhaps they did.

Both Jeff and Sunil were promoted to FIFA's ExCo and pocketing at least $250,000 a year. Sunil is going to fight for more transparency – perhaps. He says he is willing to disclose what payments and expense money he receives from FIFA – as long as he isn't breaking any confidentiality agreement. Jeff has gone, arrested in Zurich and extradited to the USA.

On the day the Simmons report was published, Blatter tweeted, '*Opened CFU Congress today. Said it is a new Era for CFU & Concacaf with a charismatic leader. They can play a key role in world football.*' The next day he tweeted, '*Great leadership and vision shown today by Jeffrey Webb shows bright future for Concacaf.*' Webb was so struck with this praise that he described himself on the Concacaf website, as 'a natural and charismatic leader.' Tame reporters repeated this, unquestioningly.

A month later, in August 2013, a whining sound was heard from Trinidad. It was Warner's lawyer, 'My client's good name and reputation has been and continues to be damaged' and with that, he filed an official notice of intention to sue Simmons.

This silliness was perhaps because publication of the Simmons report had forced Warner to resign from the Trinidad government and he was fighting a by-election to get back into parliament. In the previous two years the UNC had given him two cabinet positions. The first had the whole of the Caribbean laughing in disbelief. Warner was made minister of works with the power to allocate contracts.

The second had Trinidad groaning. Warner was appointed minister of national security, in charge of the police and army. The Trinidad police have never convincingly investigated how Mohamed Bin Hammam smuggled $1 million in cash through the national airport from his private jet. They show no interest in probing Kenny Rampersad's role in Warner's CoE frauds.

On the evidence of Simmons, FIFA should be suing Warner – and The Belly – for the return of the millions they stole. The problem is, the Deadly Duo have a perfect defence: 'You always knew – you never interfered. This was not thieving, it was Sepp Blatter's way of obtaining loyalty.'

It was a typical organised crime structure. Blatter and Havelange used the money from the profits of the World Cup to give to Warner, who delivered the votes that kept them in power to take more. Further down the feeding chain Warner looked after the little men from the islands, nominating them to FIFA committees which meant long-distance travel, good hotels, $200 a day cash per diems – all paid for by Blatter – and a fistful of World Cup tickets to sell to the Black Market. We begin to understand why Blatter has always been re-elected. He is a great president!

11

Hildbrand's Game of Two Halves

Investigating the Bribe Master and the Bagman

The arrogant old man in Rio, now aged 94, refused to admit his guilt, refused to say sorry for his quarter century of stealing millions from world football, refused to give back those millions. Castor Andrade never said sorry. Why should he? And what a great deal he had got from the Swiss cops. His crimes would be kept secret, all he had to do was hand over half a million Swiss francs – peanuts. He had lied his head off about how little money he had – and those nosy investigators in Switzerland were powerless to challenge him. They would have been bogged down forever in Rio's legal mud. The lawyers in Zurich had done a great job, fighting every inch. And Blatter, who had his own secrets to hide, got FIFA to pay the legal bills.

Never mind the tens of millions extorted from ISL, never mind the shady accounts with big black holes when he was head of Brazilian sport during the dictatorship, FIFA had made João a very rich man. He had leeched so much money out of FIFA in massive expenses and mysterious payments, had received fabulous gifts from gas- and oil-rich billionaire Gulf sheikhs that half a million Swiss francs was a pinprick in his vast wealth.

Ricardo had paid back a little more – maybe 20% of what he had embezzled from FIFA via ISL. But he still had the Nike money to play with. Blatter and those expensive Swiss lawyers had also promised that the legal settlement with the prosecutors in Zug would forever be a secret. And he was still boss of the CBF and still on FIFA's Executive Committee. Whole new possibilities of corruption were opening up around the World Cup. Lula had been a pushover and Dilma dare not confront him. She loathed him – but he was the one with the power, not her.

IT WAS ALL BLATTER'S FAULT. He had panicked when ISL collapsed in 2001, bankrupted by the huge bribes the Brazilians had demanded. Those whining troublemakers at UEFA saw a new battlefront to open. They had lost the election in 1998, outbribed by Blatter, Havelange and their paymasters in the Gulf.

Now Lennart Johansson and the Europeans were demanding action over FIFA's losses. Worried about the next election, due in 12 months' time in Seoul in 2002, Blatter capitulated and made a complaint to the cops in Zug. Even Hayatou was backing the Europeans. Hayatou! What a hypocrite! He had taken ISL money but with European support, he might oust Blatter for the top job.

Of course the Europeans hoped that a police investigation would prove what they believed; that the Brazilians, with Blatter as their link man to ISL in Zug, had trousered millions in kickbacks in return for contracts. In May 2001, Blatter reluctantly filed FIFA's complaint with the economic crime investigators in Zug.

Then it went quiet. Zug seemed slow to act. At first that was good news. Maybe the complaint would be buried. The FIFA thieves began to relax. That was a mistake.

Seventeen months later the crooks learned a new name, one that would torture them as the years went by. The Zug authorities had brought in Thomas Hildbrand, a skilled fraud investigator, to dig into the ISL scandal. He arrested Jean-Marie Weber and other former ISL directors. They were held for several days for questioning. Their offices were searched. The FIFA crooks could not be sure what Hildbrand's purpose was; was his target them – or the managers at ISL who had paid the bribes?

MEANWHILE the Zug Bankruptcy court had appointed Thomas Bauer from the auditing company Ernst & Young to liquidate whatever assets he could find in the wreckage of ISL. Bauer was doing what some of we reporters had wanted to do for a decade. He was ferreting through ISL's internal memos, bank statements and, inevitably, he was discovering some very funny payments. He wanted them back, to share out among ISL's creditors.

Bauer had a duty to the creditors to keep the costs of recovery as low as possible. It would cost a lot of money – and be risky – to tackle the well-connected Havelange and Teixeira with all their friends in Brazil's courts. But he didn't have to. Near to hand, in Switzerland, was the Bagman, Jean-Marie Weber. ISL's secret documents showed that Weber had been the delivery man; the intermediary who brought the bearer cheques to individual FIFA crooks and for others, dispatched millions of dollars to the brass plate companies in Liechtenstein.

Bauer started legal action in Switzerland against Weber – who suddenly acquired one of the most high-profile lawyers in the country. Yes, it was Sepp Blatter's lawyer, Peter Nobel. This was the solid clue that Blatter had much to fear from investigations into the contract kickbacks. Did FIFA pay his fees? In March 2004, rather than risk a public court hearing, Weber and Nobel negotiated the repayment down to 2.5 million Swiss francs. Would that bury the investigations?

In June 2004 Blatter tried to stop further investigations. In secret, he wrote to the Zug authorities telling them that FIFA had withdrawn its complaint against ISL – and goodbye. So Hildbrand could find himself another job!

He was too late. Hildbrand already knew too much to stop digging. His investigation stretched over years because he was chasing individuals and bank accounts around the world and it could take months to get agreement in foreign jurisdictions to access bank records.

The FIFA crooks did not realise that Hildbrand was playing a game of two halves. He concluded the first half in March 2005 and sent his investigation file to the Zug prosecutors, recommending the prosecution of six of ISL's top managers for the simple offence of continuing to trade when the company was insolvent, so causing greater losses to creditors. The evidence he assembled went a lot further – but this was not made public. Blatter and Havelange and Teixeira might have thought that this was the end. Phew! We got away with it.

KNOCK, KNOCK, WHO IS THAT? 'Hello, this is Investigating Magistrate Thomas Hildbrand and I have a warrant to search FIFA headquarters. Open the door please.' It was November 3, 2005 and FIFA was discovering that Hildbrand was commencing a second investigation. The authorities in Zug had agreed it was now time to target FIFA corruption. Hildbrand searched the offices and removed documents.

This was serious. Police officers inside Blatter's offices. Blatter cast around for a way, any way, to get Hildbrand off his case. He had just the man to tackle this. Swiss-Hungarian Peter Hargitay devised a strategy and planted it on David Owen, sports editor of the prestigious *Financial Times*. It was published on December 10, 2005, five weeks after the raid on FIFA.

This 'exclusive' story alleged that a deceased sister of Hildbrand had been married to a cousin of Blatter. This had been filed in a formal complaint with judges in Zug. It said, 'All of these circumstances do not seem to be conducive to the impartiality of investigating judge Hildbrand towards Mr Blatter and FIFA.' It added, 'The complainant believes that [Mr Hildbrand] tried by all available means to bring criminal charges against [Mr Blatter].' Hildbrand pointed out that he was not related to Mr Blatter. The Zug court kicked the story – and the *Financial Times* scoop – into the long grass. No more was ever heard of it. Hildbrand stayed on Blatter's case.

There was a shock for Teixeira in early 2006. Hildbrand turned up in the tiny Pyrenean state of Andorra to interview witnesses involved in managing Teixeira's secret bank accounts. He had been shipping money from Liechtenstein to an account in Andorra, the small principality high in the Pyrenees: it's nearest big city was Barcelona, where a close friend, a former Nike official and business associate, was based at Barcelona FC. An Andorran citizen would withdraw the money in cash and take it to another bank. Later it was shipped on to Teixeira.

On January 16, 2007 Hildbrand travelled to Erlangen in Bavaria to interview Brigitte Baenkler, sister of Horst Dassler. He was curious to know about a visit to see her two years earlier by Sepp Blatter and Jean-Marie Weber, the Bagman. It seems that Weber did not have the money to pay ISL liquidator Bauer's demand for 2.5 million Swiss francs.

So, says a source close to the story, Blatter had authorised payment from FIFA's accounts and now they were looking for someone to plug the hole. Apparently they told her that as a past owner of shares in ISL, she was vulnerable to demands for money from the company's creditors. If she paid FIFA the 2.5 million, they would make sure that she was not bothered again. She refused to pay and the Bagman returned to Zurich empty handed.

12

Jean-Marie Weber
Must Not Be Sacked!

Why do Blatter and Havelange need him?

Tuesday March 11, 2008, Zug: Here they come, smartly dressed in their businessman suits, pretending it's an ordinary day at the office, walking quickly past the pack of jackals with their TV cameras and notebooks blocking the glass and brick canyon leading to the court door, nodding to familiar faces, sorry, can't stop to chat, must not be late.

Seven years ago it was so different. The Big Six managers from ISL gave us interviews, smiled for our cameras, catered the vol-au-vents and waved press releases announcing new FIFA contracts! New Clients! New Sports! Global Domination in sports marketing!

We, the jackals, know that we don't know everything. We hope to learn more in the courtroom. We assume it will be incremental additions to our knowledge. We are not expecting the deafening blast coming our way.

The prosecutor here in the small Swiss city of Zug is demanding up to four-and-a-half years in jail. The six managers knew that their International Sport and Leisure company – always known as ISL – was bust and couldn't pay its debts but they went on taking credit from gullible banks and corporations who never checked how fragile the company was becoming. When ISL went down the toilet in the spring of 2001 it owed more than $300 million, the second largest bankruptcy in Swiss history.

Their biggest and best contract was the rights to sell marketing and television contracts for the FIFA World Cup in 2002 and again in 2006. With the help of substantial bank loans they had paid $1.8 billion to buy these rights from FIFA – but they could sell for lots more – and help themselves to 25% commissions on the way. How could such fantastically clever business whizzes go wrong? Where did the money go? By the end of today we should be getting some clues.

The first surprise is the square courtroom. It could be a conference room for salesmen in a no-frills business motel. At best it's down-market Swedish, designed by the guy who trucked in the ready-mix. No podium, all of us on one level. And that's hardwearing, composite flooring. The tall, lithe and quite lovely figure of 41-year-old blonde Presiding Judge Ziegler in her dark pant-suit ('I'm Carole, spelled like the French,' she purrs to me in a coffee break) sits flanked by her two middle-aged male colleagues at a table against the back wall.

Facing the judges are more rows of tables and chairs; there sit the Big Six, squashed with their lawyers and their tables are squeezed across the whole breadth of the room. At the back sit the reporters, Swiss, Germans, French – and me from an offshore island. In front of us, a dozen or so strained relatives and an attentive young man in a suit who we'll identify later.

They've plenty to worry about. The prosecutor wants to whack them for embezzlement, fraud and fraudulent bankruptcy as well as damaging creditors and falsification of documents. That's enough scandal to fill our notebooks. But we want more; we came here for bribes, not boring balance sheets. Be patient.

On the far right of the line-up is Daniel Beauvois, early 50s, living again in Brussels. With his swept-back greying hair and trim beard he's the only one who looks creative. Daniel is lucky, he joined ISL to run their television operations long after the bribery scams were put in place. But he could still end up breakfasting on Swiss-government-issue muesli because he was a director and all six are accused of keeping around £45 million they should have paid to FIFA. FIFA! At last Herr Blatter and his organisation get their names on the court record. It's 11.02 on Tuesday, March 11, two hours into the evidence.

The indictment says that most of the money came from the Brazilian Globo TV network, was an advance payment for World Cup rights and that 75% should have been sent to FIFA. The ISL Six are said to have withheld the money because the company was strapped for cash. Then they went bust and it became, allegedly, a crime.

Monsieur Beauvois tells me during a coffee break that the

allegation is 'Fucking nonsense,' the money was definitely a loan, none of FIFA's business. That's up to the lovely Carole and her two male escorts to decide. She tilts her head attentively, atop her long, elegant neck, stretches her legs and crosses her ankles. Each of the six defence lawyers make their points.

Seated next to Beauvois is The Man Who Knew Nothing And Got The CEO's Job Because He Married The Boss's Sister. When they split, Christoph Malms got a bundle of shares and this figurehead job. The Dassler family also owned Adidas but after Horst died young in 1987, sold it for a pittance to a French politician, football club owner and, later, jailbird.

Herr Malms, dark brown hair, dark face, middle height and, of course, a dark suit, leans forward into his microphone, showing his small bald patch. He can't do enough to please. He responds earnestly to every question but doesn't have any answers. We expect a verdict in July, about the time of his 53rd birthday.

Next to Malms and close to the centre of the room is ISL's former top bean-counter, Hans-Jürg Schmid. He's questioned vigorously by the judge sitting on Carole's left. It's Zug's way. There's no acid-tongued prosecuting barrister, ripping the accused to shreds. Judge Marc Siegwart wears no wig or gown, just a suit, Van Dyke beard twitching as the ramblings from the accused become more unbelievable. When he gets exasperated, Marc's eyes grow larger and rounder behind his spectacles.

Tomorrow we'll see Marc at his most lethal – but as we move towards the 6pm close of play he's warming up, leading the Six through another 15 million francs on the embezzlement part of the indictment. Again – a loan or a stage payment on TV rights? The money was from the biggest advertising company in the world who also acquired World Cup rights from ISL for resale in Japan.

As ISL teetered in late 2000, Dentsu sent money from east to west. Days later a slice of that money from an ISL offshore account yo-yoed eastwards back down that route. Even as creditors clamoured for their money, four million Swiss francs went to the Gilmark Holdings account, said to be in Hong Kong. Judge Siegwart obviously knew more than he was letting on when he went along the defendants' desks, asking them one by one what they could tell him about Gilmark. They felt unable to assist him.

(Ten days passed and Jean-François Tanda, an enterprising reporter in Zurich – with some the best sources in the business – disclosed that the money went to a senior manager at Dentsu; a Mr Haruyiuki Takahashi. Tanda has tried for comment and I have too but Dentsu's huge media operation in Tokyo is not responsive on this one.)

The Dentsu company has done business with FIFA for more than two decades. They still do. Although the ISL company has evaporated, their gleaming white offices 100 metres from the court now house the Infront sports marketing company. Infront has won, with Dentsu, a big chunk of television rights to the next World Cup. The name of the Infront CEO has a familiar ring. Philippe Blatter. What *do* uncle and nephew talk about when not doing private deals about the most sought-after football rights in the world?

Judge Carole closes the court at 5.59.

Blatter's pugnacious personal spindoctor Peter Hargitay has been calling reporters across Europe for the last few days assuring them that the FIFA president is 'relaxed' about the Zug hearings. Not worth turning up, nothing interesting will happen in court. Total waste of time.

One London paper repeated the line. They didn't see Blatter on Swiss TV the next night, after this stage of the trial ended. Pale and drawn, stress creased Blatter's face when a reporter stuck corruption questions to him. But Blatter knew exactly what was going on because the anonymous young man taking notes in the Zug court was a junior lawyer from his solicitors in Zurich.

Wednesday March 12, 2008: We barrel down the lakeside, German reporter Thomas Kistner at the wheel, and up through the cow pastures and snowy peaks between Zurich and Zug. Today has to be *Schmiergeld* – kickbacks – day. We got a taste of Japanese cuisine last afternoon; today we expect to go global. We are itching for names.

We've got the indictment; the tables in Section 12 list a dozen offshore bank accounts that were paid around 36 million Swiss francs during the last 15 months of the ISL's life. It's getting taut in the court as Judge Siegwart reminds the Six, looking more sheepish by the minute, how they shipped the money out of Switzerland to secret accounts in Liechtenstein and the Caribbean. Then it was delivered to lucky bribe-takers. Commercial bribery wasn't illegal then in Switzerland (it is now). Siegwart argues that the Six knew the company was doomed and the money should have gone to pay overdue debts.

So why was it shipped out to these accounts? Herr Malms clears his throat. At last, the pathetic admission that they weren't the brightest dealmakers on the planet, never Masters of the Business Universe, no more than a grubby bunch of machine-greasers. Anybody with a large bag of cash could have been a boss at ISL. It was a 'regular part' of ISL's business he explained, to pay kickbacks.

'I was told the company would not have existed if it had not made such payments,' Malms said. He'd discovered the truth soon after joining when he asked where the money was going. 'I do not know who the final recipients were but I was always told they were well-known decision-makers in the world of sports politics.'

(Malms knows more – but another 20 days will pass before he punches the tickets of the two biggest names in the game.)

It was usual, he admitted, in the whole sports marketing and sports political business worldwide. 'It was the style of the business. If we didn't pay, we would have had to close our company.' That's what happens when you do business with the FIFA kleptocracy.

Absolutely, chipped in bean counter Schmid. 'It is just like when you have to pay someone a salary. Otherwise they won't work for you. If we hadn't made the payments, the other parties wouldn't have signed the contracts.'

(They'll confirm who the other parties were, in another 20 days. Of course some of us know already, but it helps to have these confirmations of corruption made here and so we can report them, protected by court privilege.)

But, honestly, please believe me, Herr Malms told the

court, he intended stopping the rot. That 36 million was to be the last of the kickbacks. He never did explain why he expected the shakedown artists to halt their demands on the company. But it had to stop, he explained, because ISL was planning a stock market flotation, and they wouldn't be able to bury bribes in their books any longer.

Then he revealed that the techniques for clandestinely moving the wholesale bribe money offshore – the way drug dealers, corporate thieves and thuggish dictators hide their dirty money – were dreamed up by one of the most senior and still very active partners at their Zurich lawyers, who we reporters at the back of the court know also represent FIFA.

This racket was then signed off by their auditors KPMG, who we at the back remember present FIFA's accounts the way the client likes them; cloudy and lacking key information. What a small world these rich men inhabit. And they had friends in high places. The scam was given the kiss of life by the Swiss federal tax authorities.

Those offshore accounts had some pretty names; Nunca, Sunbow, Taora and now . . . Sicuretta. Jean-Marie Weber also distributed the kickbacks in traditional suitcases of cash, sometimes more than $500,000 a time – and won't say who he bunged. All he would ever admit was that it was cash for 'the acquisition of rights.'

In an off-hand comment to investigators, and quoted in the richly detailed indictment, lawyer Guido Renggli, who managed the Sicuretta account and doled out the bundles of cash, remembered being taken to Paris for the World Cup in 1998 by Jean-Marie to meet the newly-elected FIFA president

Blatter. Mr Renggli never did disclose why Mr Blatter was so pleased to see him. We can only guess.

OK, said Judge Siegwart, *I want to know who got the money?* Five of the Six insisted they had no idea. Like us at the press tables they knew the names of all the top decision-makers in world sport – there's not that many of them – and had lunched and partied with them – but they didn't know who had taken their money. Hadn't a clue. We were asked to believe this fantasy.

The man who distributed the goodies, Jean-Marie Weber, is the fourth stooge in the line-up in front of us and Jean-Marie knows everything. He was once Horst Dassler's assistant and took over delivering the bungs when Dassler died. His job description at ISL was 'cultivating relationships' and he carried his two black briefcases everywhere, stuffed full of these private agreements to kickback.

For years Jean-Marie's tall frame and bouffant silver hair has towered above every FIFA meeting and the congresses of other wealthy sports. Today he's looking scrawny, his voice is reedy and his hair suddenly cut short, is he hoping to avoid the prison barber?

Judge Siegwart asks him, who got the money? Jean-Marie begins the mantra we hear repeated through the rest of the morning, 'On the advice of my lawyer I have no statement to make. My lawyer will address these matters.' At other times he says 'these payments were confidential and I must respect that confidentiality.'

Siegwart's getting testy. These clowns are taking the piss. He fixes on a modest kickback, only $250,000, the indictment says it went to a Mr Abdul Muttaleb of Kuwait. When it was paid in 2000 he was director general of the Olympic Council for Asia. And yes, ISL obtained a contract with the OCA. In 2004 the BBC's *Panorama* programme caught Muttaleb discussing how bribes could be paid to his friends on the International Olympic Committee. End of the big earners for Abdul.

Why have you paid so much money to that person in Kuwait, demands the Judge. Here, we have to show our companies and tax officials documents for every meal we have with business partners – and you give away $250,000 without any notice, any documentation, any contract, any memo, any letter?

The certificated accountant Schmid states. 'We wouldn't get any receipts from those persons.'

Next for shaming is FIFA Executive Committee member Nicolás Leoz. He's not in the room, he's back home in faraway Paraguay and he did not steal a lot but he's the first FIFA official to be named. The fact that he trousered $130,000 from ISL was leaked to a London newspaper by Blatter's fixers in the autumn of 2006; damage limitation when this trial seemed imminent.

(Days after the leak Blatter was in Asunción and brazenly backed Leoz, challenging investigators to produce hard evidence of any wrongdoing. Blatter would have had this evidence in the prosecutor's report in his desk drawer in Zurich – he probably leaked it. A month later Blatter was telling reporters, 'There is no need for me to reaffirm my confidence in Leoz.')

Siegwart's had enough: He pulls a hand grenade from the files on his desk, flips the pin and rolls it across the court-room floor. *BOOUUM!*

When our ears stop ringing we realise what he's said; he's got evidence that over the years they'd paid out – wait for it, hold tight – a stunning *$100 million in bribes.* No wonder ISL dipped south, never to return.

Judge Siegwart tries yet again for names. Malms says he doesn't know them. But announces, astonishingly, that a handful of reporters do. And, *Yes!,* Jean-François Tanda from Zurich, Jens Weinreich from Berlin, Thomas Kistner from Munich and I grin at each other. But Jean-Marie still will not name names. The others repeat their mantra, only Jean-Marie knows.

The hearing ended at 11.20. The lawyers will be back on March 31 to submit their arguments and verdicts are expected in three months. We went away to think about the wider implications of the evidence.

Back in 1995 the mighty IMG group promised FIFA they would top any offer from any company for World Cup televi-sion and marketing rights. Their starting price was $1 billion and there wasn't a ceiling. They were given the bum's rush and wrote angrily to Blatter, then FIFA general secretary, that 'preferential treatment [is] being given to other parties such as ISL' and that the bidding was merely 'a cosmetic exercise.'

ISL got the rights.

Monday March 31, 2008: Back in court, it's the turn of the defence lawyers to attack the prosecution case. The hearing lasts for most of the week.

The second grenade was tossed into the courtroom by Herr Werner Würgler, the lawyer for Christoph Malms. While his client really, really, honestly didn't have proof of who got the kickbacks, he had been given two huge clues. Herr Würgler claimed that FIFA President Sepp Blatter had approached Christoph Malms and told him in no uncertain terms that if ISL wanted to keep FIFA's business, Jean-Marie Weber had to keep his job at the company. If not, 'It would be bad for ISL.'

Making sure that Jean-Marie, the man who delivered FIFA's bribes, kept his job at ISL seemed to be a priority for FIFA presidents because Herr Würgler also told the judges that during the World Cup in France in 1998 retiring President Havelange had made the same demand.

Blatter and Havelange. What more do you need to know about corruption at FIFA? The two top men implicated in the biggest bribery scam in world sport.

Würgler added that, 'because of these ultimatums made by the two FIFA presidents, it was made economically impossible for the ISL group to move away from the system of commission payments.'

(Commissions? We thought they were bribes. Calling the kickbacks 'commissions' made the ISL guys feel better about themselves. And it is being made devastatingly clear in court that Blatter knows as much as Havelange.)

Würgler hadn't finished with Blatter. The lawyer made the sophisticated point that anybody at FIFA who knew about the bribes – and who was getting them – could exercise great power over fellow officials. And in case the judges hadn't yet got the point, the ISL company had become a private source of money for FIFA – virtually their private bank.

Judge Marc Siegwart gave Jean-Marie one last chance to cough the names. 'No,' he says, 'I make no statement.' But his lips were dry, he's lost weight since the trial started and a strong wind might break him into parts.

As the first stage of the trial ended in mid-March FIFA executive members were flying into Zurich for their first meeting of the year. But tragedy had struck Nicolás Leoz – he needed some unspecified surgery – and he wouldn't be coming. The surgery was brilliant, his backbone implant was successful and within days he was attending official football meetings in Latin America.

At his press conference after the ExCo meetings Blatter fended off questions, saying he could not possibly comment on the Zug disclosures until after the verdict. That's non-sense. There was nothing to stop him commenting on the documented evidence of Leoz taking money, the money going to the company owned by Havelange and Teixeira – and Malms' electrifying claim that both Blatter and Havelange forced ISL to keep Weber in place to ensure bribes were delivered on time.

Five of the Six were acquitted. Jean-Marie Weber was con-victed of helping himself to 90,000 Swiss francs in cash, although we all believed that the money had been wrapped in a brown paper bag and ended up in the hands of a FIFA official.

Blatter was now in serious trouble. He had been named in court along with Havelange by ISL boss Christoph Malms;

they were both involved in the vast bribery scandal. And there was Nicolás Leoz as well. There must be an investigation. Who could do this?

Step forward Lord Sebastian Coe, British Olympic God. Coe had been appointed by Blatter in September 2006 to head FIFA's Ethics Committee, following my story that Jack Warner, the FIFA vice-president from Trinidad, had traded more than 5,000 World Cup tickets into the black market in Germany in 2006.

Coe accepted he could not investigate anything before the date he was appointed. He was prevented from investigating FIFA's bribe takers, ticket scalpers, expenses fraudsters and energetic thieves at the Executive Committee safe and untouchable. Decades of crimes against sport – untouchable. Total amnesty.

In late 2007 the BBC *Panorama* programme wanted to ask Coe about his investigations. Despite two requests, Coe refused to grant an interview. Our editor agreed that I should go and find Coe. We discovered he would be in a remote village in the north of Scotland the next day. We flew overnight from London to Edinburgh, drove through the mountains and soon after dawn, arrived in remote Grantown-on-Spey, where Coe was due to make a public appearance at the local sports centre.

We set the camera high on its tripod, well back from the front door and fitted a long lens. A row of local council and sports officials, dressed in their best Scottish kilts, lined up as a welcoming committee. Coe stepped from his car and began shaking hands as he worked along the row.

It was the funniest sequence I ever filmed. I ducked in and out of the kilts politely asking Coe for an interview – but Coe was blind to me. He refused to admit that I was close enough to touch him. He didn't notice the microphone clipped to my coat or my camera crew.

The kilted officials took their cue from Coe and pretended I was invisible. Millions of viewers laughed when the programme was screened.

13

How the FIFA Crooks
Got Away With It

In secret, they confess

Zug, September 21, 2009: FIFA President Sepp Blatter swallowed his pride and travelled in his chauffeured black Mercedes from his luxurious office high above Zurich to the austere lakeside office in Zug of the chief prosecutor, Christian Aebi.

Blatter's driver was probably wise enough not to point the president's gaze to the adjacent building, home to the Cantonal courtroom where the previous year the six ISL executives had performed their own version of the FIFA Theatre of the Absurd. Blatter did not need reminding that Christophe Malms' lawyer had revealed the ultimatum by him and Havelange that the Bagman Jean Marie Weber must keep his job at ISL – or they lose FIFA's contracts.

Waiting for Blatter in Zug was Investigating Magistrate Thomas Hildbrand. The last – and only – time Blatter had met him was when Hildbrand led the unexpected raid on FIFA House four years earlier in November 2005. Alongside Blatter was lawyer Dieter Gessler, paid by FIFA, but appearing to represent Blatter as well.

Chief Prosecutor Aebi took Blatter and Gessler through the evidence of embezzlement by the two Brazilians and the benevolent set-up at FIFA that made it so easy for them to steal. Blatter must have realised that all his lies and wriggling in the previous few years had not deterred the investigators; if anything it would have hardened their attitude. Over the years they were learning that Blatter's public pronouncements about his 'mission to the world' were a smokescreen concealing the looting of FIFA's wealth.

Havelange and Teixeira had now been indicted formally – all kept secret of course – and the investigation was moving slowly, but inexorably, to endgame. Yet all the participants in the swindling seemed confident they would get away with it.

THE BAGMAN, Jean-Marie Weber, was still welcome at the IOC (how many of its members did he bribe over the years?) and in August of 2009 had been a guest in Berlin for the joint meeting of the executive councils of the IOC and the IAAF before travelling on to Copenhagen for the IOC congress and decision on which city would host the 2016 Olympics. Lamine Diack, president of international athletics, had been on Weber's bribe list. In Berlin it must have been like the good old days – comradeship and rich living– all paid for by sport.

(An ISL executive – one of the clean ones – told me years earlier that Italian Primo Nebiolo was bribed by ISL in the

1980s and 1990s because marketing and television rights to track and field championships were very profitable.)

HAVELANGE STAYED AWAY while his expensive Swiss lawyer tried to protect him. Havelange wasn't risking coming to Switzerland and being arrested – as Weber had, back in 2002. Early in 2009, he phoned associates at FIFA to tell them that he was staying home in Rio where he felt safe.

Great efforts were made to slither around Swiss law so the two Brazilians could keep their stolen money. Who fought for them? FIFA's lawyer! It was Herr Gessler who argued that there was no law banning commercial bribery when the bribes were paid. Hildbrand tossed this away, pointing out that the two Brazilian scoundrels were accused of embezzlement, not bribery. The crime was stealing from FIFA. All three men had betrayed FIFA and world football.

FIFA lawyer Gessler wouldn't give up. He was being paid by FIFA to get the money back but ended up as good as doing the opposite to fight to prevent Teixeira and Havelange repaying anything. But, extraordinarily, Gessler argued at the hearing that if action had been taken against the FIFA crooks in South America or Africa, rather than Switzerland, the money could not have been reclaimed because bribery was a way of life in those countries.

Will FIFA dare to go public and tell the football associations – and all the people – of those two continents that in private they sneer at them, stereotyping them as crooks? Don't hold your breath.

Hildbrand found Havelange and his successor Blatter

guilty of 'disloyal management.' At last, a deal was agreed. Under Swiss law the Brazilians could repay some money, FIFA pay the legal costs of the prosecution and the case ended. But FIFA – that's Blatter – had to admit disloyal management and Teixeira and Havelange had to admit the betrayal of world football. The Brazilians also had to admit they had embezzled from FIFA and on condition that the verdict was kept secret forever, they agreed to repay some money. Teixeira handed back .5 million Swiss francs

THERE WERE STILL details to haggle over. At the beginning of February 2010 Havelange submitted a declaration of his wealth and income. It was a transparent fantasy. Had he gambled away the $45 million he stole from ISL? Through his lawyer Havelange claimed that all his assets were jointly owned by him and his wife and totalled only 5.2 million francs. The liar got away with handing back 500,000 francs.

FIFA paid more of football's money to a Swiss professor who gave them the opinion they wanted: that FIFA didn't lose any money because 'There are no indications that better offers were made by other sport marketing agencies.' Blatter must have forgotten to tell this scholar about the IMG opening bid of $1 billion for 2002 marketing and TV rights and the promise to top any other offer. It seems unlikely that Aebi and Hildbrand paid any attention to this nonsense.

Blatter agreed that FIFA would pay 91,970 Swiss francs towards the costs of the investigation of the Havelange and Teixeira rackets. Football lost, again. The case was closed on May 11, 2010.

14

Blatter's Fingers Crossed Behind His Back

Says he wants to publish damning report

June 24, 2010: THE TIMING was brilliant. I don't believe the prosecutors in Zug conspired with FIFA to release their statement as the first round of the World Cup in South Africa was ending and the eyes of fans were on teams advancing to the second round – and who was going home. But it helped. The world's football writers were busy.

Blatter put out a mendacious statement; 'The FIFA President has been cleared of any wrong-doing in this matter. As the investigation and the case are now definitely closed, FIFA will make no further comment.' It appeared they had got away with their crimes.

Later that year, somewhere in Central Europe, I talked with a policeman. Deliberately, to wind him up, I showed him Blatter's statement 'The FIFA President has been cleared of any wrong-doing in this matter.' It worked. The policeman

– who had knowledge of the investigation – exploded. 'That is not true!' he said. We talked for many more hours. I asked, 'How do I get my hands on the confidential investigation report, locked away in Zug?' 'They cannot and will not leak it to you,' he said. 'But there is another way.'

I listened. 'You have to convince a court that it is in the public interest to publish the report.' As dark fell over a nearby lake, I returned to my hotel room to write notes of the secret meeting into my laptop. The policeman gave me a name and wished me well.

The next day I called my friend Jean-François Tanda in Zurich. He had trained as a lawyer before becoming a top-class investigative reporter. 'Yes,' he said. 'There is a precedent case in Switzerland. I am looking at it already. A former army chief paid compensation to a woman who accused him of harassing her.' Zurich newspapers went to court and eventually the judges agreed that the public had a right to know and the name of the army chief was published with the evidence and the amount he paid her to conclude the case.

I was working on a new BBC *Panorama* programme investigation, to be screened at the end of November 2010, a few days before the FIFA lowlifes announced to whom they would give the World Cups of 2018 and 2022. I had acquired some sensational information – and a document. But we were not alone in hunting down FIFA corruption.

WORLD CUP VOTES FOR SALE! This was the headline in the London *Sunday Times* on October 17, 2010. A team of reporters posed as lobbyists for a consortium of American private companies who wanted to get the World Cup to the United States. They had secretly filmed Amos Adamu from Nigeria, a member of FIFA's Executive Committee, offering to sell his vote for £500,000.

(Thirteen months later the *Sunday Times* published documents revealing that the Qatar bid team had contracted to pay $1 million to Amos Adamu's son, Samson, to host a lavish dinner and party in South Africa, during the World Cup. The dinner took place but the Qataris claimed they had second thoughts and denied paying the money.)

The *Sunday Times* Insight Team also fingered another ExCo member, Reynald Temarii from Tahiti, requesting £1.5 million for a sports academy. This broke FIFA's elastic bidding rules.

The journalists secretly recorded hours of conversation with knowledgeable FIFA officials who discussed past bribes. One ExCo member was named as 'the biggest gangster you will find on earth,' who profited from World Cup bids. 'I can imagine that the total of what he would receive in money and in other advantages would be as a minimum, half a million.' Another one was happy to sell his vote. 'We can go to Rio and talk with him on a terrace, no problem. Openly, openly,' said a football official. Yet another of the 23 ExCo members preferred girls to money. Lots of girls.

Former executive committee member Amadou Diakite from Mali revealed that one of the countries bidding to host the World Cup in 2022 was offering $1.2 million to members for 'personal projects.'

*

IN THE YEARS that followed we witnessed Blatter's sordid attempts to dissemble and divert attention from the embedded corruption in his own boardroom. They were the actions of an organised crime boss, scorning every reasonable standard of public behaviour, protecting his loyal lieutenants, never critical when they were caught stealing. With exclusive access to confidential sources and documents I can reveal how Blatter twisted and lied to stop the world discovering the truth about the rottenness of FIFA.

Blatter's immediate response to the *Sunday Times* evidence was to announce he had banned ExCo members from talking to the media. Then he went on the attack. 'I do not think there is anything wrong with the voting procedure. We have come to expect it to be carried out morally and ethically based on good judgement and on what has been presented by a bidding committee.'

Was he smoking that stuff? Did he think we were? No, the bigger the lie the better. And Blatter had more lies. 'By having a small body decide where the World Cup will be held, you also can identify the people responsible for choosing the World Cup venue – the Executive Committee – because they are the same people responsible for making it work.'

Firstly, this was not true. It was a secret ballot, so we could never 'identify the people responsible for choosing the World Cup venue.' Secondly, they would not be 'the same people responsible for making it work.' Thirdly, few of the aging ExCo would be alive, never mind in power, when responsibility had to be taken for awarding the World Cup to Putin's police state and the feudal set-up in Qatar.

Hoping to bury the bribery disclosures, FIFA's Ethics Committee took only a month to ban Adamu for three years and Temarii for one. Claudio Sulser, Blatter's obedient glove puppet and chair of the Ethics Committee attacked the media, criticising the *Sunday Times* as 'sensationalist.' The crooks were in no mood to be remorseful. Blatter was aware there was another scandal about to break over FIFA. But he didn't know what it was. And Havelange could not care less.

November 22, 2010, Soccerex, Rio: Six months after he secretly confessed conspiring with Teixeira to embezzle FIFA's money, João Havelange was guest of honour at the Soccerex trade show in Rio. He had a special announcement to make; everybody please listen. 'Ricardo Teixeira would be a good president of FIFA. He speaks English and French and runs the CBF well. This would give me great joy.'

Shameless. The cluster of Brazilian thieves around João and Ricardo had always lamented losing control of FIFA in 1998. Teixeira might have been nominated as a candidate in that year. He and his former father-in-law had enough money to bribe delegates to the FIFA congress in Paris. So why couldn't Havelange force Blatter to stand aside? The answer is probably that Blatter desperately wanted the job and he had too much dirt on the old man to give way. There may have been a deal. Did Blatter promise Teixeira, as he did with Mohamed Bin Hammam, that he would stand down after two four-year terms?

November 29, 2010: 'TONIGHT – CORRUPTION at the heart of world football.' These were my first words as I launched the BBC's latest primetime investigation. I continued, 'We reveal the three senior FIFA officials linked to an extraordinary list of secret payments worth around a hundred million dollars.' Then came the question I was to hear repeated back to me again and again in every bar or meeting I go to in Brazil, 'Mr Teixeira. Did you take your bribes through the Sanud company?' It's funny now.

Two days before transmission of *FIFA's Dirty Secrets* I collapsed from exhaustion and was rushed to hospital. I was back on my feet 24 hours later in time to record the commentary for the film.

We were completing this complex film under intense political and media pressure on the BBC to kill the film, scheduled for transmission three days before the FIFA ExCo voted on 2018 and 2022. Prime Minister David Cameron said that our determination to screen was 'frustrating.' The brainless tabloids screamed every day that whatever was in our programme – and we had stayed tight-lipped about the $100 million bribes list – we would undermine England's hopes of hosting the World Cup in 2018.

The rightwing press hate the BBC. They went quiet after England got only two votes and it began to dawn on them that England lost an excellent bid because they would not pay bribes. Six months later I was cheered by England fans as keynote speaker at their annual fans' parliament.

One day passed and Issa Hayatou's Cairo-based spokesman was claiming that the 100,000 French Francs I disclosed was not a bribe from ISL. It was a 'donation' to celebrate the 40th birthday of their organisation. It was not explained why the money had been paid in cash to him personally.

The usually tepid Jacques Rogge stepped up to the Olympic plate announcing an investigation into the naming of IOC members Hayatou, Havelange and later Lamine Diack from track and field, who was also on my ISL bribes list. 'It will not, in my humble opinion, last for months,' Rogge told journalists. In fact it lasted 12 months – because of Havelange's devious delaying.

The world noticed that Blatter and FIFA were not launching any investigation. A week into the new year, surrounded by love in Doha, Blatter launched a deranged assault on the IOC, saying FIFA was more transparent than the IOC and 'Our accounts are open to everyone . . . We've done it since I'm the president.' Before reporters could chorus, 'How much do you earn at FIFA?' the demented Blatter insulted 50% of the planet's population.

The IOC, he stumbled on, handles its finances 'like a housewife.' A few days later he apologised to Rogge in a private call. The IOC leaked this, gleefully, off-record, to the news agencies. But Blatter was the real winner; the silliness diverted media attention from the bribes and dirt at FIFA.

Blatter won another battle in Doha. A flood of money from his friends in Kuwait and Qatar at the regional congress of Asian football ensured the removal of longtime opponent Chung Mong-joon, the Hyundai billionaire from Seoul, from his vice-presidency, replaced by Prince Who? a little-known princeling from Jordan. Prince Ali asserted, baffling me, 'I continue to believe in the power of unity to develop football.' His contribution to the bleak global concerns about FIFA corruption was to call for an end to 'politics.'

Prince Ali was elected by the 46 member countries of Asian football. The voters seemed impressed most of all by his proposal for an easy-to-access development fund. Since then he has said he wants 'transparency, openness and integrity' at FIFA. Herr Blatter's salary and perks remain a secret.

If Asian football politics were a joke, so were South America's. Nicolás Leoz, the Paraguayan vacuum cleaner, now aged 82, was re-elected president of Conmebol. It was a unanimous vote by all 10 member countries. The highlight of the ceremonies was Leoz hanging a medal around Teixeira's neck. You wonder where they stole it.

WE WERE BUILDING up to another FIFA exposé at BBC *Panorama*. I slipped into UEFA's congress in Paris and managed to confront Blatter about the bribes ('No Comment') and Issa Hayatou ('No Comment'). I tried Nicolás Leoz and he gave an unintelligible grunt and fell asleep in the front row of the convention. Other welcome guests were the two biggest bagmen in world football. Jean-Marie Weber, now on the payroll of Issa Hayatou, and Fedor Radmann, as ever with his close associate Franz Beckenbauer.

Our new programme, *FIFA: Football's Shame*, used some of the secret footage filmed by the *Sunday Times*. Former ExCo member Ismail Bhamjee, forced out in 2006 over re-selling a mere 12 World Cup tickets, had told the undercover reporters that Qatar was offering up to $500,000 for ExCo members' votes. I also revealed that despite the secrecy, the two big bribe-takers named in the Hildbrand investigation report were Havelange and Teixeira.

The crucial issue then – and would be for the next year – was Blatter's devious manoeuvres to avoid publishing the Hildbrand investigation report. From May 2010 he always had a copy in his desk drawer and could have made it public at any time. There was no law to stop him. Every time he said he was blocked by Swiss law – he lied. Another lie was his pretence that he didn't know the contents of the report. Blatter and his lawyers had argued every point with the Zug authorities in the previous few years. They knew everything.

By now my colleague James Oliver at the BBC and Jean-François Tanda in Zurich had begun legal action to have the report released, arguing legitimate public interest. They applied to the court in Zug and won! There were no objections from the authorities. This was a disaster for the crooks.

The lawyers for Blatter, Hildbrand and Teixeira fought back, sending appeals to the court. From the beginning Blatter – or FIFA – used their own identities. But Teixeira and Havelange insisted on hiding behind the codenames 'B2' and 'Z.'

On May 23, 2011 the lawyer for 'B2' – who we soon realised was Ricardo Teixeira – sent a 13-page letter to the Zug court. He stated, 'B2 has a right to have his private life protected . . . disclosing the identity of B2 would lead to negative reporting in the press which would have a disproportionate pillory effect. The public reputation of B2 would be harmed in such a way as not to be reparable.'

If this claim had been known in Brazil there would have been a national screech of laughter from Belem to Porto Alegre. Teixeira's reputation was already wrecked at home.

The lawyer continued, 'There also exist considerable security risks in the country in which B2 resides. Locally important figures such as B2 are subject to strict security measures. B2's house is surrounded by a security fence and is guarded by security staff day and night.'

The same day another letter arrived from the lawyer representing 'Z' – of course we knew immediately that this was João Havelange. He had a new point; publication, 'would result in personal information regarding Z (name, profession, criminal charges, family details and social contacts, finances) being released which is not required to meet the public's need for information.'

There was more. 'There are also considerable security risks in the country in which Z resides. Locally important figures such as Z are subject to strict security measures. Z's house is surrounded by a security fence and is guarded by security staff day and night. Personal information on the complainant such as his address or information on his financial circumstances are not publicaly [sic] available in the country in which Z resides since such information encourages kidnap, burglaries or robbery. Should the identity of Z, as well as the amount of the indemnification paid, become publicaly [sic] available, the consequences for the personal security of Z would be difficult to foresee.'

The third letter that same day was from the offices of Blatter's longstanding defender, lawyer Peter Nobel. How would he combat free publication? He argued that his clients on the hill above Zurich were protected by the Swiss Federal Constitution, the European Convention on Human Rights and the International Covenant on Civil and Political Rights.

These legal campaigns to suppress the dirty truth about FIFA were undermined in public by their latest scandal as ExCo members Jack Warner and Mohamed Bin Hammam were suspended following revelations of a plot to buy votes against Blatter in the upcoming presidential election in the Caribbean. Within the month Warner resigned from FIFA, to escape investigation. His accuser, Chuck Blazer, beamed with pleasure – but within two months was in trouble himself and his FIFA career soon over.

Behind the scenes the collapse of FIFA's image was concerning their paymasters. The sponsors – or 'partners' as we have been brainwashed into calling them – were worrying that they had paid millions to buy into an organisation that now smelled globally. Adidas, who publicly and privately had supported Blatter for 40 years, said the corruption allegations were 'neither good for the sport of football nor for FIFA as an institution and its partners.'

Coca-Cola followed, describing the revelations as 'distressing and bad for the sport.' They added, 'We have every expectation that FIFA will resolve this situation in an expedient and thorough manner.'

Again, in August 2011, the Zug authorities ruled that the Hildbrand report should be published. This was immediately appealed, again, by lawyers acting for Blatter/FIFA, Havelange and Teixeira. Blatter was incorrigible. In late October his briefers fooled the always compliant BBC Sport into announcing that he was 'making a U-turn' and would push for publication. In private he and the other two continued fighting but were again rejected by the court in Zug.

Blatter came up with a new PR trick. In secret he agreed with the other two that they should continue fighting disclosure. He would terminate his legal campaign – but claim that because of their legal opposition, he was not permitted to publish.

Blatter put out another false statement to the media. 'FIFA has been working intensively over the past few weeks with its lawyers and legal team to be able to publish the ISL file at the next meeting of the FIFA Executive Committee in Japan on 17 December 2011,' he lied.

'It was my strong will to make the ISL file fully transparent at this meeting. I have now been advised that as a result of the objection of a third party to such transparency it will take more time to overcome the respective legal hurdles.'

More lies were rolled out: 'This does not change my stance at all. I remain fully committed to publishing the files as soon as possible as an important part of my many reform plans for FIFA, which include handling the past as well as preparing the future structure of the organisation.' It was hard to tell where the clouds of smoke ended and the mirrors began.

BBC *Panorama* took more independent legal advice in Switzerland. It was absolutely clear. Blatter was free to reveal his copy of the Hildbrand report. He could have gone further and denounced the two Brazilians. But heads of criminal organizations do not denounce their fellows for criminal activities. It's their job description.

Blatter was careful to avoid meeting any critical reporters. But he was safe with the online newsletter *insideworldfootball*, dependent on funding from sports federations, promoters of mega-events and other sources. They reported that 'he has promised to leave no stone unturned and, for the first time, name names as part of his anti-corruption drive at the heart of world football.'

Blatter was quoted that he wanted only 'solutions that bite' and 'It takes time to shake the tree until all bad apples have fallen to the ground.' He was upset by criticisms that 'occasionally degenerates into personal and below the belt attacks.'

There was one more humiliating blow to come in 2011.

15

Havelange Kicked Out of the Olympics

The IOC did what FIFA would not

December 8, 2011, IOC HQ, Vidy: I was shocked. I had not seen President Jacques Rogge for two years and this late afternoon in Lausanne, as he settled in his chair at the press conference, he looked like a cadaver and spoke like he would be one sometime next week. Was he told today he has cancer? I asked one of his aides. 'No, he's always like this when there's bad news.'

The first part of Rogge's bad news was already public. Four days earlier João Havelange, the longest serving member of the Committee had resigned, in disgrace, to avoid further public humiliation. To avoid having to kick him out, the IOC had briefed reporters off the record that the recommendation on the table in the IOC boardroom was a two-year suspension for taking ISL's money. Havelange got the message and quit.

I had travelled by train from the north of England, through the Channel Tunnel, stopped off for a meeting in Paris, on to Geneva and finally to Lausanne. Snow was on the mountains, the lake gleamed in the winter sunshine, retired couples walked little dogs in the parkland of this most bourgeois of cities. I wanted to see what the IOC would have to say about the ISL bribes list. Even though Havelange had been allowed to creep out of the back door, we had named IOC member Issa Hayatou and fellow member track and field boss Lamine Diack was also in play.

A week after we transmitted the list on BBC *Panorama* we were visited by an official from the IOC's Ethics Commission. They wanted a copy. Blatter and his degenerate FIFA would not, dare not, investigate – but the IOC would. This needed careful planning. The source had to be protected. In the weeks that followed my producer James Oliver negotiated with the source and the IOC and a handover was agreed.

An Olympic source called me saying, 'I think you would want to be here!' So here I was, entering the glass and marble palace, greeting familiar faces and heading for the room where Rogge would hold his press conference.

Rogge welcomed us and announced, 'We had the proposal of the Ethics Commission and the Executive Board upheld the proposal of the Ethics Commission and issued a warning to Mr Diack and a reprimand to Mr Hayatou.'

That was it! All over. Thirty-two words in twelve seconds! Where was Havelange, the big fish in this tiny pond?

A reporter asked, 'How seriously do you take this case?' Miserably the IOC president responded, 'It's always sad if you have to discipline colleagues. Another enquired, 'What did the Ethics Commission say the two gentlemen had done wrong? That hasn't been made clear to us yet and is there any possibility we can see the reports of the Ethics Commission so we can see for ourselves the process that was gone through and the thinking behind it?'

Rogge would not answer such a direct question. But I hadn't travelled hundreds of miles for this cold jelly of a meal. I heaved myself upright; 'Just over a year ago the BBC transmitted the documents showing that João Havelange had taken a million dollars from the ISL company, a kickback on a marketing contract. Please, can we see the report of the Ethics Commission and what their recommendation was before he resigned?'

Rogge appeared to be slipping into a terminal coma. 'The reports of the Ethics Commission are confidential – the proposals to the Executive Board are public. And are published.'

I had another go. 'Did you see the one on Havelange, did it disturb you, did you have any emotional reaction to it?'

'Mr Jennings, I have no emotions on this day, I have a task to fulfil, I have duties to respect. I am not there to display my emotions.'

I tried again. 'What did you think of that report on Havelange, please?'

Rogge: 'I keep my thoughts to myself. Thank you very much.'

Another reporter took up the struggle to prise open this oyster. 'Were you disappointed that Mr Havelange resigned and therefore you were not able to be seen to be doing justice to his case?'

'As I said before, I am not here to talk about my feelings and my emotions. I received the resignation of Mr Havelange – it was endorsed by the IOC Executive Board. As a result of that Mr Havelange was no longer an IOC member. For us he is a private person.'

The presidential monotone continued. 'May I, even without a question, the IOC has shown it respects its rules, that we had a high respect of ethical behaviour and that we do not hesitate, when needed, and when the evidence is brought to us.'

I had one final go, 'The wider world, President Rogge, is now very well aware of the $100 million bribery scandal from ISL into sports organisations. Are you confident that, after announcing today's decision, that Havelange is off the hook, that the wider world will believe that the IOC is facing up to its responsibilities dealing with corruption?'

Rogge interrupted me. 'I am sorry, Mr Jennings. I think the wider world will agree and acknowledge that the IOC means business and that the IOC is accountable and transparent.'

That was it.

December 17, 2011, Tokyo: Lobster time again! Blatter and his ExCo are at the Ritz-Carlton for their annual Christmas party. The lobster sushi, a special favourite of Chuck Blazer, who chairs the organising committee, is catered at the conclusion of the Club World Cup. Corinthians won. The Belly knows it will be his last free banquet. Investigators are closing on him and his two decades of helping himself to football's millions.

They gather around Hayatou, drinks in hand, laughing, congratulating him. His escape at the IOC with only a tiny wrist tickle from Rogge is hilarious. More drinks! FIFA's paying! Blatter is triumphant! He tells a press conference, 'As for Mr Hayatou, there is no action required there. He was issued with a reprimand by the IOC regarding a very old case, but he is still a member of high standing with them and with FIFA too. There is no need to instigate any kind of inquiry because the executive committee trusts and supports him fully.'

Blatter mourns that he is not yet permitted to publish the Hildbrand report – 'a subject dear to my heart.' He doesn't tell the reporters that he is still fighting *against* disclosure. Neither does he reveal, five days later, the rejection, again, by the Zug court of the attempt by him and the still not named Havelange and Teixeira, to block publication.

January 8, 2012, Rio: Havelange, now isolated and disgraced, is reported saying, 'Until the end of my life I will never forget what that British journalist did to me.' But he doesn't stop fighting disclosure of the Hildbrand report. Blatter has now dropped out, advised by his lawyer that they can't win – but leaving the Brazilians to continue the stalling. The next month, Havelange and Teixeira now sharing a lawyer to reduce costs, appeal again. They win more months of delay while we have to waste time and money again refuting their empty arguments.

Blatter gives an interview to a German football magazine and blames FIFA's problems on 'Investigative journalists in England.' He adds, 'I've been trying to release this exasperating ISL dossier for a long time. I'd be ready to do that today if only the court would allow it.' Separately he comes up with a new plan to block the revelations. Apparently it is a complex document and would first have to be studied by 'legal experts.'

Fortunately, we never hear any more of this gambit.

Into the New Year and Blatter is off in his executive jet to Paraguay to prop up Nicolás Leoz at Conmebol's congress in Asunción. The main theme is 'the independence and autonomy of the member associations.' That is their code for opposing governments or police officers investigating their corruption.

With Leoz safe, Blatter directed his jet to fly across the Atlantic to Libreville in Gabon to give similar support to Issa Hayatou at the CAF congress. Hayatou runs African football with an iron grip and not surprisingly the gathering passed a somewhat odd motion attacking the IOC.

It began, 'The general assembly denounces the strategy by which the African sports movement and its officials are used as scapegoats by those who seek by all means to cover their tracks.' Hayatou would have drafted this gibberish; what on earth was going on in his mind? It went on, 'We note the president of CAF has in the past been the target of an unpleasant campaign.'

Again, the visiting Blatter plugged his demand for the autonomy of his corrupt associates. He told puzzled reporters, 'As you can see, "Work hard, love football" continues to be my motto.' Raising his voice he declaimed, 'For the game. For the world.' Then he got back on his ozone-busting jet and returned to Zurich.

THE LAWYER acting for the two Brazilians came up with a final, derisory argument. Maybe the report should be revealed to the media – but Messrs Tanda and Oliver were 'private persons' so it could not be given to them. Both men of course were journalists working for major media organisations and both had been reporting on FIFA corruption for years. The dispute was now on its way to be decided finally by Switzerland's Federal Court.

But Teixeira would not be around when judgement was delivered. On March 12, 2012 he resigned in disgrace from FIFA, the CBF and the 2014 World Cup organising committee. Years of investigations by the Brazilian Congress, Senate and more recently BBC *Panorama* had forced him out. Romário tweeted, 'Today we can celebrate. We exterminated a cancer from Brazilian football.'

The international debate about FIFA corruption moved to Paris. In December the previous year, three days before Rogge's embarrassing press conference, I had testified to a committee of politicians at the Council of Europe offices in Avenue Kléber. Earlier I submitted a report, at their request, analysing FIFA as an organised crime syndicate. In my presentation in Paris I named the Brazilian embezzlers and stressed that Investigating Magistrate Thomas Hildbrand knew the truth and that some of us were battling to have his report published.

The committee listened carefully. Then, in secret, they invited Hildbrand to come and testify to them. He was given permission by the Swiss government and was heard in Paris on March 6, 2012. Six weeks later the Council of Europe published their report. Their *rapporteur* François Rochebloine, a member of the French National Assembly representing the Loire constituency, highlighted a crucial statement by Hildbrand; that the order ending the Zug proceedings 'was not subject to an absolute secrecy requirement.'

He went on, 'It would therefore appear that FIFA is able to publish the document in question (which it must have in its possession as party to the proceedings) without waiting for a decision from the Swiss Federal Court.'

This was the same legal advice we had been given at BBC *Panorama*. Blatter had no justification for sitting on the report. He had lied again and again, month after month. Naïve reporters had parroted this to the world.

M. Rochebloine spotted that Blatter pays his most senior people massive bonuses. He commented, 'The suspicion is that these payments are to keep employees and Executive Committee members quiet about the corruption.'

THE END came on July 11, 2012 when the Swiss Federal Court ruled that the Hildbrand report could be published. Blatter immediately tried to divert attention from the disclosure that he had been a 'disloyal manager' and not taken action when he knew about the embezzling by the Brazilians.

He tweeted, 'Pleased by the Swiss Fed. Court decision on ISL. It confirms as I & the court in Zug said: I was not on the list.'

Blatter could not stop lying; the court in Zug had not said anything of the sort. Neither Blatter nor any FIFA officials had been on trial. It was only ISL managers, accused of trading while insolvent. Bribes were part of the evidence – but only to show that ISL managers had paid them when they should have closed the company and instead sent the money to their creditors.

Blatter continually briefs dimwit reporters that he was

'cleared' by Hildbrand's investigation. One hilarious exchange was with a reporter at Sky News who had an 'exclusive' interview with the boss of world football but had not bothered to read the Hildbrand report, or had any idea what the Swiss Federal Court had said – and not said.

Question: 'How did the allegations affect you personally? Was it very disturbing for you to read these allegations?'

Blatter: 'Absolutely, absolutely, because also it put into question my probity, my independency, [sic] but I was very happy then, even the high court in Switzerland has made a decision that the FIFA president was not personally involved in any matter where money was distributed and he had no clue in this matter, but it affects the person, it affected my family, but it will not affect my energy, my heart and my soul to go through this process until the end.'

DURING MY RESEARCH for this book I spoke with a trusted source who was very close to one of Horst Dassler's closest aides. They told me that they asked him, did Havelange ever take money from Horst Dassler?

He also said that for more than 20 years, Ricardo Teixeira and Jean-Marie Weber met to settle the 'account' – which means Teixeira received money. Two years before Dassler died he gave a confidential file to his aide. It contained a contract for 60 million Swiss francs to be paid to Havelange over 12 years. Horst would travel to see Havelange in Rio to discuss the details and at these meetings money was also paid over.

16

Marin Pointed the Finger at Vlado

Now he leads Brazilian football

Asunción, December, 13, 2013. The men who disfigure Latin American football are gathered at the Conmebol offices to celebrate surviving another year in power. Assisted by tall, beautiful young women in above-the-knee skirts, Brazil's Marco Polo Del Nero, born in 1941, is wrapping around the neck of Brazil's José Maria Marin, born in 1932, the organisation's highest honour, the 'Collar Extraordinario.' They appear utterly indifferent to the ferment in Brazil and the anger towards the CBF and FIFA.

After the ceremony Marin sits at a table with former FIFA ExCo member Nicolás Leoz, born 1928. We had been told six months earlier that Leoz had quit football, disgraced by bribery allegations. The news has not yet reached his old friends. It is a tight little world. Leoz has been replaced at FIFA by Eugenio Figueredo, born 1932, for 20 years a vice-president of Conmebol and big in Uruguay. Both are now indicted by the Feds, they deny everything.

When Ricardo Teixeira, born 1947, was forced from the president's throne at the CBF, José Maria Marin replaced him. Teixeira also had to leave his seat at FIFA's ExCo – and Del Nero stepped up. The world of football was not a better place.

Rio, December 10, 2013: Some of the old men of Brazil's football clubs gather around the CBF boardroom table together with Del Nero, who may be their choice to replace Marin in 2015. Above them on a wall is a portrait of a young, almost angelic-looking Teixeira, ousted the previous year and now living in his $7 million home on Sunset Island in Biscayne Bay, Miami, purchased from Russian tennis star Anna Kournikova. His spirit lives on in Rio. Little changes.

Brasília, December 11, 2012: Congressman Romário slips quietly into the committee room. A hundred pairs of eyes follow the iconic *Baixinho* as he heads first towards the press benches. With both hands he clasps one of mine. 'Andrew Jennings, my friend, how are you today?'

He's on great form, light on his feet, relaxed, smiling, the glint in his eye signals that one of football's greatest goalscorers intends to net another one this morning. As ever, we the spectators won't see it coming, he doesn't do build-up, Romário just does it. Boum!

'All the better for seeing you, mate,' I reply. He laughs and walks away, weaving around the tables to take his seat among the members of the Sport and Tourism Committee.

Romário is patient for a few minutes. Then the chairman on the podium throws him the ball, it's his turn to speak. He's not smiling now.

'People stop me in the street. They say, bring back Teixeira, this new guy is worse.'

In 16 words, he's turned on the ball and, Boum!

For 23 years Ricardo Teixeira embezzled millions of dollars from FIFA and the CBF. The BBC discovered documents proving his corruption, he was finally forced out of football nine months ago and the fans put away their '*Fora Teixeira*' banners.

How can the new guy heading the CBF, 81-year-old José Maria Marin, possibly be worse? Sure, he's deep in the historic looting of Brazilian football but Marin couldn't match Tricky Ricky's decades of thieving.

It must be something off the pitch, something vile, something from the past, from the era of the military dictatorship. The rage is boiling up in São Paulo, demonstrators are on the streets outside José Maria Marin's home, there's anger in the papers, he is accused in the State Senate of having 'blood-stained hands.' What's he done?

March 31, 1964: In the early hours the tanks roll. Rightists and fascists, some trained by the Americans, with more braid than brains. Generals who never led their troops into real battle where they might die.

But these generals have their nasty toys; guns, aircraft, battleships and upright steel chairs plugged into the electrical supply. They are restless. It is 14 years since they relinquished their last 20-year spell of military rule. They watch, horrified, as Leftist politicians are elected and free workers associations grow in strength.

Their friends in the CIA and the Pentagon don't approve either. New President João Goulart is from a wealthy land-owning family but he is taxing foreign companies, limiting how much profit can be exported and plans to redistribute land. Education is being expanded, adult illiteracy tackled.

In those days the American Dream was a Latin America that bowed the knee to Washington. Independent foreign policies south of the border were not permitted. When President Goulart opposed sanctions on Castro's Cuba the White House dusted down their coup blueprint. Opposition groups were bankrolled.

An aircraft carrier and destroyers carrying guided missiles sailed but weren't needed. It took the generals only 72 hours to destroy Brazilian democracy.

Brasília, December 13, 1968: The generals took four years to get round to making a law – famously known as Institutional Act Number 5 – that gave whoever happened to be their puppet president at the time the power to do any damn thing he wanted. The Congress was mothballed, most political parties banned and human rights extinguished. In passing, their censors were let loose on the press, music, films and theatre.

The Generals, knowing they were illegitimate and facing popular hatred, declared war against opponents. There was an even darker war that became known as *Operation Bandeirantes* – the OBAN – police and military officials secretly funded by Brazilian businessmen and American corporations, who paid bonuses to eradicate trade unionists in their factories.

These units tapped phones, kidnapped dissidents, interrogated, tortured and murdered political prisoners at will. In São Paulo their Death Squad was notorious.

In 1970 one of the thousands captured was a 22-year-old student, Dilma Rousseff, who had joined a clandestine urban guerrilla group. Over two years the torturers went to work on her in São Paulo, Rio and Juiz de Fora. Interviewed by investigators a decade ago Ms Rousseff described beatings, being tied up naked and given electrical shocks to the most sensitive parts of her body, at one session her uterus haemorrhaging.

'I remember the fear when my skin trembled,' she said in 2001. 'Something like that marks us for the rest of our lives.'

There is an astonishing photograph of Ms Rousseff in court being sentenced to six years' jail. She is expressionless, but doesn't cower. Up on the bench are two military judges, both covering their faces, shamed by their service to the dictatorship.

São Paulo, March 15, 1971: As the OBAN operatives were wiring up Ms Rousseff to their generators in São Paulo, again, José Maria Marin became a member of the State Congress. If he had wanted to listen, Marin could have heard her screams. He would have known of the torturing but was comfortable with it. The military made no secret of their brutality; they needed a cowed and intimidated population.

Senhor Marin had joined the ARENA party, created to front for the dictatorship. He liked them because they gave him political power close to the community cashbox – and they liked him because he was their jukebox. Press Marin's button and he would deliver a speech in the State Congress denouncing communists or anybody else the OBAN wanted an excuse to arrest and hurt.

From time to time Marin would encounter Sérgio Fleury in the political backrooms or the fashionable restaurants of São Paulo. Fleury was a world-class sadist, an artist in torture. The Prince of Pain, he oversaw interrogations and operated a network of private prisons, farms and houses, where political prisoners were hidden and tortured for days. Many died – or just disappeared.

His gangsters in civilian clothes would smash through a front door at any time and, if it amused them, begin beating the suspect. Sometimes he would be pinioned while they warmed up on his wife and parents. Children would watch, terrified. Guns might be fired. Marin thought highly of Fleury.

São Paulo, January 2013: 'After the dictatorship was installed it was a very unhealthy proposition to be a journalist. I had got out six months earlier and was in London, working for the BBC Brazilian Service,' recalls Nemércio Nogueira. 'With a colleague we lobbied the BBC to offer a job to our friend and former colleague Vladimir Herzog. In 1965 they hired Vlado, he brought his wife Clarice and they had two boys in London, Ivo and André.'

Maybe Vlado Herzog thought the dictatorship would soon wither and die. After three years with the BBC and training in television production, he took his family home and was appointed editor in chief of TV Cultura, a public station, belonging to the São Paulo state government. He was now within the rangefinder of State Congressman José Maria Marin, mouthpiece of Sérgio Fleury and the generals.

Divisions had opened in the dictatorship. The armed struggle launched by a handful of revolutionary groups had been defeated, the guerrillas eliminated. Some generals favoured a cautious return to democracy. The hardliners didn't and to stay in power they needed a Red Scare. The footsoldiers of torture agreed wholeheartedly; a lucrative sideline was stealing money, whatever they could loot from prisoners.

They got help from outside. The security services of Argentina, Bolivia, Chile, Paraguay and Uruguay launched the notorious Operation Condor, synchronised from a CIA base in Panama, arresting and assassinating Leftists and opponents of dictatorship throughout Latin America.

Vlado was more than a respected former BBC reporter and producer. He was a philosophy graduate, a successful documentary film-maker and taught journalism at the University of São Paulo.

Another colleague remembers, 'Vlado had a very straightforward and unadorned style to speak and write, as journalists do, and wasn't given to bouts of rhetoric. One phrase that he used frequently and represents very strongly his thought – and is engraved on his tomb – was "When we lose the ability to become indignant with atrocities committed against others, we also lose the right to consider ourselves civilised human beings."'

His Jewish family knew about fear, the fear of atrocities. When he was a boy they'd fled Croatia ahead of the Nazis. Ivo

Herzog told me, 'Yes my father was a member of the Brazilian Communist Party. But it wasn't an armed group. It was like a club, a discussion group.' Denunciations were what Fleury and his sadists craved. They began arresting suspected communists and torturing them for names.

São Paulo, September 1975: Claudio Marques was a cheap-shot rabblerouser writing in a free sheet delivered to households in the city. 'I knew Claudio in person, as a journalist, and to me he was a weasely little prick. I felt he was just your opportunistic hack, who saw a chance to fawn to the government and to the powerful, possibly carrying some favour, sponsorship for his column and TV programme, a job, whatever.' That's the recollection of Vlado's friend and colleague at the BBC, Nemércio Nogueira.

Claudio did all he could to ingratiate himself with the generals and the torturers. Sérgio wanted Reds? Claudio would oblige. He began typing his 'Column One.'

Look at yesterday's news on TV Cultura on Channel 2! An item about that Vietnamese Commie, Ho Chi Minh! Never mind it was supplied by the BBC's Visnews, here was the proof the TV station had been taken over by the Reds! Was the government going to stand by and do nothing?

This was the first week in September 1975. Claudio was back two days later with another poisonous attack.

Arrests of suspected communists began in the last week of September. Strapped naked into the Dragon's Chair, Sérgio Fleury's version of Old Sparky, with electrodes clipped to nose and penis and doused with buckets of water, they were soon screaming names.

The campaign moved to the state congress.

São Paulo, October 9, 1975: The stooge chosen to do the warm-up was Congressman Wadih Helú, another creation of the dictatorship. He sat on the ARENA benches, was president of Corinthians football club and provided discreet buildings to Sérgio Fleury's torturers for private interrogations.

Helú had shocking news for fellow congressmen.

Get this: the state government had just opened a new sewage system but if you watched TV Cultura, you wouldn't know. They hadn't sent a camera crew. (At this point you might laugh. Don't, the ending is dark)

Puffing himself up in faux rage, Congressman Helú continued, 'Their absence did not surprise us because we have been reading every week, in Claudio Marques' "Column One," denunciations of infiltration by Leftist elements.'

Helú racked up the volume. They only showed negative news, nothing positive. They were, 'Proselytising communism and subservience, becoming, as Claudio Marques says, "São Paulo's Vietnam *Cultura Television*," maintained by the peoples' money, disserving our government and our Motherland.'

Cue the headlining act: ARENA Congressman José Maria Marin launched a widowmaker.

'I find it strange that the press has for a long time been raising this problem, asking the competent agencies for measures towards what is happening at Channel 2, and nothing has happened,' squeaked Marin.

'It's not just a question of what they publish but the disquiet not only talked about here, not only commented on in political circles, but commented about in almost all São Paulo homes.'

Something *had* to be done.

'I wish to call the attention of the secretary for culture of São Paulo State and of the state governor, that they should publicly and definitively look into the denunciations being raised by the São Paulo press and, particularly and coura- geously, by journalist Claudio Marques.

'And it's not only Marques that has been observing the neg- ative facts. There is nothing positive to be seen, it [TV Cultura] shows only miseries, presenting problems but no solutions.'

'I appeal to the state governor: either the journalist is wrong, or the journalist is right. What cannot persist is this omission, both on the part of the Secretary for Culture and of the governor. More than ever action is required, in order for tranquillity to reign once again not only in this House, but especially in the homes of São Paulo.'

Sérgio Fleury and his OBAN thugs now had a licence to go to work. José Maria Marin had greenlighted them. The clock was ticking down on the life of Vlado Herzog.

'From that time, we lived in the eye of the hurricane,' remembers Vlado's friend and colleague, Paulo Markun. Eight days later Markun was arrested. 'I was tortured and confessed that I was a member of the Communist Party'.

On the evening of October 24, 15 days after the ravings of congressmen Wadih Helú and José Maria Marin, policemen arrived at TV Cultura wanting to take Vlado away. Vlado's colleagues argued that he was at that moment closing the evening's newscast and if they took him away the programme couldn't be broadcast. So Vlado offered to go to the police voluntarily the next morning for questioning.

Was Vlado reckless? Was he naïve? A colleague and friend told me, 'My interpretation is that, living in a well-known address, being a well-known journalist, in a well-known, high-profile job in a state TV station, and not being involved in any armed or revolutionary activities, he had nothing much to fear.'

(*There are several published stories dealing with the horrible events of this day. I have tried to edit them together.*)

São Paulo, October 25, 1975: Vladimir Herzog, aged 38, woke up earlier than usual that Saturday morning. He shaved, showered and kissed Clarice, still in bed, goodbye. She wanted to get up and make breakfast, he said not to worry, he would stop at a cafe and take a coffee with milk.

Hidden in the back of the mind of anybody who didn't count themselves a supporter of the regime was always the fear of 'disappearing.' It happened. Vlado arranged to meet a colleague who accompanied him to the front door of number 921 Rua Tutóia, in the neighbourhood of Paradiso, now the 36th Police Precinct. They arrived around 8 am.

Behind high walls guarded by armed sentries, was the home of OBAN. Vlado entered through the front door and told the attendant his full name, profession and ID number.

After that he waited, sitting on one of the wooden benches that lined the wide hallway leading to a glass and steel door. Minutes later he was taken in for questioning.

Inside Vlado was told to remove his clothes and change into prison overalls. Already in the interrogation room were two prisoners, their heads covered in black hoods. One of them Rodolfo Konder, recognised his friend: 'I pushed the edge of the cloth and recognised the shoes, Vlado's black loafers.'

Vlado denied being a Communist Party member. Konder and the other prisoner were taken out. Soon they heard Vlado's screams as the electric-shock machine was put to work. 'The screaming lasted until late morning. The shocks were so violent that Vlado howled in pain,' says Konder. 'A radio was turned up loud to drown out the sounds.' Half an hour later, around 11 am, Vlado was taken to the interview room.

'About an hour later, they took me to another room where I could remove the hood and I saw Vlado. The interrogator, a man of about 35, slim, muscular, with an anchor tattoo on his arm, told me to tell him that it was useless to resist,' recalls Konder. 'Vlado was stuck with the hood on his head, trembling, haggard, nervous. I had to help him write a confession saying he had been lured by me to enter the PCB and list other party members.'

At this point, Ivo Herzog tells me, 'They stopped the electric shocks and dictated a note for him to write. He obeyed and wrote it and then reflected and tore it up. They increased the voltage, his screams were heard again, and it killed him.'

He hesitates and stops. 'The family doesn't like to remember the torture. They had no need to kill my father – it was unintentional.'

Was Sérgio Fleury in the room, I ask. 'We don't know,' says Ivo. 'But I know that Marin was quite prepared to put my father's life in jeopardy to ingratiate himself with the military.'

Late that night Clarice Herzog was told the news of her husband's death.

October 25, 1975, later in the day: The torturers hurriedly dressed Vlado in his street clothes, looped his trouser belt around his neck, strung him up from the bars of a cell and photographed him, claiming he had killed himself. It was unconvincing. Vlado's feet were touching the floor and his knees bent.

His body was handed to Jewish authorities who would be expected to bury the corpse – and the evidence – swiftly. The Jewish tradition is that suicides cannot be buried in their cemetery. But when the *Shevra Kaddish* – Jewish burial committee - prepared the body for the funeral, Rabbi Henry Sobel noticed the marks left by torture. He ordered Vlado be buried in the centre of their cemetery. The suicide story disintegrated.

Rodolfo Konder had been released and was at the funeral. He insisted on wearing the clothes he was tortured in. 'I took the dirty clothes with urine, faeces and blood. That's how I attended the funeral of my friend.'

As the news of Vlado's death spread across São Paulo, media workers took to the streets. Armed police glared at them. But the tragedy brought home to the middle classes what was happening in their country. Slowly – although it would take another decade to return to something resembling democracy – the military grip was weakened. Rabbi Sobel said later, 'Herzog's murder was the catalyst of the eventual restoration of democracy.'

São Paulo, October 7, 1976: Two days short of a year after his savaging of TV Cultura – and triggering the murder of Vladimir Herzog – José Maria Marin was on his feet again in the São Paulo Congress.

Again, Congressman Marin was complaining. Not about the Reds. This time he was upset by the lack of public respect for Sérgio Fleury, police commissioner for São Paulo. A man who had recently ambushed and gunned down guerrillas brave enough to take on the dictatorship.

This is extracted from the official record of Marin's speech. 'We who know him closely know he is an exemplary family man, but most of all, he fulfils his duties as a policeman in the most praiseworthy manner.

'We cannot understand why a policeman of such calibre, a man who has devoted his life entirely to fighting crime, a man who has several times put at risk not only his own life, but also the lives of his family members is not receiving the admiration he deserves.

'Knowing his character as I do, there is no doubt that Sérgio Fleury loves his profession; that Sérgio Fleury dedicates himself to it most tenderly, measuring no effort or sacrifice to honour not only the São Paulo police, but above all his title of police commissioner. He should be a source of pride to the people of our city.

'Therefore, Mr Speaker, in the certainty that we are reflecting the thoughts of the São Paulo population, we wish to tell of our pride that we have in the São Paulo police commissioner Sérgio Fleury.'

Ilhabela, near São Paulo, May 1, 1979: The Generals hadn't bothered to tell José Maria Marin that his hero the torturer was becoming obsolete. Fleury was a liability. He had been useful but he knew too much, was now past his sell-by date and had to go. Less than three years passed and Marin's accolade became Fleury's obituary.

Fleury had 'an accident.' The official story was that he was drunk, 'fell' from his yacht at the island resort of Ilhabela, and drowned. There was no autopsy, he was rushed into the ground. The battered Left in Brazil could savour a tiny irony; Fleury was disposed of on May 1, 1979 . . . Labour Day.

St Helier, Jersey, November 17, 2012: Former friend of the generals, still a friend of José Maria Marin and still wanted by Interpol for money laundering, Paulo Maluf laughs at the court judgement that he's a thief who siphoned $10.5 million from a road construction contract in São Paulo.

Why should he care? He's 81 now, the government will never get the money back in his lifetime and they will never find enough evidence to claw back the estimated $1.7 billion he stole over the years.

Maluf will be remembered for three things. Maybe the most corrupt politician in Brazil's history; and a comment during his failed 1989 presidential bid that he supported capital punishment for rapists who murder their victims so, hey, 'If you have sexual urges, that's okay. Rape, but do not kill!'

Then there are the stars on the badge of the São Paulo Military Police. There are 18; one more was added in 1981 by Maluf, honouring their support for the 'revolution' of 1964.

The generals made him Mayor of São Paulo in 1969 and Maluf began looting the public purse. He levered himself into the throne of São Paulo state governor in 1979, made José Maria Marin his deputy and handed him the keys to the state treasury in 1982.

The most memorable event of Senhor Marin's ten months in the governor's chair was being booed in the Legislative Assembly after the discovery of suspicious loans from a federal bank. He realised he would not make his fortune in politics and turned to football. Friends appointed him president of the São Paulo region of the national CBF.

Marin performed well enough to impress Ricardo Teixeira, who made him a CBF vice-president in 2008. When my disclosures of Teixeira's bribes forced him out of the CBF (and FIFA) in March 2012, Marin was the pliable replacement. He'd proved that he shared Teixeira's view of football; if it can be stolen, steal it. Marin was caught on television stealing a medal at a youth championship.

Three months later Brazil's splendid football reporter Juca Kfouri dug out Marin's speech to the São Paulo Congress in October 1975, fingering Vlado Herzog. Juca blamed Marin for the journalist's arrest and death. Juca also took his readers back to the barely believable speech a year later when Marin praised the repulsive torturer Sérgio Fleury.

Marin was interviewed on TV. Reporter Fernando Rodrigues put the Big Question: 'Some people think that some speeches that you made, very acid, tough, eventually led to the imprisonment and then the death of journalist Vladimir Herzog?'

Marin: 'Sheer scheming, sheer scheming, sheer scheming . . . a lie, a lie, I had nothing, absolutely nothing to do with that.'

Rodrigues: 'It's really a very big coincidence, your speech at the Parliament and later his death?'

Marin: 'Again, I insist, it's all scheming, I had nothing to do with it . . . I was always a man known for conciliation, for harmony and for conciliation.'

A São Paulo journalist who observed Marin's political 'career,' says. 'He was and is a non entity. Marin's a mouse, not even a rat'.

São Paulo, Saturday November 11, 2012: A few hundred demonstrators, alerted by articles in the city's newspapers, are outside the home of José Maria Marin at Rua Padre João Manoel, 493, in the Jardins district, at the corner with Alameda Franca.

Armed with banners, drums, tambourines, microphones and a sound truck, the demonstrators sing songs composed especially for the occasion, one asking, 'See Marin's dirty record, is he, is he, a snitch?'

Among them is Adriano Diogo, a member of the Workers' Party now led by President Dilma Rousseff. Diogo, now aged 63, was also arrested and tortured by the OBAN in 1971 and jailed for a couple of years.

São Paulo, Tuesday November 27, 2012: Adriano Diogo is on his feet again, but this time in his weekday job. He is a São Paulo state congressman, as was José Maria Marin 37 years earlier when he attacked TV Cultura. Congressman Diogo sings from a different songsheet.

'Ladies and gentlemen, first I want to congratulate this new generation of young people who make *escrachos* [name and shame] at the door of the torturers, who had this brilliant idea of going to the door of the apartment of José Maria Marin.

'Senhor José Maria Marin, the snitch of the dictatorship, is responsible for the imprisonment and death of Vladimir Herzog,' said Diogo. 'He has bloodstained hands. He is not fit to be the president of the CBF.'

Wednesday January 23, 2013: Official announcement. 'The Inter-American Commission on Human Rights of the Organization of American States will investigate the state's responsibility for the death of journalist Vladimir Herzog in 1975, during the military dictatorship, 1964–1985.'

According to the complaint, Brazil still has not complied with its obligation to investigate, prosecute and punish those responsible for the death of Vladimir Herzog.

'The case of Herzog illustrates the failure of the judiciary during the Brazilian military dictatorship as well as democracy,' said Viviana Krsticevic, executive director of the Center for Justice and International Law, based in Washington, who came to Brazil on Tuesday to announce the acceptance of the complaint.

'We want to know who is responsible for what happened to my father,' said Ivo Herzog. His mother, Clarice Herzog, campaigns to name the names *and* to expose the ones still on the public payroll, employed by the police or security services. 'I pay taxes to support torturers,' she tells me.

Will José Maria Marin be invited to testify to the human rights investigators? Tell what he knows about the death of Vladimir Herzog? Marin once boasted of how well he knew the torturer Sérgio Fleury. Surely he asked him about the day Herzog didn't come home?

Marin ignored a request to attend the meeting of the

Congressional Sports and Tourism Committee in Brasília, leaving an open goal for Romário.

Rua Victor Civita, Barra da Tijuca, Rio, April 1, 2013: Former superstar Romário, now a congressman, leads a demonstration outside the CBF offices. With him is Ivo Herzog. Romário hands in a petition with 50,000 signatures, calling for Marin to quit because of his connection to the military dictatorship. He holds up a poster headlined '*Fora Marin!*' They call for an investigation into Marin's possible connection to the death of Vlado Herzog.

Port Louis, Mauritius, May 30, 2013: FIFA's 63rd congress opens; delegates endorse President Sepp Blatter's 'reforms.' They welcome Brazil's delegate José Maria Marin to their party. Many of them hate journalists anyway.

New York, June 5, 2013: Ivo Herzog asked FIFA's ethics investigator, American lawyer Michael Garcia, to investigate Marin's involvement in his father's death. Garcia replies, 'Your petition addresses events of paramount importance, and the sincerity of your interest in this matter cannot be questioned. The allegations you raise nonetheless appear to fall outside my jurisdiction, which the FIFA Code of Ethics restricts in both scope and time. My authority extends only to violations by football officials of applicable provisions of the Code of Ethics, the first version of which was enacted in 2004.'

17

Blatter Hires His Own Investigators

Big money to be earned, no need to hurry

November 18, 2010: Zurich: 'I cannot tolerate the way they presented the truth,' fumes Blatter's ethics chief, Claudio Sulser. Journalists revealing that ExCo members were in the business of selling their World Cup votes were 'sensationalist' and 'twisting the facts.'

Blatter, sitting next to Sulser at the press conference, looks uncomfortable. He had appointed this clown, once a Swiss national player, to sedate the reporters, not insult them. The whole world knew that the secret cameras of the London *Sunday Times* had caught Amos Adamu and Reynald Temarii behaving corruptly and that they would have to be thrown out. Sulser wasn't being smart, attacking the reporters.

Why could he not keep his stupid mouth shut? But . . . the truth was that Sulser's rudeness accurately reflected the private rage of Blatter and the ExCo. How dare some reporters, outside the deferential, timid cabal that regularly attend Blatter's press conferences, expose how business was really done in the private world at FIFA! But this was not the time to be aggressive.

A few weeks earlier Sulser had refused to answer questions about the ISL scandal from a German television reporter, saying it was 'historic.' Again, everybody knew it was not and would soon be back in the headlines. The sooner Sulser was given a one-way ticket back to his home in Lugano, the better.

Now Blatter had to move forward, bringing to a conclusion the most determinedly corrupt World Cup bidding process ever. He commanded Sulser to send a letter to all the bidding countries telling them they must not be naughty! Surely that would warn them to do any deals in secret, where hungry reporters could not catch them.

Claudio did not copy his warning letter to the ExCo members, the ones who could, and some would, sell their votes. When there were allegations of improper collusion between Qatar and the joint Spain and Portugal bid, the malleable Sulser admitted that Spain's Executive Committee member Ángel Villar-Llona and Qatar's Mohamed Bin Hammam had been contacted – but by letter and not interviewed in person.

It made no practical or moral sense that both 2018 and 2022 would be voted on simultaneously. In 2010 there could be no reliable predictions of the value of sponsorships or TV rights a dozen years ahead. Never before had FIFA or the IOC allocated two of the mega-events at one go.

So how – and why – did Qatar win the vote? We have all guessed, haven't we? Some evidence came in March 2014 with the disclosure that Jack Warner, and his crooked sons, took big payments from Qatari businessman Mohamed Bin Hamman around the time of the vote. Greedy old men at FIFA did secret deals – fearing they might not be active in four years time for the next vote. Now football has to sort out the mess. How many of the other seven ExCo members forced out since the vote were involved in questionable activities?

There will be a few more years of pointless discussion. Blatter knows the event cannot possibly be held in the European summer in Qatar – too hot – nor in the winter. The European leagues, clubs, fans, TV rights holders and the football industry cannot afford to accept the huge financial and sporting losses of a suspension of at least six weeks. Will Blatter threaten to suspend Manchester United or City, Chelsea or major European clubs for refusing to shut down and release players?

The bogus 'investigations' commissioned by Blatter are cosmetic and expensive delaying tactics. We can respect the right of the people of Qatar to their own culture – but we did not ask for a World Cup on the terms of their unelected government and built by slave labour. Blatter frequently announces that the tournament should be more widely spread – and that Indian football should grow. So let's give it to the Indians, with their acceptable temperatures, growing national fan base, diverse cultures – and splendid beers!

Once the old boys were given what they wanted, Blatter turned his attention back to himself and plotting to block

Mohamed Bin Hammam from contesting the 2011 presidential election. He went to Saudi to check that the money was available to fund his campaign.

Sulser was told to get rid of the *Sunday Times* problem speedily. The reporters handed over hours of tapes and notes and memos. Four weeks after their disclosures, he announced his judgments. Adamu was banned for three years, Temarii for one. For both of them it was only a brief holiday from the game. By the summer of 2013, Temarii was active again in football in the Pacific, running the Beach Soccer World Cup in Tahiti. In November 2013 Adamu was meeting Nigeria's sports minister to discuss future plans.

For Blatter these two were not the problem. It was the lower-ranking officials who enraged him, who had committed the biggest crime in Blatter's world; the sin of breaching *Omertà* – organised crime's code of silence. They had *talked* to the undercover reporters! They had *talked* about the huge private world of FIFA bribery and corruption, the legacy of mobbed-up Havelange. Some *talked* about who was offering bribes in return for the right to host the 2018 and 2022 World Cups. An example had to be made of them.

Slim Aloulou from Tunisia got a two-year ban, Amadou Diakite of Mali was out for three years and Ahongalu Fusimalohi from Tonga was also kicked out for three years. The biggest punishment was a four-year ban on former ExCo member Ishmael Bhamjee from Botswana. He was recorded saying that Qatar was offering 'anything from a quarter to half a million dollars' for ExCo votes. All four were also fined 10,000 Swiss francs.

I interviewed *Sunday Times* reporter Jonathan Calvert for the BBC about the FIFA probe and the punishments. He was scornful of FIFA. 'They should have done a proper investigation. They should have employed proper detectives, an outside company, someone independent, someone professional who could go through the allegations in detail.

'And the outcome of that would have been that they would have had to postpone the votes for the two World Cups. Because there were some serious allegations in there which have never seen the light of day.'

Monday November 29, 2010: Two days before the vote for 2018 and 2022, BBC *Panorama* broadcasts the ISL Bribes List. We name Havelange, Teixeira, Leoz and Hayatou. Sulser does nothing. The ExCo huddle together. These are old friends. Temarii and Adamu were new boys, not missed. These four must be protected! Their time among us totals more than 100 years! The IOC takes a different view and begins the investigation that will lead in another year to Havelange being forced to quit the ranks of the Olympians.

Two days later Teixeira, Leoz and Hayatou cast their votes and the World Cup is awarded to two secretive petrodollar dictatorships. FIFA's ExCo departs Zurich's finest hotels, flies to Abu Dhabi along with Jack Warner, Chuck Blazer and Mohamed Bin Hammam, who do not know this will be their final lobsterfest paid for by football. The gang check into more of the world's most luxurious hotels for the Club World Championship, the most unimportant tournament in soccer history. Then it's Christmas.

Blatter kicked off the new year on January 2, 2011,

announcing that he would set up an anti-corruption committee. Seven days later this was undermined by the resignation from Sulser's Ethics Committee of Günter Hirsch, one of Germany's most senior judges, saying that 'FIFA has no real interest in playing an active role in the resolution, pursuance, and prevention of violations of FIFA's ethics code.'

Lamely, Blatter told Swiss newspaper *SonntagsZeitung*, 'I will take care of it personally, to make sure that there is no corruption at FIFA. This committee will strengthen our credibility and give us a new image in terms of transparency.'

I had heard this puffery a decade earlier. Speaking at the FIFA congress in Seoul in May 2002 President Blatter insisted, 'We don't just want to talk about transparency, I believe in transparency, we have started to build transparency brick by brick from 1999 onwards.' His then general secretary Urs Linsi, singing from the same hymn sheet had no doubts. 'FIFA is a healthy, clean and transparent organisation with nothing to hide.'

Blatter's Grand Plan to portray his FIFA as publicly committed to reform while privately doing the opposite was almost derailed by the scandal in May of Warner and Bin Hammam, then worsened with the revelation in July of Chuck Blazer's intriguing offshore self-enrichment and tax arrangements.

Blatter then suffered an attack of verbal diarrhoea and he babbled about a 'committee of the solutions,' possibly including former US secretary of state Henry Kissinger and the opera singer Plácido Domingo. That was soon forgotten. But, yet again, a crazed diversion was sufficient to distract compliant reporters from his crimes against the game.

The president wasn't going to take personal responsibility for rampant corruption in his ExCo, telling the FIFA congress in Zurich that 'I am the captain, we will weather the storm together.' His period of office, unchallenged with the banishment of Bin Hammam, was extended for a further four years. As long as Teixeira and Marin and Del Nero controlled Brazil and delivered the World Cup, he would sweep through to re-election in 2015.

The flood of diversionary news stories was cranked up. They would run non-stop for the next two years. Ordinary fans with real lives were never going to keep up with the barrage. So many sound bites, interviews, press releases. We couldn't keep up.

The news agencies, overwhelmed by 'reform processes,' road maps, task forces, concept papers and interim reports, gave in and faithfully and uncritically pasted the press releases from Blatter and his hired hands into 'stories' and wired them to the world's media.

NOW CAME THE MASTERSTROKE – a breathtaking act of deceit. Behind closed doors Blatter set to work re-writing FIFA's Code of Ethics, its Statutes and their Regulations. Two hundred pages of legalistic and sometimes obscure language. The compliant reporters would never read them and if they did, they would not comprehend what Blatter was doing. Drafted cleverly, they would build a high wall to protect wrongdoing and dilute investigation.

There would be a new Ethics Committee, but twice as big as before! It would have two grandiosely-named 'Chambers.' The

Hard-Men-of-Football-Crime-Busting at the 'Investigatory Chamber' would be led by tough former super-cop Michael Garcia.

FIFA wanted us to know that Garcia had been US attorney for the area of New York covering Wall Street and had tangled with fraud, insider trading, terrorism and national security. Wow! That was vibrant stuff for a great FIFA press release. We are serious! Death to corruption! Would there be waterboarding?

But law professor Scott Horton, writing in the *Daily Beast* four years earlier when Garcia left public service, didn't share Blatter's boosting of the former prosecutor. One source Horton quoted said, 'Garcia had a knack for knowing what would make the politicos happy and he played that very effectively.'

What about Garcia's time keeping a watchful eye on the bankers and smooth talkers of Wall Street, the conmen who brought us the great financial crash? Professor Horton considers that, 'Garcia ignored his mandate to enforce discipline in the nation's financial industry [and] ignored years of chicanery on Wall Street.' Horton added, 'In his 39-month tenure as U.S. Attorney Garcia can claim no high-profile enforcement effort – not one.' Finally, he thought Garcia was too close to the world of George W. Bush.

Garcia now lived a different and richer life. No more jacket off, sleeves rolled up detective, eyeballing deviants in austere, grey-painted interrogation rooms. Five years after leaving public service and comfortable with multi-million dollar earnings at New York law firm Kirkland & Ellis,

Garcia often represented the wealthy targets of law enforcement – the people he once pursued. Was Garcia hired to be FIFA's corruption buster? Or defence attorney for Blatter?

Garcia, accompanied by his junior Sherlock Holmes, David Abramowicz, also from Kirklands, would supposedly lead his investigation team deep into the mucky world of FIFA and then send devastating reports to the impressive sounding Adjudicatory Chamber. This was headed by Munich judge Hans-Joachim Eckert, a specialist in financial crime. Judge Eckert did not seem disturbed by fellow German judge Günter Hirsch's warning that Blatter had no interest in reform. Each of the Chambers had six other members, drawn from sport and sometimes sports law.

Briefly on the FIFA stage was Transparency International. They produced an excellent report insisting there must be an independent investigation delving into the past management of FIFA, external people on key committees, term limits for senior officials, disclosure of Blatter's pay and bonuses and a declaration outlawing conflicts of interest. That romance didn't last long and TI left the stage three months later, slamming the door behind them. But Blatter had bought more time.

'I AM CONVINCED FIFA will get it right.' Another new voice, the eminent corruption expert, Professor Mark Pieth from the Basel Institute of Governance. He is introduced at a Zurich press conference in late 2011 by Blatter. It is a bit sticky. 'I'm happy and proud that you have accepted the call

– my call and the call of FIFA,' gushes the president and you wonder what has been going on in the back room.

Pieth was to head what he and Blatter called an 'Independent Governance Group' and substantial fees would be paid to members who wanted them. They included ambitious American football official, Sunil Gulati, a vice-president of sponsors Hyundai, a French publisher who did business with FIFA, four experts on governance from the Americas, a representative of professional footballers, the former British attorney general who gave the Blair government the legal go-ahead to invade Iraq – and Ms Lydia Nsekera, a football official from Burundi and also an IOC member. 'She's a lovely lady, she's a tough lady,' said Blatter. 'She's a princess, the daughter of a sultan. She was really the best choice.' Six months onwards, in November 2013, Ms Nsekera was ousted from the presidency of Burundi football. She retains her seat, probably for several decades to come, at the IOC.

An invitation to join Pieth's group was rejected by Football Supporters Europe, an organisation supported by fans in 38 countries. Ms Daniela Wurbs, their chief executive, said they could not accept the invitation 'because of concerns over Fifa's credibility.'

Professor Pieth, who has advised the World Bank on integrity, did more body swerves than Romário in front of goal. The difference is that Romário always scored. On that great day when Blatter and Pieth embraced each other the professor stated, 'I have to take a decision, whether I look at the past or the future. My answer is that I'm looking to the future, other people will look at the past. A week later he was reversing, stating that he would address previous allegations of wrongdoing and that looking at FIFA's past is 'necessary' to understand the 'risk scenarios.'

By late January 2012 Pieth was talking tough again. 'We must see to it that the gangsters do not escape in the wake of reform detractors. Many of those who now sit on the Executive Committee will not be there much longer.' Those that did leave were not forced out by Pieth's feeble efforts.

Two weeks later he was not so sure. 'We will decide at the end of March, whether there should be an investigation into the more serious allegations of the past.' Seven months onwards Pieth was still concerned about the past. 'They have skeletons in the cupboard, that's true' he said. By December 2012 Pieth was flailing around for support. 'It would be most welcome if the committee of the Council of Europe could add its voice to those demanding urgent change.' It did not seem to occur to Pieth and his group that they should threaten to walk out and call a noisy press conference revealing that Blatter and his ExCo had no interest in reform.

In April 2012 Blatter made his agenda clear: he visited Havelange in a Rio hospital and a month later at the FIFA congress in Budapest, led a standing ovation for their bribe-taking honorary president and discredited former member of the IOC.

At the London Olympics Blatter told a news conference that his reform campaign was working. 'We are not a corrupt or a mafia organisation. It is always a question of perception and the question of reality. We are in a good mood and in a good moment, and I am sure that we will be able to succeed.'

Fast forward into 2013 and Pieth's Group announced, 'The lack of transparent structures and culture of nepotism affect the organisation's reputation and undermine its ability to show the way to ethical governance of the sport.' By now Blatter knew he could safely ignore them and told reporters, 'The reform process is on the way to conclusion.'

That was enough for one member of Pieth's group. As FIFA's next congress, in faraway Mauritius, neared, Ms Alexandra Wrage, a Canadian expert on good governance who had declined fees, walked out. 'It's been the least productive project I've ever been involved in. There's no doubt about that. None of our items made it onto the agenda,' she said. 'I don't need a trip to Mauritius to have them not vote on our issues.'

A day later American member Sunil Gulati – the economics teacher who never spotted Chuck 'The Belly' Blazer looting regional football and was now hoping to be selected for a seat on FIFA's ExCo – saw things differently. 'I think the reforms that have been achieved are a very good first step.'

On the eve of the Mauritius lobsterfest far out in the Indian Ocean which, because of the expense, would be attended by only a few reporters, most of who would say thank you for press releases, a now confident Blatter said the congress would 'bring FIFA up to the highest standards of good governance, as befits an organisation such as ours, which plays such a fundamental role in society.'

He told delegates, 'As the captain, I am pleased to say we

have weathered the storm. We have emerged from the troubled waters stronger and now we can look forwards to the future and waters as calm as the beautiful sea around us in Mauritius and I think the boat can now go slowly into the harbour.' He added, 'FIFA is now setting the highest standards for governance in world sport.' Not true, but this is what his national associations wanted to hear.

Pieth remained on the margins, popping up at conferences and arguing his group had had its successes. Sometimes you had to wonder if his governance group did anything more than advise how many silver knives, forks and spoons, glasses for aperitifs, wine, champagne and sherry and FIFA embossed napkin rings should decorate each place setting at the ExCo banqueting table.

TOUGH GUY Garcia arrived at a Zurich press conference beating on his chest and making the same noises we remembered from the early days of Professor Pieth. 'If there is conduct in the past that warrants investigation, I will do it. There are no limitations at all on what we will be looking at.' And there was a huge step forward in the history of corruption investigations . . . they would set up a special telephone line to record allegations! Later there would be a website and an online complaints form. Is that how Garcia intended to catch the ExCo members who took bribes from bidding countries? There was another diversionary sprat tossed to the reporters. Garcia would be looking at how the 2006 World Cup was awarded to Germany.

The world wanted to know what Garcia was doing about

the biggest story; in what circumstances did Qatar win 2022? That struck at the roots of FIFA's reputation and the future of the World Cup.

Meanwhile he appeared to have more urgent concerns. Who was the biggest threat to President Blatter? Qatar's Mohamed Bin Hammam. FIFA was having difficulty getting rid of him. Might Garcia's report achieve something?

In December 2012 Mo was banished, forever. Garcia later alleged he had been doing naughty things with the money he controlled at the Asian Football Confederation – and Judge Eckert was quick to agree. Soon Mo's sidekick from Sri Lanka, Super-sized Manilal Fernando, who buys his trousers from the same store as Chuck The Belly, was exiled from football for eight years. Garcia used an investigation report by forensic accountants PricewaterhouseCoopers against Bin Hammam, alleging conflicts of interest.

They had dug into the AFC's accounts and found some big numbers moving around the world of Mo and the sale of marketing rights. Bang! Mo was gone. But buried in the lengthy report were some curious numbers that Blatter and the ExCo have not pressed to be investigated. In March 2008 Bin Hammam slipped $250,000 to Jack Warner. Then there was around $180,000 to the Luxembourg account of the Brazilian racehorse owner.

Mo paid $4,950 for suits made by the world famous Kuala Lumpur Lord's Tailors for African soccer boss Issa Hayatou. Lord's also design suits for hunky Mel Gibson, shoemaker Jimmy Choo and, long ago, Muhammad Ali. Another beneficiary of Mo's generosity was Sepp Blatter who, in February

2008 got $2,000 worth of shirts, again from Lord's. These would seem to be breaches of FIFA's ethics code, old and new. We may never be told. All Garcia would say was, 'It's not appropriate to get into a debate over what the PwC report says.'

THE HAVELANGE BRIBE in March 1997, known about by Blatter, could not be avoided. Once Garcia had read the IMG correspondence and how Blatter blocked their $1 billion attempt to oust ISL, then inspected that *'Garantie JH'* payment and heard the statements by FIFA's two top officials who had witnessed the kickback mistakenly sent to FIFA – Blatter would be out, finished, disgraced.

There would be an election for a new president, the new leadership would sort out the other scandals and Garcia would be needed no longer. His bill would be settled sooner than expected, thank you and goodbye, back to New York. It could not end any other way.

I broke the story 12 years ago and never gave up on it. I owed it to the fans who bought my books and watched my films and who trusted me. Knowing about that bribe was always Blatter's Achilles heel. So . . . here's the chronology of the scandal. It began with a phone call from the other side of the globe.

18

Blatter Rewrites His Ethics Code

Now he can never be caught!

Seoul, May, 2002. 'A big bribe for Havelange arrived accidentally at FIFA, it was a nightmare for us all and Blatter had to sort it out it.' The phone call was from Korea, the caller one of FIFA's most senior executives, in Seoul making final arrangements for the World Cup and FIFA's congress. Five years had passed since he witnessed Blatter's shock when the bribe for Havelange landed accidentally at FIFA instead of in one of the Brazilian's personal accounts. Only now did he feel safe to tell me.

He had spent half a lifetime working at FIFA and had seen the blatantly corrupt partnership between Havelange and ISL's bagman Jean-Marie Weber. The official had no doubt what had happened. Of course Blatter knew about the bribe from ISL to his boss. Say what you like about him, nobody ever thought Blatter was stupid. He had been trained by Horst

Dassler in the 1970s to put world football at the disposal of Adidas and later ISL; he had rescued ISL in 1996 from the IMG billion-dollar overtures, it is unbelievable that he didn't know it was a bribe. What else could a 1.5 million franc payment from the ISL company to the president of FIFA be about?

The call from Seoul in May 2002 came as FIFA was being torn apart. UEFA was leading the charge to unseat Blatter but, by the end of the month, Blatter would split his enemies and retain the president's throne. But at the beginning of the month I was having a brilliant time, being offered exclusive stories from FIFA's dark underbelly.

I asked the source if he had any documents. No, he said, he couldn't get to the archive of bank statements and did not recall a precise figure. But he had been in the office of then General Secretary Blatter when the kickback arrived and watched his boss panicking as the biggest corruption scandal in world sport unravelled before their eyes.

He recalled that the amount on the bank payment slip was in Swiss francs. The kickback made sense. Two weeks earlier I had published exclusive documents revealing how Blatter and Havelange had blocked the $1 billion dollar bid from the American sports marketing company IMG, who were trying to prise ISL's fingers off the wonderful World Cup contracts. Havelange could be expected to get his payback.

I talked with my editor and we published, in the London *Daily Mail* on May 25, 2002, a cautious story not naming Havelange or Blatter but saying that a bribe of around £500,000 had arrived accidentally at FIFA from ISL for 'a senior FIFA official' and that attempts had been made to persuade FIFA's bank to erase any record of the payment.

We had put the bribe story into play. Another eight years would pass before I got my hands on the evidence, the list of bribes paid, and discovered the payment on March 1997 to Havelange, recorded in the ISL secret payments as '*Garantie JH.*' Meanwhile it was too important a story to let go. It was the key to proving the corruption of Havelange and knowledge of Blatter.

Frankfurt, Friday December 5, 2003: Today is the qualifying draw for the 2006 World Cup. All week a thousand FIFA officials and delegates from national associations worldwide have been partying in Germany. I thought I might add something to the party, bathed as it was in self-congratulation. That morning I published the bribe story again, substantially similar to its first outing 18 months earlier. I now had a second source who had also been in Blatter's office and was certain that the general secretary knew the payment was a bribe. He did not want to be quoted.

Without a document I still could not publish that the payment was to Havelange. But I nosed the story, 'A senior FIFA official received a huge secret payment from the Swiss company who were awarded the lucrative TV and marketing rights to the 2002 and 2006 World Cups.

'The payment should have gone direct to the official, whose name is known to us, but accidentally ended up in a FIFA bank account, causing panic in the upper levels of the organisation.' We wrapped the story – most of a page – around a big picture of Havelange with the World Cup. President Blatter did not call to ask us who got the money.

Tunis, January 23, 2004: Here we go again. I have now been banned for a year from Blatter's press conferences but I've travelled to the African Nations Cup and a Nigerian friend smuggles me in. Halfway through Blatter's 'meet the press' session I stand up and eyeball him.

'After the last marketing and TV contract was signed with ISL for 2002 and 2006, a secret payment of one million Swiss francs from ISL arrived by accident in FIFA's bank account.

'It is alleged that you, as general secretary at the time, instructed it was to be moved immediately to a private account of a FIFA official. Who was it to?'

Blatter is traumatised. His face goes flat. His dirty secret is being aired in public, again. Then, he says, frostily, 'I will not enter into discussion here in this press conference and I think also it is totally out of the matter we like to discuss today in Africa together with the African journalists.' The exchanged filmed by a German TV crew, was screened internationally.

London, May, 2006: My book *Foul!* is published and is soon in 16 languages. The first chapter opens with the bribe arriving at FIFA and then my question to Blatter in Tunis. I get phone calls from Swiss reporters; 'Blatter says your story is completely untrue,' they tell me. 'No payment of this kind ever arrived. He says you have fabricated the story.'

London, June 11, 2006: The BBC screens my first TV investigation of FIFA corruption. The bribe story takes centre stage. First, we show the clip from Tunis two years earlier. Then, still banned from his press conferences, I step from behind a tree in the gardens at FIFA House and catch him on a footpath. My two cameramen spring into action and I try yet again with the FIFA president.

AJ: 'Let me just ask you this, do you know which football officials took bribes from the ISL marketing company?'

Blatter: 'Sorry, I don't speak about that.'

AJ: 'Do you know which football officials took payments from the ISL marketing company?'

Blatter: 'I don't answer these questions.'

AJ: 'Will you tell me who took the 1 million franc bribe? . . . I'm told you ordered this bribe should be moved to the man whose name is on the payment, can you tell me who it went to, was it President Havelange?'

Blatter fled into the FIFA building and ordered his functionaries to guard all the doors, in case we pursued him along the corridors of FIFA power.

REPORTERS do not work to be loved. Our responsibility is to put hard questions to the rich and powerful. I raised that same question about Blatter and Havelange and that bribe in more BBC *Panorama* programmes in 2010 and 2011. At the Senate *Comissãode Educação, Cultura e Esporte* in Brasília in October 2011, I showed the document proving the bribe to Havelange and repeated the exercise a month later in Paris at a meeting of the Committee on Culture, Science and Education of the Council of Europe's Parliamentary Assembly.

At last, in June 2012, we got our hands on Investigating Magistrate Thomas Hildbrand's long-suppressed report of his investigation into FIFA corruption. There was the official proof! Page 33, point 6.6 confirmed with beautiful clarity:

'*The finding that FIFA had knowledge of the bribery payments to persons within its organs is not questioned.*' (My italics.) That was it. FIFA – that is Blatter – knew! No surprise to me but great to see independent confirmation.

Hildbrand continued, 'This is firstly because various members of the Executive Committee had received money, and furthermore, among other things, it was confirmed by the former chief financial officer of FIFA as a witness that a certain payment made to João Havelange by the Company (ISL) amounting to CHF 1,000,000 was mistakenly directly transferred to a FIFA account; not only the CFO (Chief Financial Officer) had knowledge of this, but also, among others, P1 (President Blatter) would also have known about it.'

Unlike the private Pieth Group and the private new Ethics Committee and its two Chambers, all selected by Blatter, this report was from an independent, public investigator, working strictly to Swiss, public law. He was stating, clearly, that Blatter knew this was a bribe to Havelange.

In the public world outside FIFA, any politician or member of a company's board of directors would have been forced to resign in shame. Shamefully, only one football official in the whole world called for Blatter's sacking; the ExCo were silent, all 209 national associations were silent, as were the sponsors. So was the Brazilian government, which could have used this judgement as a lever against FIFA demands for tax and other privileges.

Blatter found an uncritical reporter from Reuters and told him, 'I did not know until later, after the collapse of ISL in 2001, about the bribery.' This lie was published globally.

The only football official to scorn Blatter was Reinhard Rauball, president of the German Football League. 'Blatter should hand over his duties to someone else as soon as possible,' he told *Die Welt*. 'For the sake of credibility of the reform process, FIFA needs someone who is willing to make a fresh start. It is always difficult when someone who was part of the problem seeks to carry on when change is necessary.'

Blatter ignored Rauball and diverted attention with a poisonous comment about Havelange. 'He is a multi-millionaire. That he received bribes beggars belief for me. He does not need it.' Of course Blatter knew that Havelange took bribes – but by confirming that Havelange was a rich man, he was undermining the Old Man's claims to Hildbrand that he was not wealthy enough to make a substantial repayment.

A week later Blatter publicly approved the appointments of Michael Garcia to be FIFA's Top Cop and Hans-Joachim Eckert to be his judge. Garcia was given the job of investigating the ISL scandal and especially Blatter's knowledge of the big bribe to Havelange on March 3, 1997. Eckert would pronounce judgement on whatever evidence Garcia chose to submit to him. Would this be the end for Blatter?

MORE THAN HALF A YEAR passed before Garcia submitted his report to Eckert. What does Garcia's report say? They will not tell us. It has been suppressed. Who did Garcia interview? We are not permitted to know. What documents did he discover, hidden in dusty archives? That's a secret. Did Garcia go back and look at the scandal of Blatter blocking the $1 billion bid from the IMG company, to preserve the flow of

ISL bribes? That cannot be revealed. I could have supplied Garcia with the correspondence. He will know from my past book, articles and films that I have them. He didn't call.

Disgracefully, the supposedly independent Eckert and Garcia have bowed to Blatter's demand for *Omertà*, his culture of non-disclosure and his ban on transparency. All 4,200 pages have been locked away in Blatter's safe in Zurich. That has been approved by all the members of the FIFA ExCo. The timorous 209 national associations are silent. The reporters have not noticed.

The most crucial document in the Garcia bundle must be the transcription of his 'interrogation' of Blatter. What was the date of this interview? Where did it happen? Was it in the comfort of Blatter's office? What questions did Garcia ask? Was he as tough on his wealthy paying client as he was in his past life as a prosecutor investigating organised crime, terrorists and murderers in New York? That's all secret. We will never be given answers to any of these questions.

Garcia's report was sent to Judge Eckert in Munich. Eckert's 'verdict' began by telling us what we had known for years. 'It is certain that not inconsiderable amounts were channelled to former FIFA president Havelange and to his son-in-law Ricardo Teixeira as well as to Dr Nicolás Leoz.' They were 'bribes.' Then Eckert gave us his opinion on Blatter's involvement in the vast corruption at FIFA.

'It must be questioned,' Eckert ruled, 'whether President Blatter knew or should have known over the years before the bankruptcy of ISL that ISL had made payments [bribes] to other FIFA officials.

Was Eckert serious? Everybody working at FIFA, in the battalion of reporters who covered FIFA, in the army of sports managers, agents and rights salesmen in the football world had known for many years that ISL were lubricating their relationship with Havelange and FIFA. The sun came up in the morning; the micro-manager Blatter knew all about the bribes. What else did he talk about during Jean-Marie Weber's visits to FIFA House and the long spells they spent together in the same hotels at FIFA's tournaments?

In past years Blatter admitted spending holidays with Weber and, amazingly, once compared their relationship to 'a Venetian night of love.' But they didn't ever talk about the $100 million of bribes. Sepp says so and we are expected to believe him. Weber doesn't say anything.

We will never know if investigator Garcia interviewed Weber or former ISL boss Christoph Malms about the demand by Havelange and Blatter that Bagman Weber kept his job at the company. Several ISL employees in their finance department organised and dispatched the bribes to FIFA officials. Did Garcia talk to them? That's none of our business.

Finally, Judge Eckert ruled that when the Havelange bribe came in, Blatter 'may have been clumsy . . . but this does not lead to any criminal or ethical misconduct.'

As Garcia has 'cleared' Blatter, despite massive evidence to the contrary, let's guess how the interrogation went.

Garcia: 'Is Seppy-weppy sitting comfortably?'

Blatter: 'Get on with it.'

Garcia: 'You had no idea that the payment from ISL to Havelange was a bribe, did you?'

Blatter: 'Of course not.'

Garcia: 'Can I have my cheque now?'

Blatter: 'This is all secret, right?'

Garcia: 'Anything you say.'

Blatter: 'Christine, outside, has the cheque ready for you. Or would you prefer cash? Grondona will fix it.'

How did they get away with it? It's time to go back and study Blatter's artfully constructed new rules.

IT LOOKS LIKE another of FIFA's routine documents. But it is crucial in Blatter's underhand campaign to suppress the truth. Dark blue cover, 56 pages of 'FIFA Organisation Regulations.' Approved by Blatter's ExCo on March 21, 2013, it marked the final step in his destruction of reform and transparency. The document is there on fifa.com. Who has bothered to read it?

On page 8 we are told that all ExCo meetings are 'confidential.' On page 12, the mantra is repeated for all FIFA's committees; they are 'confidential.' How about the supposedly independent Audit and Compliance Committee? You guessed: 'Committee meetings are confidential.' Salaries, bonuses, expenses, whatever they talk about at the 'Compensation Sub-Committee' is none of our business.

It was Blatter's final lockdown. He was safe. The regulations ensure that how he spends FIFA's money, his private deals, the ticket deals, luxury trips to the world's finest hotels, his imperial travel in chartered jets, his salary, bonuses, expenses, car and housing allowances, every item of him milking FIFA for himself, his family and his girlfriends, remains confidential. To keep his ExCo happy, they can submit their sometimes extraordinary expenses claims without receipts, sometimes fantasy sagas, trips they never made; they get the money – in cash if they want it. It doesn't come out of Blatter's pocket and it keeps them loyal – and silent.

What debates do they have in the committees? We cannot be told. Do they ever argue? *Omertà*. How do they arrange distribution of World Cup tickets? Don't dare ask! What discussion before lucrative contracts are awarded? Go away. Blatter's tight circle of associates own football and the fans, players and clubs are excluded.

Blatter has had an astonishing, amazing, privilege going all the way back to the days when he was Havelange's general secretary. He could sign cheques without the consent or knowledge of other officials. He could give FIFA's money to anyone. It was not a total secret; you could discover this online at the Zurich companies registration office. But only one other reporter ever thought to look; Zurich investigative reporter Jean-François Tanda.

How was FIFA's money spent? Who checked Blatter's spending? Only Finance Committee chairman Julio Grondona and his deputy, Jack Warner, probably the least trusted men in world football, the co-conspirators who agreed Blatter's secret salary. FIFA claim, belatedly, that they have now changed so Valcke has to co-sign cheques. Do you find that comforting? Will we ever be allowed to see the years of bank statements, revealing who Blatter was paying? Don't hold your breath.

Then there are the statutes: they lay down the FIFA law that Blatter is above the law in any land in the world. Try and sue him or any official in the civil courts and you are banned from football! On page 50 national associations are instructed that any appeal against this rule must be 'strictly submitted to arbitration, and not to ordinary courts of law.' Blatter of course appoints the officials who control FIFA's arbitration procedure.

'THE GENERAL SECRETARIAT of FIFA shall provide both the investigatory and adjudicatory chambers with a secretariat with the necessary staff.' This bland statement at the heart of the revised Code of Ethics, produced by Blatter in July 2012, strikes down the claim that the two 'Chambers' are independent. Check it at page 26, regulation 33.

Blatter has organised his Ethics Committee so that is inhouse and that he employs its bureaucrats, secretaries and filing clerks. He chooses them from among his most trusted staff. They owe their jobs, salaries, promotions, bonuses and pensions to Blatter. They are based a few doors from his presidential office so he can keep tabs on the evidence being assembled by Garcia and Eckert.

The Code of Ethics specifies their responsibilities. They have control of 'facts of the case, contents of the investigations and deliberations and decisions taken as well as private personal data.' Individuals wanting to approach the Ethics Committee with secret evidence about corruption may be deterred by Regulation 62 (1) on page 41: 'The secretariat of the investigatory chamber shall carry out an initial evaluation of the documents submitted with the complaint.'

Regulation 62 (2) of Blatter's new rules makes clear that his staff will know of complaints before Garcia or Eckert. 'If there is any indication of a potential breach, the secretariat shall conduct the appropriate preliminary investigation.' There can be little doubt that if Blatter was being named by informants, he would have early warning from his own staff.

The Code pretends to offer protection to vulnerable witnesses. Page 74 (4) says 'Oral statements shall always be heard behind closed doors.' But they will be transcribed to an archive that can be accessed by Blatter and Jérôme Valcke.

Secrecy and silence – or *Omertà* as they call it in Palermo – is the FIFA rule all the way to the end of the 'investigation' process. Then we are told, on page 78 (1) 'The Ethics Committee may decide not to communicate the grounds of a decision and instead communicate only the terms of the decision.'

That translates as 'we have executed somebody but we will not reveal why. Why not? Because we have made a rule that says we don't have to.'

Blatter wrote the new rules. His ExCo waved them through. Was there any discussion, any argument? We are not allowed to know. All the minutes are 'confidential.' None of his members resigned in protest. It must have been lunchtime.

There may be one file of evidence that the Secretariat will not see. I asked someone with an intimate knowledge of Garcia's investigations how he could possibly get hold of private bank accounts to see who was paying and receiving bribes, now he was no longer working in law enforcement and did not have legal powers to seize documents. 'That's easy,' laughed my source. 'He'll get XXXXX YYYYY to do it.' He named a well-known private investigator that has worked for FIFA and who has strong connections to American law enforcement.

I checked with the Code and yes, at 66 (3) it permits, 'In complex cases, the chief of the investigation may request the chairman of the investigatory chamber to engage third parties – under the leadership of the chief of the investigation – with investigative duties.' There is no rule banning illegal enquiries. So Mr YYYYY will almost certainly be blagging bank accounts. That will be covered by *Omertà*.

Blatter's PR machine claims this 'improved' Ethics Code was produced by one of Blatter's task forces to 'strengthen the powers and independence of the judicial bodies.' It appears to have done the opposite. But Garcia and Eckert are entirely happy to have their work constrained by FIFA's chief. In March 2013, both men congratulated FIFA on 'the quality of the FIFA Code of Ethics and the support and cooperation received from FIFA.'

What did the members of their two teams, investigators and Adjudicators, think? There are 16 members of the two 'Chambers.' I wanted to know if they had been involved in the ISL investigation – or were they just decorations on FIFA's ethics tree? I found email addresses for 10 of them. I asked five of Garcia's investigators, were they shown the IMG correspondence? Was IMG's boss Eric Drossart interviewed? Were they convinced that Garcia gave Blatter a tough enough interview about the Havelange bribe? Were they happy that all the evidence was being suppressed?

I put similar questions to the members of Judge Eckert's Adjudicatory Chamber.

Only one had the courtesy – and honesty – to respond. Mr Nicholas Davidson QC, of Christchurch, New Zealand emailed me, 'Due to litigation commitments in New Zealand, I did not attend the Plenary Meeting in 2013 and I have not been, and am not, involved in any specific investigation, including the matters about which you enquire.'

Tucked away on page 63 of FIFA's 2013 Financial Report – rubberstamped at their Congress in São Paulo – is the reality of Blatter's bogus 'reform process.'

Garcia has called only two meetings of his impressive sounding Investigatory Chamber. Three members, Robert Torres of Guam, Jorge Iván Palacio from Bogotá and Ahmed Yahya from Mauritania got to both meetings. Deputy Chairman Cornel Borbely, who lives a short drive from Zurich, only made one meeting. Same with Vanessa Allard, Cayman lawyer. Noël Le Graët from Paris, president of the French Football Federation, failed to attend either meeting. Nick Davidson from New Zealand was only a member for one meeting – which he was unable to attend.

It was not much better at Judge Eckert's Adjudicatory Chamber. His two meetings were both attended by Jack Kariko from Papua New Guinea, Juan Pedro Damiani from Uruguay and Abdoulaye Diop from Senegal. The deputy chairman, Alan Sullivan from Australia got to one meeting, as did Norway's Yngve Hallen and China's Liu Chi, The abrasive Alan Rothenberg from Beverly Hills has still to make it to Zurich.

Will the world ever be allowed to see the minutes of these

meetings? Where were they held? How long did they take? Who was late? Who left early? Was there any debate about the 'evidence' produced by Garcia? Had everybody read the thousands of pages allegedly compiled by Garcia? Or were they merely handed a Garcia summary?

Was Eckert challenged at any point on his ludicrous verdict, the one Blatter so desperately sought? None of them will say. It is *Omertà* again. Information that is too important to share with the wider world of football, which is paying for this insulting, dark farce.

COMEDY NOTE: I asked FIFA why they had not published the report of Garcia's 'investigation' into the ISL scandal – including a transcript of Garcia's alleged 'interrogation' of Blatter. Let's not forget that this is about Blatter's knowledgeof the big bribe to Havelange. It is very, very serious. It is one of 175 bribes paid. What happened that morning in March 1997 is morally offensive and in many countries criminal, carrying jail sentences and public disgrace.

If Garcia and his Investigation Chamber are to have any credibility we have a right to know what questions Garcia asked – and what answers Blatter gave?

There is surely an audio tape of this confrontation which could be uploaded. Surely Blatter and FIFA want to dispel suspicions that it might have been a sweetheart interview with the man paying Garcia's bills?

I wrote to FIFA's media department. Nothing changes. Blatter has written a set of rules that shield him and his interrogator from scrutiny. How can we trust Judge Eckert's opinion without seeing the evidence – as we would in a public court? The answer came from Ms Delia Fischer, who for many years, has stonewalled for Blatter.

Dear Mr. Jennings,

In line with article 28 of the FIFA Code of Ethics <http://www.fifa.com/mm/document/affederation/ administration/50/02/82/codeofethics2012e.pdf> the investigatory chamber is preparing a report on final investigation results for the adjudicatory chamber only. One or more members of the investigatory chamber will then present the case before the adjudicatory chamber if a hearing is conducted.

If a recommendation is made for sanctioning, the relevant party's sanctionable conduct and possible rule breaches are to be indicated in the final report. In accordance with article 36, paragraph 2 of the Code of Ethics only final decisions already notified to the parties involved can be made public. As such FIFA published the final report by the chairman of the adjucatory chamber, Hans-Joachim Eckert, on 30 April 2013 which is available on FIFA.com, direct link: http://www.fifa. com/mm/document/affederation/footballgovern- ance/02/06/60/80/islreporteckert29.04.13e.pdf

Kind regards,
Delia Fischer

19

Blatter Digs Up His Family Coffins

He refuses to be buried near Hildbrand

The chairs look uncomfortable and no doubt that is deliberate. The President doesn't want you to linger too long because he doesn't give a shit who you are and why you are here. He may have already forgotten your name. He has his survival plan configured, the voters are already paid, and nothing you say or do can change it. He's got all he needs; billions of World Cup dollars, Putin and the emir. If you have a vote at his congress, here's more money for 'development.' May it rest in peace in Cayman, Cyprus or property investment in Dubai.

The press release, already written – just fill in the date and name – will stress the harmony, the positive nature of your meeting. Then, Mr or Ms Visitor, will you please fuck off and leave me to calculate who in my electoral machine currently needs additional lubrication.

Oh, before you go, we must be photographed with me

handing you one of our cheap blue-and-gold pennants with the exhortation, *'FIFA: For the Game. For the World.'* No, I don't know what it means but some expensive PR agency suggested it. We had to dump the old one, *'FIFA: For the Good of the Game,'* for obvious reasons.

In the outer office, blonde Christine is gossiping on the phone with her husband, Charly Botta. Christine is the president's executive secretary and keeper of the secrets. Her father, an international ice hockey player, was a friend of the president, they are both from the little town of Visp in the Valais. Sepp's first job in sport was general secretary of the Swiss hockey federation. In 1975 Horst Dassler spotted Blatter's ambition and took him to FIFA alongside new President Havelange as the reliable bag-carrier to help protect the future for Adidas and his marketing contracts.

Christine met Charly when he was overseeing the building of the president's glass palace on the hill above Zurich. The former Mrs Botta departed and Christine, formerly Ms Salzmann, claimed half the duvet. What do they do under the duvet? Charly says 'Creative real estate management is our great passion.'

Charly is a busy chap. He holds the grand title of FIFA's chief consultant on Stadium Design and Construction and had a hand in all the stadia built or upgraded in South Africa for 2010. Charly was heavily involved in the Brazil 2014 stadiums and so Sepp was always better informed on the state of construction than Valcke. Charly is consulting on the stadiums for the 2018 event in Russia and was busy in Sochi, supervising the new Central Stadium and Bolshoi Ice Palace.

The other fixture of the presidential waiting room is Guy-Philippe Mathieu. His work on Blatter's claims for per diems and other expenses is legendary, even surviving an inquiry from a Zurich prosecutor. His father, like Blatter, is from the Valais and runs a vineyard.

Decorating the presidential suite is a display case of 'honours' bestowed by people and organisations you may sometimes have difficulty tracing. From the list Herr Blatter helpfully supplies at fifa.com he wants you to know he has received one 'For Humanity in Football' from somebody. Then there is the 'International Humanitarian League for Peace and Tolerance'; if it has a website, it may be in the Dark Web. That hasn't prevented whoever they are lauding him not once – but twice! When Sepp isn't 'International Humanitarian of the Year' he is receiving their 'Golden Charter of Peace and Humanitarianism.'

The 'American Global Award for Peace' from 2003 was awarded by another organisation lost in the deeper recesses of the web. Apparently it is the International Amateur Athletic Association – *not* the one that runs world athletics and not a fulltime panel. Then there is the IOC's Olympic Order; Blatter is well-qualified for this one. Look who else has been honoured; Manfred Ewald, who developed East Germany's doping programmes, his political boss Erich Honecker; the butcher of Bucharest, Nicolae Ceauşescu, and Bulgarian dictator Todor Zhivkov, father-in-law of Ivan Slavkov, crooked Bulgarian football boss and member of the IOC.

On the same list of sporting heroes is deceased Primo Nebiolo, who protected doping in athletics, Boris Yeltsin, who gave Russia to his oligarch backers and 'Mr One Per Cent' Mitt

Romney, who ran the 2002 Olympics. Blatter has also been named the 'Dove of Geneva' – whatever that is.

The politicians in South Africa, who ignored poverty among their own people to let FIFA loot their land – while a few well connected pocketed huge profits and kickbacks – gave him the 'Order of Good Hope,' and an honorary doctorate in philosophy from the Nelson Mandela Metropolitan University in Port Elizabeth. Those baubles could be ignored. The betrayal was President Zuma giving the shifty Blatter the Order of the Companions of Oliver Tambo, one of the heroes of the apartheid liberation struggle.

The display becomes sinister: Blatter seems proud of awards from thug regimes in Uzbekistan, Kazakhstan, Kyrgyzstan and a couple from Azerbaijan. Then there's the tokens of admiration from Sudan, Yemen, Morocco, Tunisia, Bahrain, UAE and the Central African Republic. Blatter covers up his Humane Order of African Redemption from Liberia's Charles Taylor, since his old friend was jailed for 50 years by the international court in The Hague for unspeakable tortures inflicted on children, women and opponents.

This display is much more than the vanity of a man surrounded by sycophants. They signal to would-be regicides; 'These may be gifts from thieves and murderers but because I never criticise them, I have their gratitude and their votes and I will keep them. Challenge me at your peril.' The awards also signal to visiting businessmen that Sepp can open doors.

IT IS NOT TRUE that the president is mocked by the entire Swiss media. There are loyal exceptions and one is the

Aargauer Zeitung newspaper in a modest town to the west of Zurich. After the president's coronation in 2011 he made himself available for interview. The President liked the result so much he uploaded it to fifa.com.

The first tough question was, 'Mr Blatter, you have said that you would like to set a few things straight about you as a person by the end of your term of office. *Please go ahead!*'

This was followed by, 'Do you receive too little recognition for your achievements?' and 'Does the criticism hurt you?' Manfully, the president dealt with these – and then revealed where he gets his inspiration. 'I was brought up a Catholic, so of course the Catholic Church has an influence on me.'

The president says he is 'Profoundly religious,' adding that God talks to him. 'From time to time he tells me "You have to fix that on your own. I cannot help you with that."'

Three weeks earlier the president had made the traditional annual pilgrimage to his family grave in the small town of Visp. 'My father said to me, "Don't lose your grip. Do not lose heart. Keep going".' Blatter senior died 35 years ago.

The president forgot to mention something else about his father, his faith and the family grave in the cemetery in Visp. Beware: some may find this spooky, if not downright smelly.

After many decades the vault has been opened and all the Blatter family coffins moved to another part of the cemetery. Why would the President, when his time comes, not want to be interred at this spot, chosen by his forebears?

Across the pathway from the Blatter family's final resting place is the vault of another Visp family. It is that of Thomas

Hildbrand, the investigating magistrate who pursued the ISL bribes with such determination. It appears that the president could not tolerate the thought that, bearing in mind the two decades difference in their ages, the investigator, when paying respects to his own late father in the years to come, would inevitably cast his gaze across the pathway at the tomb of the former FIFA president.

Worse still, one day, the two adversaries would forever lie within a few metres of each other. The gravediggers were summoned and the Blatter family uprooted.

THE HOLE IN the ozone layer personally created by Sepp Blatter has increased in size overnight as his chartered jet lands in São Paulo after the long flight from Zurich. The most important person in world football forgot long ago what it is like to fly scheduled. It flatters his vanity and imperial delusions to command his own plane. Leave when I am ready! Yessir! There's another reason. With all the FIFA scandals it is best not to risk being accosted in airports by angry fans. Ask him about his carbon footprint? He'll think he stepped in something. In South Africa he and the ExCo had two chartered jets to fly from game to game.

There's an unexpected coldness about the airport staff. Maybe they were among the million protestors last summer. The president had thought it so smart to have said of the anti-FIFA protests. 'It's a spontaneous movement without purpose or reason. People just want to use the World Cup to be heard. Football is like potatoes: it goes with everything.'

*

EVEN WITH HIS POLICE ESCORT the journey from the charter terminal to the hotel takes time; time to reflect. If the riot police and their cavalry can club and gas the protestors away from his congress and his 64 games, he might survive as President. Is it too late to move next year's congress to Pyongyang?

BUT NOW, the ExCo dinner. And here's the first slobbering embrace of the evening. It's my closest ally at FIFA, Don Julio Grondona from Buenos Aires, five years older than me but still with an iron grip on our Finance Committee. His deputy used to be Jack Warner – *Stop laughing!* – but I have replaced him with the equally reliable Issa Hayatou. *Stop it!*

Julio agrees my salary – and I sign his expenses. Valcke is supposed to be involved in this decision and some time, we may tell him how much I earn. Maybe not, he would be jealous. The only other person who knows is Markus Kattner, he was at McKinsey with my nephew Philippe when I paid them all that money in 2000 for reports I threw away. Now Markus is our finance director – that helps with giving all those World Cup TV rights to Philippe's company Infront. Markus is also deputy general secretary and Valcke dare not lay a finger on him. We are indeed the true family of football.

Don Julio is senior vice-president. If anything nasty happened to me he would become president. It's a scary thought and it makes me feel safer. Julio makes a point of not speaking English so he's never had to answer directly for his comments about Jews. Or about how we spend FIFA's money. The Don has been an ExCo member since 1988 after forging an extraordinarily good relationship with the generals who rescued Argentina from the Reds in 1976.

Four years older than me and half a year younger than Don Julio is the new boy from Uruguay, Eugenio Figueredo. He replaced dear old Nicolás Leoz, fingered by the BBC bastards for being on the ISL payroll, but we let Nicolás stay on our gravy train until last summer, picking up the best part of a further $1 million in fees and expenses. It has been a bumpy time for our old friend. In Chile they stripped his name off a seaside boulevard because the local politicians thought his name disgraced their city. But the good old boys in Paraguay have stood by him, naming this year's challenge tournament the 'Dr Nicolás Leoz Cup.'

It was sad to see Ricardo Teixeira go but sitting in his chair at the ExCo is another old friend from Brazil, Marco Del Nero. I can look down on him, he is five years younger than me. Julio and Eugenio and Marco – 230 years experience between the three of them! Just the people to represent a vibrant young Latin America.

Marco has brought his lovely young Carolina with him. No, she's not his granddaughter! When she dances down the Sambódromo in a few feathers and not much else it makes us all feel young again.

Marin is along as a guest. He is running the CBF just as Ricardo taught him. If Ricardo had wanted to spend the money, he might have fulfilled João's ambition and taken my seat – one day. I was preparing the way in 2002 when I gave him a place on our new Internal Audit Committee. A few were shocked but they did not have votes so that was that.

*

JOINING US at the top table is another of my favourite
vice-presidents, Issa Hayatou from Cameroon. He spends a
lot of time at his African Confederation presidential office in
Cairo. He is not looking well, I'm told he has some kind of
transfusions in Geneva. I wonder who pays? But after 24 years
on our ExCo he will not stop serving football.

I think it excellent that Issa's son Ibrahim is a senior manager with that French media company that buys the TV rights
to African football from his dad. Again, in the family of football
we trust each other as I do my nephew Philippe.

Issa still has the guts to stand up to interfering governments.
Look at those nobodies from Togo. When their national team
was ambushed by gunmen in 2010 in Angola the government
in Lomé called for three days of national mourning for the
three who were killed and the nine injured. Then they pulled
the team from the Africa Cup of Nations.

Issa would not have that! Our sacred rules must be upheld.
So he banned Togo from the next two championships and
fined them $50,000. Issa was upholding FIFA's sacred rule that
governments are not permitted to interfere in our affairs. Later,
I had to step in and reverse this decision but it sent the message
that we play by our own rules.

I don't believe the rumour that Issa took $1.5 million to vote
for Qatar. It cannot be true. Issa knows that his vote and influence in Africa is worth a lot more. He's got the best adviser in
the business. One of us had to provide a safe home for Jean-
Marie Weber and Issa has made him a consultant to the African
Confederation's marketing committee. That way Jean-Marie

gets accreditation for all our events and because Issa is an IOC member, he joins his entourage and gets plastic to hang around his neck for all Olympic Games and conferences. Isn't that neat?

I don't like Jean-Marie being called the 'Bagman.' He's a cultured man determined to maintain the legacy of Horst Dassler. The accusation by those detectives in Zug that I was assisting my Brazilian friends embezzle FIFA's money is despicable and I am not going to go into it. Jean-Marie will join us later for a nightcap and tomorrow he will be in the congress hall, seeing all his old friends.

Over there, look, is Jacques Anouma. Issa got a lot of stick for changing the rules and making it impossible for Jacques to challenge him for the African presidency. Critics didn't realise that Issa cares passionately about maintaining continuity for the sake of African football. And, I must keep my voice down, there is a possible problem with Jacques. You know he was chief financial officer to President Laurent Gbagbo in the Côte d'Ivoire? You know where Gbagbo is now? Locked up in The Hague awaiting trial, accused of murder, rape, sexual violence, persecution and what they call 'other inhuman acts.' I think these human rights people go too far sometimes – there was civil war. I don't believe this gossip about misappropriation of millions from the cocoa and coffee farmers.

GIRL'S HYMENS! Such slander! We had this nice young man, Prince Ali from Jordan, keen to be elected as one of our vice-presidents, helping me get rid of that uncontrollable Korean billionaire from Hyundai, Chung Mong-joon. All looked good, the prince was backed, like me, with the money from Saudi, and then women's football in Saudi became an issue. A religious scholar condemned the game because it 'could damage a girl's hymen,' followed by those unnecessary jokes about 'How does he know?' It's their culture and we shouldn't interfere.

In Zurich we helped Prince Ali with some sound bites for his script. I liked, 'I continue to believe in the power of unity to develop football,' because none of us knows what it means so you cannot argue with it.

Hopefully the prince will not be a problem because we have now found him a day job. Let's hope he doesn't turn out like Makudi. How Worawi keeps his football job in Thailand baffles me. The accusations come from everywhere. We can all learn about survival from him. Since we got rid of Bin Hammam there are new faces in Asia but we will hopefully get them voting the right way. David Chung from Papua New Guinea is slotting in nicely, and so is Zhang Jilong from China. We don't know much about them so there's little on the ExCo website.

I LOVE THE BRITS! They have a tradition of providing FIFA with vice-presidents who never cause ripples. The last one, Geoff Thompson, refused to give interviews to the press.

The crowd from UEFA, all eight of them on my ExCo, could be, should be, trouble but they can never agree on anything. I hope Michel Platini is listening to me. If I do stand for re-election I expect to pick up a majority of the match-fixing countries of central and Eastern Europe.

Back in 2002 I was able to persuade Spain's Villar-Llona to back me against the rest and I doubt he has changed.

D'Hooghe from Belgium is never a problem, Lefkaritis from Cyprus seems wrapped up in UEFA and his own businesses. I hear he is popular in the Gulf.

Warner and Blazer have gone but Rafael Salguero from Guatemala, who was chosen by Warner, joined us in 2007 and says he is crazy about football. The two replacements are Jeff Webb and Sunil Gulati, the banker and the economics teacher who never spotted the industrial-scale thieving of their predecessors.

I admit, I miss Ivan Slavkov. A man loyal to Bulgaria's Stalinist regime, and then to me, represented a world I felt comfortable with. A true entrepreneur, Ivan organised illegal arms consignments to the apartheid regime, was a natural fixture at the IOC and had his hand out for bribes from cities bidding for the Olympics.

This qualified Ivan to be a member of the IOC's '2000 Reform Commission' after the Salt Lake scandal of 1999. He sat next to me and to our Dear Former Leader President João. We got to know more men representing the best of the Olympic Ideal like Sheik Ahmad from Kuwait, René Fasel of Switzerland, Ireland's Patrick Hickey, Henry Kissinger, Carlos Nuzman and Hungary's Pál Schmitt.

I stood shoulder to shoulder with Ivan to the end. In 2004 those bastards at the BBC *Panorama* programme secretly filmed Ivan on the eve of the Athens Games with his hand out for a bribe in the competition to host the 2012 event.

(The IOC had to suspend Slavkov so he didn't make it to Athens. 'We regret he isn't here,' said Blatter, 'we believe in the concept of innocent until proven guilty. For FIFA, he remains president of the Bulgarian FA and we are going to send a letter to him confirming that.' Eventually everybody had to dump toxic Ivan.)

WHEN I PLANNED our new FIFA headquarters, I made sure that the chairs for the ExCo members were the most expensive money could buy. The old boys, and our new girls, I forget their names, love them.

After a long flight to Zurich they are soon falling asleep. Few of them care about the agenda because little of it affects them. Some of them have their own rackets in their own confederations and I think most of them come to get away from their wives and charge stupendous expenses – which I am happy to pay. I wake them up for lunch and after that even more fall asleep. A couple more hours later I wake them up again and the fleet of FIFA Mercs takes them to their plush hotels to change and dine in some of the world's most expensive restaurants.

THIS WRITER hears another voice, whispering to him from the Finance Department. 'You remember me saying that many of the members were cheating with daily allowances and travel costs. They claimed to have been somewhere and requested travel costs first class without presenting tickets. XXXXXXX and Warner did that also on a regular basis. XXXXXXX even claimed twice!! When he was travelling for the IOC he passed through Zurich in order to be able to claim money again!

'Most of these guys never informed their tax authorities about these extra cash payment and additional income which could amount to easily 30 to 50 thousand extra dollars per year – and I speak only of daily allowances!'

*

THE MOST-WATCHED football in the world is the English Premier League. It is always on a TV screen near you. Whoops, I have got the name wrong! It is called the Barclays Premier League. Barclays say they bring football to the fans. What else does Barclays bring to the world?

In recent years regulators and judges in America and the UK have fined Barclays more than $2.2 billion for ripping off customers, breaking sanctions laws, rigging markets and avoiding paying taxes. Offences include insider trading, overcharging and mis-selling. It is going to get worse. Barclays have put aside a stunning $5.1 billion for customers ripped off on other deals.

They are also being investigated in America for potential breaches of the Foreign Corrupt Practices Act. That could lead to very big fines. But they have no comprehension of public shame. On the day I am writing this Barclays have announced they are cutting 12,000 jobs *and* increasing bonuses to already highly paid senior managers.

To divert attention from their anti-social activities they bought a new image. For a mere $40 million a year they own the English Premier League. Their logo is everywhere, it is on every screen in every sports bar in the world. How can you hate a bank that, as they claim, brings you the game you love? The Italian Marxist philosopher Antonio Gramsci scored with, 'How can you have a revolution when the enemy has an outpost in your head?'

The Barclays tentacles reach every outpost of the game. Their official Barclays Premier League Trophy Tour kicked off in Manchester in August 2011 and glided its way around the world through Kuala Lumpur, Bangkok, Hong Kong, Doha, Dubai and Abu Dhabi. More sightings are promised in North America and Africa. Fans were offered 'a once-in-a-lifetime experience!' getting 'up close to the official Barclays Premier League Trophy.'

If you cannot get up close to the 'Barclays Premier League Trophy' there is always the 'The FIFA World Cup™ Trophy Tour by Coca-Cola.' Have your photo taken with it in 90 countries. It was launched in Rio up close to the statue of Christ the Redeemer, implying a Christian blessing. It's now in a country near you, transported by a very large jet aircraft painted red and loaded with tons of equipment and what is claimed is the one and only World Cup trophy, accompanied by the smiles of the boosters.

Photos of the Tour are distributed globally and again, every-body is smiling. There are dancers, bands and singers, again, non-stop smiles. Some of the female teeth are accompanied by big feathers and small bikinis. Well-rewarded former football stars appear, their smiles well coached. You realise after a while that the advance team for the photographer excluded any adult with a fang or two missing and kids with braces on their teeth (one did slip in at a stopover in Colombia). What began as the Coke tour becomes the 'We don't need dentists Tour.'

That could be misleading. Coke are so sensitive to endless accusations of the damage their fizzy drink does to teeth that they have produced a special website. The answer is 'a sensi-ble, balanced diet.' How that counters sugar and phosphoric acid is not explained. Worries about obesity and diabetes have yet to be addressed. Keep smiling.

*

THE GOOD OLD BOYS at the Coca-Cola factory in Atlanta have ruthlessly promoted their fizzy sweet drink as a global brand. They are among the smartest businessmen on the planet. Did they ever wonder where ISL found the money to bribe FIFA? The ISL company in Switzerland did not have any other sources of income, only auctioning sports rights. They did not sell motor cars or real estate. Only launder big cheques from business clients to FIFA.

Year after year Coke spent millions buying the rights to be FIFA sponsors – or 'partners' as we must say. They paid the money to ISL. Did they guess that some was leaking out of the side door in kickbacks to crooks at FIFA, to keep those contracts coming? Did the Boys from Atlanta never smell the stench of bribery and corruption when they were in the same room as Jean-Marie Weber, Blatter, Teixeira, Havelange? Many others, not as clever as them, did.

As global players Coke will have encountered every kind of attempted shakedown by corrupt businessmen and politicians. What blinded them to FIFA–ISL bribery? For a decade before ISL collapsed in 2001, I was discussing this in bars around the world with sports officials, marketing people and other reporters. We knew – but didn't have the proof.

OK, let's be kind to Coke. They never guessed their dollars were being siphoned off by the crooks that sold them rights. But once ISL collapsed in 2001 the media was full of corruption allegations. The bribery stories surfaced again when the Havelange–Teixeira–Blatter case was settled in Zug. And they soared again in November 2010 when I revealed the $100 million Bribes List – and named names. Coke and the other 'partners' were silent. But they have what they want – the World Cup logo on all those cans, bottles, cartons and advertisements

FANS JOKE that FIFA is a 'mafia.' It is not a joke – the evidence shows that Blatter's leadership group at FIFA has all the elements of an organised crime syndicate. It has a strong and ruthless leader, a hierarchy, a strong code of conduct for its members and, above all, the goal of power and profit, much of that entangled in illegal and immoral activities.

Blatter and his ExCo *never* criticise their fellows when they and their crimes are exposed publicly. The eight that went out of the door in recent years? Not a word of condemnation. The rest of the world attacked these thieves and fraudsters. Not a whisper from Zurich. Not a word of upset about Jean-Marie Weber, who handed out the bribes. He is always welcome at conventions. This is the key to understanding Blatter's ExCo: In their collective view the only thing the crooks did wrong was get caught.

Blatter has never criticised Warner or Blazer – both men sitting on devastating evidence against him and his complicity in the theft of tens of millions of dollars from FIFA. Blatter looked away when Judge Loretta Preska in a Manhattan courtroom accused both Blazer and Jérôme Valcke of lying in the Visa case in 2006.

There was international howling and eventually Valcke was 'sacked' – so said Blatter. Valcke went off to work with Teixeira in Brazil for a few months, choosing the cities and their new stadiums, negotiating the political and business alliances and contracts for 2014. How is it possible that Jérôme Valcke did not realise what all of Brazil knew: that Teixeira was a 'great bloodsucking vampire squid wrapped around the face of football, relentlessly jamming its blood funnel into anything that smells like money.' *(Thanks, Matt Taibbi!)*

The job done, Brazil's taxes flowing freely from the national treasury into dark places that may never be explored in Brazil and abroad, Valcke went back to Zurich and was promoted to FIFA general secretary, to spend the next few years liaising closely with the Brazilian Squid as the cost of 2014 accelerated upwards.

But still we ask; why was Jérôme Valcke happy to work closely with such a mega-thief and, never, ever voice a syllable of criticism? Is there more to discover about their relationship? Is there a reporter brave enough to ask questions at Valcke's press conferences? I cannot, I have been banned for more than a decade because they don't want such questions on their international video feed, upsetting the bland, unchallenging silliness from most of the friendly press corps.

Amos Adamu was a major thief of football money in Africa, long before he was welcomed into the arms of the ExCo. Leoz was first named in the ISL scandal in 2006 but allowed to stay for another seven years ripping off FIFA. Fedor Radmann was involved in what ended up being a rip off for Australian taxpayers – FIFA travel office books his flights. Teixeira was thoroughly exposed in 2001 – and Blatter gave him the World Cup to steal from. The president has never distanced himself from these crooks but that must be expected; he profits from leading a regime of crooks. They are blood brothers.

I am asked frequently; 'You have exposed so much FIFA corruption, how come Blatter is still in power?' Here's the answer: it doesn't matter what fans, reporters or politicians think or say about these crooks, Blatter is untouchable.

He controlled six families scattered around the globe. These are the continental confederations. Blatter has huge powers of patronage, funded from the billions earned by the World Cup. He uses this to lubricate the affiliated 209 national associations who happily vote to keep him in power. The grease is barely audited multi-million dollar 'development grants' and access to immense quantities of World Cup tickets to sell for cash into the black market, frequently for secret tax-free profits. All he asks in return is loyalty at the ballot box and silence in the Congress.

For many presidents of national associations Blatter is the finest president their money can buy. There is no reason to change him. Blatter forever!

It is defining that dissent is rarely heard in this huge international organisation. Blatter claims their congress is a 'parliament' but, with one short-lived exception – the contested presidential election of 2002 – FIFA is essentially an anti-democratic organisation.

When there are a few problems Blatter calls his hand picked flacks to the podium, often from tiny countries where football is marginal, to hurl abuse at his critics. That takes it slightly up the democracy scale from the Peoples' Congress in Pyongyang. My favourite headline from the Korean gatherings is 'Perfect unity between leader and people.' You could find that on fifa.com.

20

Remember to Wave Goodbye

The President's game will soon be over

Banned as ever for the last eleven years by Sepp Blatter's thought police I couldn't make it to his Congress in Sao Paulo on June 10, 2014. He knew the FBI were working with worrying diligence, hints were coming from some of the middlemen selling TV and marketing rights in the Caribbean and Latin America that they feared good friends were now wearing wires.

Jack Warner's oldest son Daryan was co-operating with FBI – that had been in the papers. The word on the touchline was that Chuck Blazer was telling all he knew. My colleagues who did get places on the press benches saw a President strained, distracted, gazing around, nostalgia already setting in.

Could he sense there would be empty chairs at the next congress, that some of his executive committee would be behind bars? That never again would they all be gathered in self-indulgence, fine food and wines?

The President is nearly ready to step into the spotlight. A few moments left to chat off-stage with his personal guests. Last time he fronted a Congress in Latin America was in July 2001 in Buenos Aires. A platoon of speechwriters, dressers and makeup-artists flown in from Europe at considerable cost by nephew Philippe and his colleagues at McKinsey prepared him for his performance. That day he routed his critics.

Herr Blatter gazes around. His sad thoughts are now carved across his face. He can't be sure that all his delegates and their buses made it here through the protests and the banners, and the chanting 'We want schools and hospitals FIFA style.' It is going to look terrible on the global TV news shows. Mounted police charging demonstrators, batons flailing. Some of his national association presidents have stayed in their hotels with bundles of tickets, waiting for the foreign traders and their bags of cash.

He looks lonely. Is the political protection ebbing? From the White House to the Elysée, Downing Street to Berlin's Kanzleramt, politicians once bowed to this organisation. No policeman – outside Zug – dared meddle with them. Putin should be here, the next tournament is in Russia. But will he instruct his doctor to write him a 'sorry not to be with you' sick note?

Problems everywhere. There must be a press conference later. Will a reporter throw a shoe?

The President gazes at his family. He smiles. Are his lips moving? As his era is ending, he's talking to himself. Is this what he is saying?

Where are the delegations from Israel and Palestine? If

they don't sit next to each other, at least for a photo-call, that's goodbye to the Nobel Peace Prize. And those wild cops outside don't help.

I hope Nephew Philippe could make it – the son I never had. Isn't he doing well! You would not believe he is stroking 50! Philippe's a tough guy, he does the Iron Man. Philippe learned so much from me when he led a McKinsey team to shake up FIFA's accounting and management systems a decade ago. I paid McKinsey millions of Francs for that. Philippe moved on to Infront and, remember, his friend and colleague Markus Kattner left McKinsey to become our head of finance. We call it synergy in our football family.

Philippe learned a lot when McKinsey were contracted to advise Morocco's bid to host the World Cup in 2010. I have never accepted the rumours that Morocco's government paid bribes to my ExCo colleagues. If they had, Philippe would have told me. So would Alan Rothenberg from Los Angeles who was also promoting their bid. It is not believable that Morocco actually beat South Africa in the secret ballot by two votes. I would have been told.

We gave Infront the contracts to sell TV rights in Asia, America and Canada to the World Cup until 2022. We gave them another contract to televise the tournament, supplying the pictures to the world's networks, and more contracts involving hospitality and stadium management. They handle sales of our World Cup film archive – and they are not cheap! Why does nobody believe that I wasn't in any way involved in awarding those FIFA contracts? What do we talk about at Blatter family gatherings? That's family business.

Continuity is so important and so Philippe's Infront company is based in the same glitzy offices in Zug where Jean-Marie Weber did the distribution of bribes in the good old days. Three years ago Infront, highly valued because of its exclusive deals with us at FIFA, was bought by the Bridgepoint private equity group. They also own a Polish biscuit baker, a chain of clothing stores, motorcycle racing, sandwich makers, education crammers and a chain of dental clinics. They are trying to take over publicly owned hospitals in Britain. Then there's marine engineering, refrigeration in Austria – and paying huge amounts to politicians to speak at their conferences and they have hired a BBC TV presenter to write for their glossy company magazine.

The smile fades, then returns as he sees the man he hopes will be his saviour if all collapses next year.

Here's another guy who understands private equity companies and he is an expert on merger and acquisitions, my Swiss compatriot Domenico Scala. He is absolutely the right fellow to be the totally and completely independent chairman of our totally and completely independent FIFA Audit and Compliance Committee. He is completely open and transparent, nobody can pressurise him – and he has promised me that he will not reveal my salary, expenses, bonuses.

Domenico gets wonderful press back in Switzerland. He has hired his own media briefer – I think that is him over there talking to reporters – and FIFA has never had such good publicity. Domenico is sold as a really tough guy, cracking down on my greedy ExCo. The reporters write what they are told. He is awesome, much more effective than Walter de Gregorio working for me. I change press officers, like my car, every two or three years. When Domenico moves on, maybe I can tempt him to do the same job for me.

Domenico heads a three-man committee I created to fix my salary. There's him, Julio Grondona and another Swiss guy you have never heard of who is a respected consultant to Citibank Private Banking in Geneva. This chap also works for another business in Geneva that claims, 'We work at the highest levels of leadership to create tangible and enduring business impact.' That sounds like the kind of guy to get me into a high earning bracket.

Over the years Domenico has been in charge of money at the big Pharm companies, Roche, Nobel Biocare, Basilea Pharmaceutica and also Nestlé. He was a big shot at Syngenta, the agrochemicals people. Domenico is a true child of vibrant corporate capitalism in Switzerland – and we love him! Ten years ago the wise people at the Davos World Economic Forum, you know them, the one per cent, named him as a Young Global Leader. You can trust those bankers, mortgage brokers and bond traders.

He is the gift from the Big Brands to us at FIFA, helping but keeping an eye on us so scandals don't get out of control. One of his first statements in a typically hard-hitting interview we organised at FIFA.com was, 'I think the financial reporting standards are very high. In fact, FIFA reports their financial numbers according to international accounting standards . . . I think we're starting at a very good level.' That made life easy for the journalists who get their news from us. Of course in the real world of international business chief executives have to declare their pay and perks – but not at our FIFA.

One cruel critic said, 'Scala offers football the public persona of an attentive and accommodating headwaiter at Blatter's feast.' I think that is unfair. Professor Pieth thinks very highly of Domenico and that's good enough for me. There is one worrying aspect of Domenico. He may know something the rest of us don't. In May last year, in a casual comment, he mentioned investigations by the FBI and the IRS. It chilled me.

It was helpful that Domenico gave his blessing to last year's Financial Report, presented at our Congress in Mauritius. There were 106 dense pages of reporting so it was a relief for delegates to read Don Julio's assurance on page 8 that he has kept costs under control so 'We can continue to invest directly in the beautiful game.' They didn't need to read any more.

I don't think every delegate understood the Analysis of Revenue, Balance Sheet, Development of Reserves, Revenue Component and Investments, small print, lots of bars and pie charts. So they probably didn't notice that the money spent on football development *fell* from $183 million in 2011 to $177 million in 2012. That was just 15.2% of total revenue. Delegates are unlikely to have realised that a few years ago FIFA spent 18.95% of its income on developing the game.

But total income increased from $1,070 million in 2011 to $1,166 million – so there was more to spend on ourselves! The 24 members of our Executive Committee, plus the handful of senior management who serve us, pocketed $33.5 million in 2012. That's *up* from $29.5 million the previous year. Football is good to us – we have nearly doubled the $18.9 million we paid ourselves in 2007!

I have pulled the same trick again in our latest Financial Report. It will be approved unquestioningly by the muppets here at the congress today.

The President turns the pages of his report. Again he smiles, a man who is reading something wonderful about himself, forgetting that he wrote it.

He has increased the size of the report, padding it with masses of boring material about our committees and what they do. It should have delegates off to sleep well before lunch. It is decorated with the usual confusing graphics, charts and tables.

His slogan, in very large type, is 'WE HAVE REACHED VERY HIGH LEVELS OF ACCOUNTABILITY, TRANS-PARENCY AND FINANCIAL CONTROL.' His letter to delegates follows on the next page. 'Dear Friends of Football,' he tells them, we have achieved, 'the completion of practically all elements of the FIFA governance reform process.'

They won't care about that. What will please them is the next sentence announcing 'that our direct financial support programmes for member associations had hit the $1 billion mark.'

On page 8 of last year's photo of Grondona the President pauses. He thinks, like his, it may be ten years old – and has more big type on an otherwise empty page; 'WE CONTINUE TO INCREASE THE RESOURCES THAT WE PUT BACK INTO THE GAME.'

That must be true because Domenica Scala, again in big type on the next otherwise empty page, insists; 'FIFA HAS DEMONSTRATED THAT IT IS PREPARED TO ADOPT BEST PRACTICE.'

On the eve of publication the president dictated a press statement. 'As a not-for-profit organisation and in line with its mission to develop the game, touch the world through exciting tournaments, and build a better future through football, FIFA shares as much of its income as possible with the global football community.'

The muppets rarely bother to read the Finance Report carefully. Spending on football development is not as rosy as is being claimed.

Income shot up by more than $200 million but FIFA increased football development spending by a miserable $6 million. That's a 3.4% increase on last time. The total percentage allocated to development has fallen again – from 17.48% to 15% – but the national associations—won't notice they are getting a smaller slice of a much larger cake!

Once football had made that sacrifice there was enough money to give the top people at FIFA an 8.4% increase, taking pay to $36.3million. Goal!

The President brightens up. His lips are moving again. Not everything is dark – for now.

Where is Ron Noble, the American boss of Interpol who has a direct line to every policeman in the world? It was the President's pleasure to hand him a cheque of $20 million for Interpol in 2012, insisting that was only to help with the fight against match-fixing.

When they gave him the $20 million at FIFA's Budapest Congress in 2012 Ron responded generously, saying, 'No objective person can reasonably question whether FIFA's leadership has taken serious steps to fight corruption, to foster good governance and to ensure greater transparency in football. Yes, the world's Top Cop said it.

The President's face clouds. Not everybody he sees is welcome. His lips are moving again. The pressure from the FBI is doing him no good.

I wonder if Fedor Radmann is here? And Peter Hargitay, his private media adviser, with his son Stevie? Those three are not popular in Australia. But Peter has done a terrific job for the last ten years diverting reporters from the ISL story. He's been a great crisis manager.

The President asked them to stay in the shadows today but the Hargitays are always looking for business opportunities. FIFA gave them money because Peter said he had a great idea for a hit movie. The best script line was 'Wow babe, with all those curves on you, and no brakes, you're liable to get rear-ended.' It was called *Chicks Dig Gay Guys*.

One last thing before going up to the stage. If he is here I must be photographed shaking hands with Jérôme Champagne. All the delegates will see he has my blessing. Keep him visible, keep him in play. He has published three serious and very boring statements about why he should be next President. A total of 9,600 words – and not a word of criticism of me. The word 'corruption' surfaces twice but it's all blamed on forces outside FIFA. That's his boy!

Platini must be blocked. If Champagne takes my place, I'll

ask him to keep the files secret. If he agrees and on my way out of the door I can organise enough votes for him to take control. Exactly the game Havelange and I played in 1998.

BACK TO THE REAL WORLD. The referees in the Department of Justice in Washington have had enough of this dirty game. It is the last congress where Herr Blatter will be in control. The following year, in Zurich, there will be empty seats on the podium, moans of self-pity coming from rich men in nearby police cells.

Eleven months and three weeks after this puffed up performance in Brazil the FBI and the Swiss cops will strike at dawn. But the last congress in Brazil had one element missing.

The custom is for the Head of State to Open the Congress. But President Dilma Rousseff had been advised to stay away. Her people hate Blatter and his parasites. Enraged demonstrators might turn on her. She was booed when she stood next to Blatter at the Confederations Cup in 2013. *Reuters* had run a story revealing the FBI were digging deep into Blatter's organisation.

Wisely, she stayed home in the Presidential palace in Brasilia. I had the privilege in November 2011 of testifying at the Senate in Brasilia about corruption in FIFA. I presented evidence revealing the corruption of Havelange and Teixeira and much of the evidence in this book.

As I finished my sleeve was tugged. It was a Presidential aide. 'Please. The President's Chief of Staff has been watching the TV feed and would like a copy of your presentation.'

My pleasure. Later I supplied more evidence, again in this book about the FIFA rogues. Teixeira was soon forced out of Brazilian football, the World Cup organising committee and then FIFA itself.

The President's intended speech to FIFA's Congress was never delivered. It remained in her desk. From my conversations with her advisors I know what she wanted to say, would have said.

Today we have been inside the head of the soon-to-be gone FIFA president. Now come inside the head of the determined woman who shared her nation's disgust at the manipulations of Blatter and his lowlifes. Here is what would have happened and now, thanks to detectives in many lands is going to happen for several years to come. Close your eyes and see the future . . .

PRESIDENT ROUSSEFF sweeps in with her bodyguards. Walking at the heart of her entourage she progresses to the platform. The football President extends his hand but the hard-faced bodyguards will not let him near this real, democratically elected President. She steps up to the podium and suddenly she dominates the room from the twin video screens high behind her. The bodyguards go to the back of the stage.

Dilma stares around the room at the rows of delegates, they expect a few bland welcoming comments and then back to selling tickets to the black market operators. She looks serious. She adjusts her glasses and begins to speak.

We hoped for harmony – but FIFA and our CBF have brought us strife and corruption. Today I want to explain to you why our nation of football lovers is not sure it wants you here. You must be told how you have poisoned our beautiful game. Your President – she turns and glowers at Blatter – avoids meeting ordinary fans. From now on he must step out of his bubble of illusions and hear the voice of the fans I speak for today.

In the dark days forty years ago when the Military ruled our country some of us fought against them and for democracy. We read a lot of political theory and gazing around this platform, and its collection of geriatrics that have held power far too long, I am reminded how Antonio Gramsci summarised all that is wrong with the people controlling football. He said, 'The crisis consists precisely in the fact that the old is dying and the new cannot be born; in this interregnum a great variety of morbid symptoms appear.'

José Maria Marin is one of the morbid symptoms and we do not wish to see him in public life anymore. Senhor Marin, will you please leave the stage.

Marin is the rabbit in the headlights. Maluf cannot help him now, Sergio Fleury is gone – and his torturers failed with this strong woman. Mesmerised by her charismatic presence – and the flinty stares of her guards – he finds himself rising and shuffling off the stage. The football officials are open-mouthed. This is not the kind of woman they would choose for their ExCo. There are outbreaks of laughter among the older reporters at the back of the hall who remember Vlado.

Her point made, Dilma turns back to her script. She has put a lot of thought into what she is going to say today.

Firstly, I want to deal with what is wrong. Then, what we

are going to do to put it right. I salute Alvaro Dias and Aldo Rebelo for the work they did in Brasilia in 2001 to expose the corruption of the CBF and Ricardo Teixeira.

The ExCo shudders. They happily co-existed with the Thief of Rio for two decades. He is still family. Blatter half raises from his seat. He must put a stop to this. A bodyguard leans over, puts a firm hand on his shoulder and shakes his head. Blatter sits down.

Congressman Rebelo and Senator Dias demonstrated with hard evidence how Nike's money had been misused by the CB to corrupt our national game.

The Senate will be setting up a new inquiry with legal powers to summon documents and witnesses, to investigate what has happened at the CBF since 2001 – and why Teixeira and his fraudsters were not prosecuted.

We will want to hear more from the good people in our game about drastic reform of the CBF, the organisation of football and the rights of fans, players and taxpayers in our country. The CBF is steeped in self-dealing and corruption and that has to end. The democratic base of the game will be widened and a much larger cross-section of citizens will be able to vote for the leadership of the CBF. All these changes will be enshrined in law. The culture of impunity will be ended.

We will require that the CBF commences uploading all current and historical documents on line. Everything; correspondence, financial deals, salaries, contracts, expenses. We have this now in government and we will have it in sport. We will appoint an independent commission to monitor any complaints. It will have the power to force disclosure.

Dilma turns to Blatter and his ExCo, now looking horrified as they take aboard that people's power in football will end their padded lives, and addresses her remarks directly to them.

Back in October 2000, Herr Blatter, you threatened to ban Brazil from the World Cup because our Congress was investigating Teixeira. Don't ever think to point your jackboots at us again. Your members assembled here do not want to forfeit games with our wonderful teams.

She turns back to the hall where it is sinking in to 1,000 suits that they need Brazil more than Brazil needs them.

I am not sure that Brazil will want to send a team to compete in the World Cup in 2022 if it is held in a country where trade union membership is illegal and the stadiums are built by slave labour.

Dilma pauses, turns at the podium and one by one, eyeballs the Exco. A World Cup without Brazil! That will halve the TV revenues! Sponsors will walk away.

Brazil is the home of modern football and so we must lead the way in real reform. The so-called reform process at FIFA has achieved nothing except protecting the geriatrics that created the scandals. Your generation gave us match-fixing, corruption, dirty play on the field, vote-rigging and bribery.

The President looks down at her notes and then up at the delegates. To regain credibility, FIFA must follow Brazil's example and put everything online. The world is entitled to see every bank statement, every expenses claim from your ExCo – with the receipts supporting them – the bill for hiring the Presidential jets and how many litres of aviation fuel is consumed. How much are the departmental Directors paid? What are their bonuses – and why do they get them? What is the cost of the Garcia investigation? The financial reports must become comprehensible. FIFA must get the message that it isn't their money.

As important are the minutes and video of every meeting from the ExCo downwards. They can be streamed online and archived forever. The vote for World Cup hosting must be transparent. We must go back to 2010 and discover how votes were cast. Then organise a transparent revote.

Another essential measure is publishing all the confidential Management Letters submitted to FIFA by auditors KPMG since 1999. And appoint an independent Freedom of Information Officer to enforce disclosure.

FIFA must instruct all 2009 national associations to follow this example. The whole world of FIFA money, policies and decisions could be online by the middle of 2015, paid for with the vast profits FIFA is taking from Brazil. Any national association not complying would be suspended.

Brazil will be proud to host a special World Football congress to debate new structures for FIFA. Then new Presidential elections can be organised.

Tomorrow I will be setting up a Task Force of forensic accountants, quantity surveyors and construction experts to investigate the contracts for the new stadiums. I expect fast results and all documentation will be put online. I regret and apologise for the white elephants. We should have seen what was happening in South Africa.

Dilma folds her notes and instead of taking a seat on the podium, leaves the stage and walks to the back. A reporter gives up their seat. The silence lasts and lasts. Blatter and the ExCo glow with silent rage. The delegates are stunned. Then a reporter starts clapping. All the Brazilians join in. Is that a reporter, bending down and taking off his shoe?

Sources

Research for my books and television documentaries investigating corruption in the international sports federations began in 1988. My collection of documents, public and private, stored in various secure locations, is unsurpassed by any sports, media or academic institution. Genuine researchers, journalists or lawyers seeking further sources or factual information are welcome to contact me at: Omerta201416@gmail.com

Acknowledgements

The greatest joy for me, researching this book and filming award-winning documentaries for the BBC about FIFA's decades of grotesque corruption, is being swept up in passion: the passion of outraged fans, clean officials, decent politicians, determined police officers and journalists in many lands, all hoping to reclaim their sport from the criminals.

Next came the physical thrill of unravelling the evidence that organised crime took over the world's most loved sport. Acquiring secret, explosive documents should be the aim of every reporter.

Thanks to my colleague Paul Greengrass at *World In Action* for urging in 1986 that I dig into corruption in the international sports federations. Paul went off to Hollywood and I dug into the International Olympic Committee, winning my most cherished award: a suspended jail sentence in Lausanne for disclosing that the IOC's President Juan Antonio

Samaranch was a life-long right-arm-waving Spanish fascist. His colleagues at the IOC avoid discussing the contradiction of a man who thought the wrong team won World War II while claiming he was a moral leader for the world's youth. It's a great story.

Colin Gibson at the *Daily Mail* kickstarted me into FIFA in 2001. From 2006 BBC *Panorama* editors Mike Robinson, Sandy Smith and Tom Giles have been rewarded with applause from the fans when our BBC investigative journalism peers into sports' dirty corners. Our goalkeepers were experienced BBC lawyers.

Director Roger 'Dodger' Corke created the first beautiful film in the sequence, 'Panorama's The Beautiful Bung' in 2006 while Andy Bell watched our backs. James Oliver took over and helmed again in 2006, then 2007, 2010, 2011 and currently in 2015. Cameraman Steve 'Rocksteady' Foote never missed a shot and always framed them beautifully, even when sprinting a step behind me, camera on shoulder, after evasive FIFA lowlifes. Same with Big Dave Langham, the calmest of all when the going gets rough. Editors Gary Beelders, Adam Richardson and Simon Thorne cut with élan, style and scored so many laughter goals.

The grassroots were watching and reading. The Football Supporters' Federation in the UK honoured me as their Football Writer of the Year in 2006. I was proud to be keynote speaker at their annual parliament in 2011.

Jan Jensen at *Ekstra Bladet* in Copenhagen gave endless support over 20 years, Ezequiel Fernández Moores, Jens Sejer Andersen at *Play the Game* and Ana May, Thomas Kistner,

Jean-François Tanda and Stella Roque, Camini Marajh and Lasana Liburd in Trinidad were there when I needed them. Denis O'Connor's brilliant forensic analysing of FIFA's opaque financial reports revealed that every year the Zurich crime family spent more on themselves and less on football development.

Claire Newell and Jonathan Calvert at the *Sunday Times*, Torgeir Pedersen Krokfjord and Espen Sandli in Oslo, Jens Weinreich and Karrie Kehoe shared more facts and often, laughs. Professors John Hoberman and Jay Coakley showed me new ways to think about sports institutions, and globalisation.

In São Paulo, Natalia Viana and her team of formidable Sisters published me in *apublica.org* and introduced me to Brazil's impressive World Cup committees and social movements. And hugs to the investigative reporters at ABRAJI, especially Guilherme Alpendre, Fernando Molica and Veridiana Sedeh for looking after me.

In Rio, Chris Gaffney, Carlos Vainer, Giselle Tanaka and Milli Legrain spared time for me. They took me to *favelas* and to the Maracanã to meet athletes evicted from the *Celio de Barros* athletics track because they were in the way of the World Cup. I will always remember the gracious welcome from the indigenous people at the Aldeia Maracanã. Carolina Mazzi and Manuela Andreoni taught me about Rio's gangsters and ticket racketeers.

In Brasília Romário de Souza Faria, Afonso and Carine Morais, José Cruz and Gustavo Castro welcomed me warmly. My thanks to Senators Paul Bauer and Álvaro Dias for inviting me to speak about FIFA as an organised crime family at the *Comissão de Educação, Cultura e Esporte* in October 2011.

Juca Kfouri made my previous book – and this one – possible in Brazil and Rodrigo Mattos and Jamil Chade shared their terrific investigations.

Thanks to Gavin MacFadyen who introduced me to Brazil and thank you to the judges, investigating magistrates and lawyers who invited me to speak at the Magistrates School in São Paulo in December 2012 about FIFA corruption. I think we educated each other.

It has been another pleasure to be associated with the wonderful reporters – the crème de la crème – at the Global Investigative Journalists Network and Executive Director Dave Kaplan.

As ever, there are special sources that cannot be named. But they know who they are and the value of the documents they gave me.

We must all thank the special agents from the FBI in New York and the Department of Justice in Washington who studied my documents and used them to launch a moral tsunami at FIFA. Moral? Some of the G-Men are soccer fans and when in London looked forward to catching a top-class match.

Thanks, and *abraços*, Big Brazilian Hugs,

Andrew

Here's Andrew:

In the late 1960s I took a story to the *Sunday Times* Insight Team and went on to spend the 1970s working in popular newspapers as a reporter and re-write man. Moved to BBC radio and then television, always specialising in investigations. Spent five happy years presenting investigations at Granada TV's *World in Action* programme. Took a break to do some war reporting: learned to duck for cover in Chechnya, Central America and Beirut. Reported Mafia in Palermo close enough to smell the garlic breath. Won some prizes, wrote a book and made three films about high-level police corruption in London, wrote three books about Olympic corruption and one about the dirty world of FIFA. That was *Foul!* in 2006.

Blatter banned me from his press conferences in April 2003 following my documented disclosure that he pays himself a huge secret bonus. Researched and presented five BBC

Panorama programmes about FIFA corruption. Freelance all over the planet. One specific Bad Guy is always messing (yawn) with my Wikipedia biography and organising massive botnet attacks on my blogs.

You can contact me at Omerta201416@gmail.com

Cannot promise replies.

I announce new stories on Twitter: @ AAndrewJennings